BROOKLYN

POETS ANTHOLOGY

BROOKLYN

POETS ANTHOLOGY

Edited by Jason Koo & Joe Pan

BROOKLYN ARTS PRESS & BROOKLYN POETS | NEW YORK

Brooklyn Poets Anthology

Edited by Jason Koo & Joe Pan.

Paperback ISBN-13: 978-1-936767-52-6
Ebook ISBN-13: 978-1-936767-53-3

Cover design by David Drummond. Interior design by Benjamin DuVall.

Published in the United States of America by:

Brooklyn Arts Press
154 N 9th St #1
Brooklyn, NY 11249
BrooklynArtsPress.com
info@BrooklynArtsPress.com

Brooklyn Poets
135 Jackson St, #2A
Brooklyn, NY 11211
BrooklynPoets.org
koo@BrooklynPoets.org

Library of Congress Cataloging-in-Publication Data

Names: Koo, Jason, editor. | Pan, Joe, editor.
Title: Brooklyn poets anthology / edited by Jason Koo and Joe Pan.
Description: First edition. | Brooklyn, NY : Brooklyn Arts Press, 2017. | Brooklyn, NY : Brooklyn Poets, 2017. |Includes bibliographical references and index.
Identifiers: LCCN 2017001333 (print) | LCCN 2017008746 (ebook) | ISBN 9781936767526 (pbk. : alk. paper) | ISBN 9781936767533 (e-book) | ISBN 9781936767533
Subjects: LCSH: American poetry--New York (State)--Brooklyn. | American poetry--21st century. | American poetry--20th century.
Classification: LCC PS549.B765 B74 2017 (print) | LCC PS549.B765 (ebook) | DDC 811/.6080974723--dc23
LC record available at https://lccn.loc.gov/2017001333

ACKNOWLEDGMENTS

Our gratitude goes out to all the poets who submitted work for this anthology, first and foremost. Thanks to David Drummond for creating this wild book cover. Thanks to Minos Papas and Cyprian Films for shooting our Indiegogo promo video; thanks to Tina Chang, Candace Williams, Robert Gibbons, and Emily Skillings for lending their brilliant voices to the video; and thanks to all those who donated to our crowdfunding campaign. Thanks again to Tina and to Dennis Nurkse for their kind words in support of the book. Thanks to our wonderful volunteer team of readers: Justin Maki, Daniel Fernandez, Lisa Muloma, Nadia Alexis, Puck Malamud, Anne Marie Bompart. Thanks to Brooklyn Poets Board Directors Gunny Scarfo, Flako Jimenez, and Tiffany Gibert for their enthusiastic support and oversight of the project. Thanks to Wendy Pan Millar, Johnny Schmidt, Daniel Borzutzky, Sam Hall, Kendra Lueck, and Ana Maria Farina for their instrumental feedback. And finally, a special thanks to Me-Young and Bon Chul Koo, Julie Koo, Phillip Sohn, and an anonymous donor for their generous contributions in support of the production of this book.

CONTENTS

BROOKLYN

POETS ANTHOLOGY

THIS SIDE OF THE BRIDGE

JASON KOO

> The impalpable sustenance of me from all things at all hours of the day,
> The simple, compact, well-join'd scheme, myself disintegrated, every one
>   disintegrated yet part of the scheme,
> The similitudes of the past and those of the future,
> The glories strung like beads on my smallest sights and hearings, on the walk
>   in the street and the passage over the river,
> The current rushing so swiftly and swimming with me far away,
> The others that are to follow me, the ties between me and them,
> The certainty of others, the life, love, sight, hearing of others.
>
> —Walt Whitman, "Crossing Brooklyn Ferry"

I came to Brooklyn in the summer of 2009, with only a couple of adjunct jobs lined up in the city and some money left over from an NEA fellowship I'd won the year before to keep me financially afloat. In other words, I was crazy to be moving here, as rents, even in Sunset Park where I settled because they were "cheaper," were high and climbing, and the teaching market, especially for full-time jobs in New York City, was basically nonexistent—you couldn't even call it a "market" anymore. But my two best friends lived here, one of whom, a writer, convinced me I could get by adjuncting as he had done, and my first book of poems was coming out at the end of the year, so Brooklyn seemed like a good place to be. If anything, my lack of a secure job anywhere else was a blessing, as it pushed me to see Brooklyn as an opportunity rather than an impossibility; if ever I was going to live here, as I'd dreamed of doing since I first dreamed of becoming a writer, now was the time.

Brooklyn existed for me first as a beacon in the imagination. I discovered the poetry of Hart Crane as a freshman in college and fell in love with the "unfettered leewardings" of his rhapsodic style, that "silken skilled transmemberment of song" he launched into American verse, the legend of his life played out against the backdrop of Brooklyn Bridge and the city, as captured so well in his magnificent letters and the famous photo of him on the roof of 110 Columbia Heights, the Bridge proudly in the background. I photocopied this photo from John Unterecker's *Voyager* biography and taped it above my desk in Cleveland, where I, like Crane, grew up. I had never seen the Brooklyn Bridge or set foot in Brooklyn before reading Crane, so they took on his own mythic proportions in my mind; the first time I walked the Bridge I wasn't pulled upwards by its cables so much as his poetry, seeing aloft his grand "harp and altar, of the fury fused." Towards the end of my first year out of college, when I lived in Astoria, I took one of my best friends to the Bridge at midnight on July 21, 1999 to pay homage to Crane on his 100th birthday: we poured out Cutty Sark at the base of the Brooklyn tower and took turns doing shots and reading stanzas from "Atlantis," Crane's ecstatic close to *The Bridge*, out loud.

Discovering Crane led me to rediscover Walt Whitman, whom I was indifferent to in high school. When I went back to *Leaves of Grass*, luckily buying an edition that featured the original 1855 text, I was floored by this poet who just seemed to be…everything. There was an *unleashing* in Whitman that felt entirely original and world-making, as if this were the first and last poet who really mattered. The poet pictured on the frontispiece of the 1855 *Leaves* seemed to believe this, standing there, fist on his hip and hat cocked, with such swagger, opposite only the title of his book in big letters and the simple "Brooklyn, New York: 1855" beneath that. This was the original Brooklyn badass, self-publishing his first book out of the Rome Bros. print shop on Old Fulton Street *without his name on the title page*, as if the reader should know who he was already.

Something in this swagger linked the poets I felt most inspired by as I got deeper into poetry; perhaps there was something natively *Brooklyn* in this, although I wasn't conscious of it at the time. Epic ambition, a wild, outlaw attitude, a give-no-fucks daring that wagered everything on the capacity of the self—these became my Brooklyn poet. Vladimir Mayakovsky, whom I discovered in grad school in Houston, brought me back to Brooklyn as he rolled out across the Bridge in his glorious homage, boasting that if "the end of the world / befall— / and chaos / smash our planet / to bits…from this bridge, / a geologist of the centuries" could "succeed / in recreating / our contemporary world." Everything was here for the Russian Futurist poet, as it was for Crane, and Whitman before them; here is where the unshackled, voyaging self could find the right magnitude. And when I heard Mos Def for the first time, I felt as if that voyager poet had been reborn in hip hop, arising like a new sun god in Brooklyn to usher in the twenty-first century:

> I'm reaching a height that you said cannot be
> I'm bringing a light which you said we can't see
> Saw the new day comin', it looked just like me
> Sun burst through the clouds, my photo ID

I see these same qualities in the 170 poets collected in this anthology, the first devoted to celebrating Brooklyn's contemporary poetry scene. As the country slouches towards bedlam, poets like these are ready to snap us to attention. Here is that same self-reliant hustle, summoned in the service of community building: look at all the founders of literary orgs, journals, and presses in this roster, from Out of the Binders' Leigh Stein to Berl's Brooklyn Poetry Shop's Farrah Field & Jared White to Oye Group's Modesto "Flako" Jimenez to *Yes, Poetry*'s Joanna C. Valente to Ugly Duckling's Matvei Yankelevich. Here is that same middle finger to the law, from Lemon Andersen,

> You want to arrest me,
> arrest me for being honest

Marina Blitshteyn,

> what good's the hand without the chance of a fist?

and Elisabet Velasquez:

> I don't know how to talk without sounding like
> revolution.

Even a Brooklyn baby is pugnacious, as imagined by Abigail Welhouse:

> I will light fires in the garden.
> Fuck plants. Long live babies.

And here is that same epic fury unleashed in a multiplicity of ways, most impressively by the women in the anthology, from Emily Skillings imagining herself extravagantly breastfeeding in public, feeding a lover and friend "as much milk / as they wanted, / one on each side, / more than a baby / could take," to Natalie Eilbert defiantly declaring her intentions to "eat the whole avocado, publish its fat on my tissue" and "spill champagne in the lap of my dysmorphia," to Velasquez channeling Crane in rewriting how gentrifiers read her stretch marks:

> these new art galleries on the block wanna
> call my stretch marks abstract, when in reality they are the strings of a harp,
> the tag name of God.

We see this epic impulse driving Sophia Le Fraga's "monuwomental" "Feminlist" of words replacing "man"/"men" with "woman"/"women"; in the "womanic" (as Le Fraga might say) cataloguing of the ridiculous things men say in Christine Larusso's "Cento of Past Lovers"; and in Morgan Parker's "Matt":

> For all intents and purposes and because the rule applies more often than it doesn't, every white man or boy who has entered and fallen away from my particular moderate life has been called Matt. Not Dan. Rarely Ben. Never Matthew. Matt smokes unfiltered Pall Malls because Kurt Vonnegut did.... Matt's in love with someone else but I can tell he's still interested in me. Matt and his girlfriend aren't really together. Matt doesn't have a condom so we can't. Matt also doesn't have a condom so we can't.

There is no one kind of Brooklyn poet, of course. This is what you learn here—quickly. To be here is to be jostled, and ultimately edified and strengthened, by difference, met by what Whitman beautifully called the "certainty of others, the life, love, sight, hearing of others." You have to respect that, enthralled as you might be by the "glories" of your own "smallest sights and hearings." If what drew me first to Brooklyn was the myth of the singular self, what I came to value more deeply was how that self could be "disintegrated"—to use Whitman's curious word—by the borough's more powerful, churning diversity, its endless crossings of other selves. And this disintegration did not feel annihilating but augmenting; you were disintegrated "yet part of the scheme," as Whitman says, the "simple, compact, well-join'd scheme," or what we might paraphrase as everyone and everything in all their differences unified in "reality." Or what Timothy Donnelly describes as "the earth itself, with the added weight of all the living on it." The "added weight" of all those differences might feel painful, but, as Parker asserts, it is a pain you absorb because it is creative:

> I knew what it meant to be wrong and woman.
> When I walk into the world and know
> I am a black girl, I understand
> I am a costume. I know the rules.
> I like the pain because it makes me.

This is why a poet would be "crazy" enough to move here; Brooklyn might hurt but it *lives*. Living here you are, as Lonely Christopher puts it in his hymn to Brooklyn, "just another crazy person quietly trying to choose life," praying to the borough:

> ravage me with bright fulfillment, when I nest in your sweaty arms
> grasp my throat and tell me this is how you leave me alone

A poet might leave at some point, but will "always come back here," as Mervyn Taylor says in "The Center of the World," to

> review things from this vantage point,
> the confluence of people and lives after deliveries
> are dropped off early in the morning by trucks
> rambling through this intersection of the world.

That extraordinary "confluence of people and lives" is the borough's true blessing, what breaks down and bolsters you, Whitman's "impalpable sustenance." I love the feeling in Brooklyn that I am constantly breaking ground because the I itself is a constantly breaking ground. Perhaps this feeling is behind the popular misconception that the original Dutch name for the borough, "Breukelen," is Dutch for "broken land"; it is not, but the myth matches the spirit of the place.

When I first moved here, I thought I knew all the poets—I thought poetry was a small world, as I often hear poets say. But looking through this table of contents, I'm struck by how few of the poets I knew when I founded

Brooklyn Poets in May of 2012—less than 20%. In other words, I didn't know shit; but as Joanna Fuhrman quips in "Brorealism," "none of us knows shit and that is the shit." The overwhelming majority of the poets here I've met while working for Brooklyn Poets over the past five years, curating and attending readings, organizing and teaching workshops, hosting our annual retreat, publishing our "Poet of the Week" feature online, emceeing the Brooklyn Poets Yawp, our monthly workshop and open mic, and teaming up with co-editor Joe Pan to put together this book, reading open submissions and learning of the many poets he knew from running Brooklyn Arts Press. This is partly the reason we wanted to publish an anthology—to meet other poets, both on the page and in person, breaking ground, breaking boundaries.

I worried when I started our "Poet of the Week" feature that we'd eventually run out of poets, a concern I now find laughable. And not because there are too many poets in Brooklyn, as the cynical among us like to think, but because there are so many good poets we have yet to read, including those who have not yet discovered that they *are* poets. The poets in this anthology I'm most proud of are those I've met through our workshops and the Yawp who have just started writing poems or returned to poetry after many years, poets who stand shoulder-to-shoulder with United States and Brooklyn Poets Laureate, Pulitzer Prize winners, and all the other big pimpin' names: Julie Hart, Patti Greenberg, Betsy Guttmacher, Dell Lemmon, Laura Plaster, Chris Roberts, Arthur Russell, Candace Williams, stand up! And here's a shout-out to those poets we may have missed or overlooked, whose work may appear in the next edition of this book, because this isn't a fully representative or definitive anthology—the very nature of this place makes that notion impossible. This book, already much thicker with poets and poems than we'd originally intended, is just a slim sampling, especially as we limited poets to a maximum of three poems (so we could include more poets). We intend this to be the first volume of a series, whose subsequent volumes will reflect the ongoing evolution of Brooklyn poets and poetry, including the "hundreds and hundreds" who will cross here "years hence," as Whitman would say. We look forward to the certainty of those others.

BROOKLYN AS A BOTTOMLESS CUP

JOE PAN

Lately I've been haunted by disembodied lines, little phrases that bubble up unexpectedly and which my mind keeps playing over. Crossing the street, I'm arrested mid-step by snippets of text, or find myself troubled by some lingering musical pairing of words at a checkout counter, wondering where they came from. They aren't of the usual kind my brain snatches from social media or my daily diet of alarming news articles, the raised warnings of a nation in crisis, but feel instead informed by a noticeably conscious effort toward subtlety and interiority, a probing inquiry into language, or some crucial turn of phrase articulating one's experience. After a few moments I'll realize it arrived from a poem in this anthology, some errant bit of wordplay I've carried with me into the city, like this line from Greg Fuchs:

My poem here on the empty black line of your mind

This intro came to me similarly piecemeal, as paragraphs and lines jotted down to remind myself what not to forget. Jason Koo and I decided the best way to tackle any sort of introductory essay was to write separate ones, so we could keep them personal and avoid treating Brooklyn as some monolithic subject; besides, the poems herein do a much better job of approaching the borough independently or ignoring it completely to tease out and define their own relationships and interests. And yet each time I sat down to write out what compelled me to co-edit and co-publish this book, a new wrenching event occurred in our nation's politics, forcing me to reconsider my work in certain aspects more broadly. Soon the personal was merging with these political concerns and a greater sense of Brooklyn's history, and where this book was arriving in that continuum. An earlier version of my introduction began: *Brooklyn is a nation of immigrants.* Another began: *I spent a lot of time in Manny's Pizza on 5th and 5th in Park Slope when I first arrived in Brooklyn in 2003. Like many mom & pop shops, it was soon shuttered due to rising rent costs.* And another: *No writing is apolitical.* And yet another: *I remember hearing about Brooklyn as a young kid growing up in the backwater pinelands of central Florida. It was this mythical land of b-boys and graffitied skateparks constructed under overpasses, a city of musicians and writers and gangs, and the poor, like me. It was emblematic of an America larger than my own, chock full of history. It had the Dodgers. The subway. Bagels. That big bridge. Coney Island's monopoly on grease fires and mermaids. The shipyards. That old cemetery. The stal-*

wart brownstones. The basketball courts. MTV and Tina Turner under the bridge, singing "What's Love Got to Do with It?" Kids running through the fanning arcs of open fire hydrants and shoes twisting overhead by their strings.

> We're at fucking Cooney Eyeland now not that fancy fuckin abandoned lake inna fuckin Berkshires dontcha wanna be the virgin mother fer me people fallin in love hey Duke what the fuck man getthefuckouttahere dat's my girlfrien's birdsnest
>
> —Bernadette Mayer

I kept rewriting, managing little scraps of info I'd jot down as I sometimes do when creating a poem, with the faith they'd eventually coagulate into some rudimentary form I could later refine in editing. I found myself scribbling at odd times, in odd places—in a van filled with protest signs en route to the Women's March in Washington, DC; in cafés and diners in Manhattan; a few hours before dawn on a hotel bed thinking back to the candlelight vigil I'd attended earlier that night behind the White House, wondering if all the writers who had attended the AWP conference were quickly making major changes to their work to reflect the changing world.

> I was a sacrificial smile burning off
> lamb's fat after midnight.
>
> —Rachel Eliza Griffiths

But I understood, foremost, and happily, that these anthologized poems would forever speak best for themselves, and in ways I could not hope to summarize; that my introduction would be merely one of a multiplicity of forthcoming gestures used to frame the experience of reading them. As one of my own gestures, I felt the need to address, at the outset, the time in which they are being published, which is an uncertain time, where aspects of our democracy are being challenged and laws rewritten and fights waged in the courts and even in our homes, among family and close friends. And all this arriving on the heels of an era marked by rising tensions, hate crimes, and violence in our streets.

> what unarmed boys down on bruised knees?
> what mad blue suits?
> *what men or gods are these?*
> *what mad pursuit?*
> [...]
> whose bloodied hands shall stain the earth?
> what eye for what eye shall suffice?
> *who are these coming to the sacrifice?*
>
> —t'ai freedom ford

It takes tremendous force
To weaken a building
And turn bricks into rubble

But it doesn't take long

—Edward Hirsch

And so—undeterred but no less certain—I went back into the book, into the poems, and listened to the voices, and ultimately chose an introduction that celebrates memory while acknowledging uncertainty. In this way poetry is a lovely affliction: by reading we become hosts to poetry, to the deeply engaged and aestheticized language presented to us, fraught as it can be with urgency and tension. And by taking these words into ourselves, perhaps some part of us becomes changed by them, we who are ourselves composed of many selves in private consultation, reacting to the world.

If I am a mouth,
let there be a chorus of raucous tongues
[...]
If I could multiply myself
I couldn't be any more lonely.

—Tina Chang

In part by rising unexpectedly through one's body with the imprint of someone else's imagination, one of the things great poetry does is shock us. It demands our attention and, in the intimacy and immediacy of reading, asks us to judge, to test our knowledge and experience against these new examples, and mitigate the friction. And perhaps cut free some old biases, or call the work out for its own. When I'm reading poetry I'm hopeful, not just that a poem might be a great one, but that it might challenge me, might undermine my sense of the expected, stir up empathy, or drop me down a well of my own memory, faults, and insecurities. Poetry excites differences, and it baffles, in the way a good argument or unexpected beauty baffles.

My name seems mysterious to me,

Is yours mysterious to you?

—Ana Božičević

So I was very hopeful—ecstatic, even—to embark upon this project with Jason in December of 2014, stemming from a shared desire to seek out and present a broader representation of the poetry being written in Brooklyn today. It was interesting to discover personally what forms and methods local poets were using to investigate and critique contemporary culture, in what ways they were choosing to express their ideas, and where exactly they were locating their emotional and psychological and musical imperatives. Also,

Brooklyn is my home, and part of me simply wanted to hear and enjoy the voices of my talented neighbors. I've personally found few greater examples in my travels of closer bonds between unlike individuals than those being forged just beyond my doorstep, few greater confluences of people in the world, with their exceptional beliefs and differing religions and ideas and prejudices, living so closely, so entirely reliant on one other, and offering each such courtesy, as to render them something akin to common-law siblings. Maybe it's just close quarters in a shared economy that allows for this beautiful something that I'd wager is culturally stickier than tolerance and more meaningful than acceptance; it's the kind of thing one experiences as an active participant in the lives of many others. Brooklyn's no heaven, but there's no arguing that it's got a whole lotta love in its heart.

When we reach the other world
We will all be hippies

—Dorothea Lasky

Speaking of community, to hear some people discuss it, the Brooklyn poetry scene is just one big community, but I've never found that to be the case. Instead it's composed of many different communities, some of which overlap, but many that operate independently, and so partly this collection was us familiarizing ourselves with writers both within and outside our immediate purview. Jason Koo's position as chief architect of Brooklyn Poets made things a bit easier, as his workshops, classes, readings, and open mics draw diverse crowds, from working-class autodidacts and MFA-ers to bar patrons at 61 Local who wander over to see what all the fuss is about. But to generate a true consensus or claim a perfect overview of poets working in Brooklyn today is a task both impossible and unverifiable—we work with blind spots, which we try to remedy, and find ourselves bring introduced to the work of new or unfamiliar Brooklyn poets every day. Which is why we decided early on that this collection should be the first of however many subsequent volumes, to attempt to account for those we've overlooked or who missed the call for submissions or didn't have any work available at the time, and to better chart the enormity of poets currently living in Brooklyn and the new ones coming in every day. Also, a reader may notice going through the bios that some poets have since moved away—to Maine, LA, Baltimore, Kentucky, or Rhode Island to become that state's poet laureate (congrats, Tina Cane!). For reasons economical and personal, Brooklyn has a high turnover rate. Many poets we hoped to include moved on, or hopped over to another borough. Our criteria for inclusion in this book was that a writer needed to reside in Brooklyn currently or have significant claim to the place, having been born or raised here, or having lived here for a significant amount of time in the past. Philip Levine is the only poet we include posthumously, as he was alive when this anthology was conceived, and because Jason and I and others here are big fans of the work of the former Brooklyn Heights resident and it just didn't seem right not to have him represented in these pages. In the end, we've gathered together a group of poets that includes Pulitzer Prize winners, authors with several books, and emerging talents, some for whom this is an early publication in a hopefully storied career.

> Brooklyn
> is covered in little
> pieces of paper
>
> —Matthew Rohrer

It's worth mentioning that when we put out the submission call, we didn't specifically ask for work relating to Brooklyn, but many sent us poems that did. Lucky us—I welcome any chance to walk the different neighborhoods under someone else's care, to get peripatetic on an East River promenade, or traffic underground with the multitudes as the G train squeals into a turn, or gaze out a dark window into the cold night and sense a lover's fear of love escaping him while his lover sleeps. Or find myself indoors, just beyond view of the beach where supposed whales are breaching the rough ocean, confronted by an intensely private moment, as in this poem by Arthur Russell, where a father on his deathbed asks something fragile and deeply human from his son:

> The next week, he said, "I asked mother to shake me like a baby. She said no.
> Embarrassed."
> Then I mounted the bed, found his shoulder blades, and did it again,
>
> strange massage for the places that his heart had ceased to serve, and this time
> he moaned loudly and shivered and dropped into a thick, robust, snoring sleep

Here we are, in various states of disrepair, needing each other; it's what some of us write from and out toward, these toothy caught-upon intensities. Finding inspiration in this city and its people is a moderately simple task—walk outside and you're confronted by a million different stories, forms, connections. The saturation can at times feel overwhelming. In the loneliest moments one is rendered faceless, claustrophobic, packed-in, perpetually underfunded. Conversely, the sheer energy of the streets can invigorate, sending you back fresh and renewed into the bustle and flow. And yet, as the new buildings rise along the waterfront, as old neighborhoods shift their identities and a new kind of metropolis finds its footing, and despite the inconsistencies and competing realities of its residents, Brooklyn somehow never stops being Brooklyn. I could talk about the abnormal density in the quality of light falling on brownstones in Park Slope in the late afternoon, and what I would be doing is adding to the myth of a place already steeped in it. There's a company that sells dirt from McCarren Park to people online who want a test tube of Brooklyn on their bookshelves, which I feel speaks to some larger stature of the borough in the collective imagination. But in speaking only of these things we can lose the reality of the place. Like anywhere, its people range from welcoming, warm, and gregarious to blithe, insouciant, and downright shitty, and everything in between. More importantly, the larger problems besetting our nation find their corollaries and worst examples here as well:

> I grow into a bright fleshy fruit.
> White bites: I stain the uniform.
> And I am thrown black type-
> face in a headline with no name.
>
> —Morgan Parker

> pigeons of every color but exactly one size
> mob, scatter, and reorganize
> to practice crash landings on the street
> that divides the black neighborhood from the white.
>
> —Vijay Seshadri

These are the realities we face, realities we must push back against daily in order to undermine and resolve them, not just as artists, but as members of our larger communities. Poetry, like any art form, is a product of the individual complicated by their time—poems speak to our values and identities, here in this second decade of a new millennium, to our fears, our injustices, our bodies, our loves and commitments, our various norms and transgressions, to our humor, to our unrests. Yet I expect a reader twenty years down the road will find that these poems speak to them as well, because although a poem is formed in one era, its broader investment is in humanity and language, and those concerns over time probably won't vanish, but more likely deepen.

> Perhaps it is natural to be giddy
> and full of dread. By giddy, I mean full
> of agitated wonder, like maybe
> I can really get things done
> because I'm organized and intelligent
> and super freaked about a lot of stuff.
>
> —Todd Colby

There's no effective way to summarize poems, thankfully—you have to go read them—and often while proofreading this anthology I'd instead find myself pulled back into the reading of the poems in full, revisiting some sense of mystery or wonder in them. The comedic ones have a special place in my heart, especially when things get bad in the news and I go looking for a pick-me-up cocktail and find something like Joanna Fuhrman's surreal, astutely funny, and deadly accurate take on bro culture:

They say inside each bro is a different
identical bro, and inside that bro is the chicken
that laid the egg that started the world,
but dude, where's your magnetic pocket knife,
your heliotropic brain extensions made
for the afterlife, you know, your poetry?

Which is different but no less effective than when Emily Skillings asks the kind of possibly revealing, possibly ironic question one might discover in one's Facebook feed:

I've always
really wanted
to publicly breastfeed
something. Ideas?

Or Sheila Maldonado's excruciatingly slow grind of the auger driven into a frenemy:

I am so jealous of how poor you are
of how you are poor
your particular stilo pobre
The way you put no cash and
no money together is uncanny

Lines that push into our sore and tender spots tend to stay with me, too, and this book is full of wonderful examples. They may take the form of open defiance against the habit of accepting received knowledge without question, or present an attempt to mitigate the very non-neutral "neutral zones" between one person and the next, the charged spaces that define othering. Sometimes a line will arrive with a particular rush of energy, fully encapsulating the immediacy of a situation, and like a shout in a small room will define through sound the boundaries of that room, while also giving us a sense of its inhabitants' histories:

"Mijo, your father is coming home soon. Hide your heels."

—Christopher Soto

We need poems that venture unshielded into our truths, our natures, unveiling wounds, charting the gray and complicated and undeveloped spaces. It took me three years before I could write a poem about the time I sat trying to keep a trapped, dying poet awake on a subway platform after he'd been hit by a train. I wrote and published a short article about the occurrence a week later, replete with facts and emotional intensity, but had to wait a good while and let things percolate and settle before I could pursue that kind of humility and pain in any poetic fashion. Same for writing about the homeless folks

I've met here in New York while handing out sleeping bags with Brooklyn Artists Helping. I'm completely emptied by the emotional strength left on the page by some of the poems in this anthology, and have to take a minute to reorganize myself back into the present, because one can sense the poet coming to terms with each part of the poem in its construction. Take for example this passage from Dell Lemmon's poem about sculptor Robert Gober, striking at the intersection of sexuality, art, mortality, and politics:

> and then those damn sinks that I didn't understand or maybe I didn't *want* to understand them because
>
> they are so fucking central to what I am saying. Because they are completely emblematic of that time / when so many people died / so young / from a disease / that nobody understood / and it didn't matter how many times / you washed your hands / in those damn sinks /

And I do realize the effect of poetry is personal, needing no justification, but that language is historical and political, and sometimes emotionally reliant on how we identify certain situations with our own experiences and empathy. My aunt died from complications of HIV—this informs my reading. But I'm also aware of and moved by the technical breakdown of the speaker's voice here, formally, how up to this point it's been annoyed with being unable to understand the basic governing concept behind these Robert Gober sink sculptures, and then is suddenly overwhelmed with understanding, a catalyst that immediately powers the voice running through a series of enjambments, these normally invisible rules effectively governing how things should end, and into a cathartic wealth of impotent fury and purging and pain. That poetry is an exceptional space for a variety of formal experiences like this to occur, and that each poem must define this space unto itself, is undeniable, and wonderful, and a reason I return to this particular art form again and again. Because rarely will you find answers and questions and mysteries in such collusion, in a place where one truth can be undermined by another truth.

> For my own strength would never suffice unaided by strength out of dark
>
> A rock, I mean, has content
>
> —Anselm Berrigan

For these very reasons, I became a poet. Started a press. And read through a bunch of poems with my buddy Jason Koo to put before you this first installment of the *Brooklyn Poets Anthology*. I can't begin to imagine what the world will look like when the next incarnation of this anthology hits the stands, but I'm certain the voices of some of these poets will be among those making waves: revealing, pushing, transgressing.

> One of two things will happen:
> our avatar will live or it never
> was.
>
> —Rachel J. Bennett

I want to thank all the poets in this anthology for giving me clarity, hope, joy; thank you for your compassion, your ingenuity, your investigations, your playfulness, your stamina.

> you are more than
>   a reflection of America
>
> —Uche Nduka

I am grateful for the sheer density of this object, for the many pages I get to return to, for these poems offering up views into so many worlds and charged language spaces. This is a gift.

> The it of love was on my mind.
>
> —Wendy Xu

And thank you, reader, for making the time to engage with their work. I hope you find some favorites here, and share them with those you think would enjoy them too. I hope you crack the spine of this book in quarters. And I wish the poets among you the very best with your own work; I can't wait to read the important poems that arise from this time we now live in.

KIM ADDONIZIO

Invisible Signals

I like it when I forget about time with its cleaning rag
and the drunken gods standing ready with their fly swatters
while I hide in the curtains. I like thinking about the friends I miss,
one with her twenty-four hour sobriety chip,
one making pozole while her dog
frets in its cage in the kitchen, one helping her sister drag
the oxygen tank to the bathroom. One is preparing her lecture
on the present moment, not mentioning me but here I am,
or was, watching this slut of a river smear kisses all over
east Manhattan, letting the ferries slide under her dress,
her face lit up and flushed. I like to think of my friends
imagining me so we're all together in one big mental cloud
passing between the river and outer space. Here we are
not dissolving but dropping our shadows like darkening
handkerchiefs on the water. One crying by a lake,
one rehabbing her knee for further surgery. One
pulling a beer from the fridge, holding it, deciding.
One calling the funeral home, then taking up
the guitar, the first tentative chord floating out,
hanging suspended in the air.

Seasonal Affective Disorder

Whoever came up with the acronym must have been happy
to think of everyone in winter walking around
saying "I have SAD" instead of "This time of year,
when the light leaves early and intimations of colder
hours settle over the houses like the great oppressive
oily scutes of a dragon's belly, I feel, I don't know,
a sense of ennui, a listlessness or lassitude
but more than that a definite undertow of dread
spreading over the waters of my already not-
exactly-sunny-to-begin-with-soul, if one can even
speak of the soul anymore, which is part of the problem,

isn't it, I mean, how do I even know if I have one,
given that I'm essentially a secular humanist and missing
whatever constellation or holy Smurf guides people
through their lives, Jesus or Muhammad and then
either Muhammad's son or second in command
depending on who you thought was the true
successor, which is only one of the problems still being
worked out by wars and car bombings just
as similar problems were solved in earlier times by flambéing
people in public after rack-induced confessions, and if
there's no immortal soul that's soon (too soon if you
ask me) to be either whirled up to heaven
like a cow shining in a tornado or else hauled screaming
into the underworld like a pig to a scalding tank,
that is, if we just, you know, stop, the filament worn out
or shooting through the glass and exploding the bulb
but either way, done, done for, pure nothing, the socket empty
for long enough to hear some prayers or poems and then
another little light bulb's screwed into place with
songs and lullabies and eventually loud music and drugs
which maybe I should be taking to overcome this thing
I hardly know how to describe, and which hardly anyone
wants to hear about since who can think too long
about such matters before all they want
is a drink or quiet place to curl up or TV to turn on
along with every light in the house," and when your lover
(if you are lucky enough to have one even if you sometimes
feel bored and stifled by him/her or that maybe you could have
done better especially in terms of having more sex
money complex conversations a heavier plinth
for your nobly woeful statue) asks *What's wrong*
you can forget all this and simply say "I have SAD"
since everyone knows that diagnosis is the first step
though on which stair or ladder is better left unmentioned
since they lead either way, but are best traveled
with someone steadying the rungs or waiting at the top
or bottom with a candle, a word, a cup of something hot
and not too bitter, that you can drink down, and proclaim
good.

The Givens

Someone will bump into you and not apologize, someone will wear
the wrong dress to the party, another lurch drunk into the table
of cheeses and pastries at the memorial service, someone will tell you
she's sorry it's out of her hands as though everything isn't already.
One day the toilet will mysteriously detach its little chain
from its rubber thingie and refuse to flush, in the throes
of whatever existential crisis toilets experience after so much human
waste, so many tampons it wasn't supposed to swallow, so many pills
washed down because someone in a fit of sobriety tossed them in, though later
regretted it but too late, they're gone, someone kneeling to empty
a meal, a bottle of wine, too many mango-cucumber-vodka cocktails made
from a recipe by Martha Stewart. Someone will have seen Martha Stewart
in a restaurant, surrounded by admirers. Sinners
will order quail, world leaders stab their forks into small countries
to hold them still for their serrated knives. Ben Franklin said
nothing is certain but death and taxes and he was wrong
about the taxes but then again, right about the impermanency
of the Constitution. No one will come to your door to give you a stack
of bills imprinted with Ben Franklin's face, but a Jehovah's Witness
will find you one day to tell you there is no Hell and that the souls
of the wicked will be annihilated. Someone will love you but not enough,
someone else send gift-wrapped pheromones to your vomeronasal organ
which will promptly destroy them like bugs in a zapper. These are but a few
of the many givens, and it's tempting to boil them down to just two
like Franklin did but I prefer Duchamp's "*Étant donnés*,"—1. The Waterfall,
2. The Illuminating Gas, water and light, as it was when God began
to pronounce those words in his marble bathroom but given how it's all
gone since then he probably should have skipped the part where clay
sits up and rubs its eyes, looking for something to fuck or kill.
The rain, the lightning. The river town, the fireworks off the dock.
Someone will run through a lawn sprinkler, someone else open a hydrant.
Someone will pull you from the fire, someone else wrap you in flames.

Kim Addonizio is the author of a dozen books of poetry, fiction, and nonfiction. Her latest are a memoir-in-essays, *Bukowski in a Sundress: Confessions from a Writing Life* (Penguin), and a poetry collection, *Mortal Trash* (W. W. Norton). She recently resided in lower Manhattan and Williamsburg, and now lives in Oakland, CA. She is online at www.kimaddonizio.com. "The Givens," "Invisible Signals," and "Seasonal Affective Disorder" are from *Mortal Trash*.

HALA ALYAN

Salat

When I asked *regrets?* you could speak only of the cement rooftops
the woman you left for Arizona

who took thirty-two Ativans and drove herself to your father's house

You give what you give to reclaim it

*

The fog a necklace around the bridge

I am possessed as in possessed by the sound of checkpoint guards whistling
they lovetap the taxi's windshield

the joke of *how many Beirut girls does it take*

*

In Girona we climb marble stairs
to find an unwashed couple sleeping in the grass

Ramadan, baba, I fast for the plastic tarps, hypothermic infants, ebola winter,

my grandfathers' names—Salim, Mohammad—

*

For the afternoon tea, we gather in the elders' parlors,
kissing their fingertips

introducing ourselves hurriedly—somewhere, a film reel unspools—

ibn Fares, *bint* Hilal, we recognize ourselves by what we belong to

Asking for the Daughter

Because she stood palm first to the sky. A raindrop,
then a dozen more. Because she is climbing tombs

with those legs of fire, stone houses to lace the gray
cypress with sunlight. Because she eats fruit with

dirt and lime salt. Everywhere the mud blossoms.
Because she can name each of the wrecked temples.

Because moon. Because ruin. Because a woman
who knows war knows deliverance, her mouth a sea

of sharks trapped in coral. Because she broke
into the flooded shopping mall and played cello in

the wet atrium. There was no one inside.
Even the security guard pretended not to hear.

Hala Alyan is a Palestinian American clinical psychologist and author of three collections of poetry, the most of recent of which, *Hijra*, was selected as a winner of the 2015 Crab Orchard Series in Poetry and was published by Southern Illinois University Press in 2016. Alyan's debut novel is forthcoming from Houghton Mifflin in the spring of 2017.

LEMON ANDERSEN

Noose York

Waiting for a Crown Victoria
on the corner of Central & Putnam
in the Bushwick section of Old Medina
Waiting here on the corner
for a Crown Victoria which finally shows up
after running past a traffic light
without the thought of a fast child
crossing the street
chasing her mother's milk
grocery list in hand.

Pulling up to a hard stop
heavy-footed brake
The car doors unlock in a dominos spill.
The driver jumps out
points his finger and barks,
"What are you doing here,
got any drugs on you buddy?"

This is not the cab
I was waiting for,
not the Spanglish taxi man
who always tells me on my way to JFK
I could get more bang
for my dollar Americano
if I spend my money in DR.

"Static, static"

His partner
who jumps out of the passenger side
with a walkie-talkie chirping
is shaped like a radio DJ
Too many crack-of-dawn diners in his blood

He grips his pistol and also barks,
"Hey big guy, where were you coming from?"

The kids up the block
take their eyes off the moon
and I am center stage
under that same moon, luminous
against the storefront dry cleaner,
shoved toward the cold glass
by the hype man behind the badge
face pressed tough against the cold glass,
needle-and-thread neon sign rat-a-tat-tatting.

I stare at the Selena-shaped tailor sewing inside.
Wanting to speak, even if I stutter,
I still have to utter the words
to these officers
for those kids who were staring at the moon,
for their older brothers,
their uncles dragging their backaches
back from a prideful hard day's labor.

Wanting to speak for them with valor
capture for these blue bloods
the beautiful confidence
snatched every day on this corner
I pull out the heart to say,
"Yes sir, no..."

An empty can crooning,
"No sir, yes..."
The rhythmless words cut off by the rattlesnakes
these nerves cut short by the quotas
because history on this corner has proven
that collars have to be made
by the end of the month
and these backward numbers have nothing
in common with real suspects
real crimes
Like outta-town gun laws and Walmart shoppers.

I go over the speech in my head
"What are you going to arrest me for, officers?"
Shit, that's easy.
"Do I look suspicious by the trends I wear
for standing on the corner waiting for a cab?
On the corner of a street you don't own…"
Damn, too liberal.
"Sir, why do these men
only get stopped for being black,
for owning their brown skin?"
That is it! That's the stinger.

But just then
the radio DJ checks my chin and my pockets
while his partner
kicks my legs wide and to the side,
and I finally yell out,
"Do you even know who Israel Putnam was?!"

Intermission…

Do you know this corner was named after
an American revolutionary
who killed the last remaining wolf of
Connecticut in a town called Brooklyn?
You wouldn't know that, hype man,
cause you did not go to school
to research the beat of your streets
to uphold the law
That's right, this same corner
where your guns make me feel like
breathing air is a felony waiting to happen.

Is it because of the way we look?
How does this deep hooded sweater
I wear over my head
come with a license for you to kill
when I wear it to block out the frozen world
while the projects are overheated.
Maybe it's my sneakers
I bought them for running,

but if I run we all know what happens next.
It can't be the color of my skin
when you both look like distant cousins
If you go back far enough, aren't we all…

Then again maybe not,
cause in my family we were raised
not to point at people
especially at officers
cause they don't point back with their fingers.

You want to stop and frisk someone,
stop and frisk the mayor
cause his pockets
are low and his money is high
and the teachers are as broke as a joke.
You will get more out of his spare change
than what you can get
out of these rabbit ears right now.

You want to arrest somebody
go arrest that new neighbor across the street,
the one right there double-timing it
with the checkers-game flannel shirt
that could be mistaken for gang colors on me.

Arrest him
for not helping the *doña* next door
with her bags of empanada ingredients
up the stairs
cause he is too busy constructing,
plotting a blueprint plan
to open up a Vietnamese restaurant
run by Mexicans,
when Doña Margo been dodging hollow tips
right here,
on the corner of Central & Putnam
right here,
when your precinct wouldn't even drive
down this block thirty years ago.

You want to arrest me,
arrest me for being honest
cause I was lying before.
The words never came out,
never blossomed.... Never.
Too scared of this new city
pushing me out
Too many front-page posts
warning me
it will be my word against yours
The truth is that you know like I know
that a law like stop-and-frisk
is built to send
more Puerto Ricans to Orlando
Blacks to Camden
and the Dominicans
to Amish country, Pennsylvania
But they will be back when it's over.
Cause they gotta go home
We all gotta go home.

Andrew "Lemon" Andersen was born in 1975 in Brooklyn, New York. A spoken word poet and actor, Andersen is the author of the poetry collection *Straightrazor* (County of Kings Publishing, 2013) and the memoir *County of Kings* (County of Kings Publishing, 2009), which was adapted for the stage and produced by Spike Lee. Andersen has also been featured as a regular on *Russell Simmons Presents Def Poetry* and was an original cast member and writer of the Tony Award–winning *Russell Simmons Def Poetry Jam* on Broadway. Andersen lives in Brooklyn.

AMBER ATIYA

New York State Office of Temporary and Disability Assistance

SSI/FOOD STAMP BENEFITS APPLICATION

Name i'm ~~hungary~~ hungry
SS# what this iz?
Address southside a union square park
Phone# no

Are you/have you ever been a drug abuser? sometimez to stop the hunger
Have you ever been convicted of a felony? yea but i only stole cuz i wuz hungry

** Felony crimes are serious crimes that include burglary and murder. Felons lose many of their civil rights: the right to run for office, join the military, and vote can be taken away. Prospective employers have the right to inquire about any felony convictions. Many insurance companies will not insure convicted felons making it difficult for felons to find work.*

Are you working? no
What is your hourly wage/yearly income? no

Do you speak English as a second language? i'm hungry
If yes please list first language: xoxo

Please punctuate the following sentence:
According to *The Huffington Post* Ray Canterbury
a politician from West Virginia believes children
should work for their school lunch
(Your ability to punctuate this sentence will greatly
impact your eligibility for SSI/Food Stamps)

Are you Muslim? i'm hungry
Are you an ~~illegal alien~~ immigrant? i ain't from across no outta space borderz

Please solve the following equation:
$3f''(x) + 5xf(x) = 11$
(Your ability to solve this equation will greatly impact your eligibility for SSI/Food Stamps)

Have you ever been diagnosed with a physical disability/psychological disorder? yea

check all that apply:

AIDS/HIV ☑
Bipolar Disorder ☑
Cancer ☑
(please list type) i still got my left titty & it iz hungry
Chronic Heart Failure from hunger? ☑
Diabetes ☑
Dissociative Identity Disorder ☑
(please list the names of your multiple identities) florence, mary & diana
Epilepsy ☑
PTSD iz this post trama slave disorder? ☑
Schizophrenia ☑

Are you hungry? i'm hungry

Do you need food stamp benefits right away? i'm very hungry

x hungry____________________________________
signature

FOOD STAMP BENEFITS (FS) PENALTY WARNING
Anyone who is fleeing to avoid prosecution, custody or confinement for a **felony**, or who is violating a condition of probation or parole, is **not eligible** to receive Food Stamp Benefits. If you get more Food Stamp Benefits than you should have (**overpayment**), you must **pay them back**.

If your case is active, we will take back the amount of the overpayment from future Food Stamp Benefits that you get. If your case is closed, you may pay back the overpayment through any unused Food Stamp Benefits remaining in your account, **or you may pay cash**.

Amber Atiya is a multidisciplinary poet whose creative practice incorporates elements of performance, book arts, and visual arts. Her work has appeared in various journals and in the *Bettering American Poetry* anthology and is forthcoming in *Dismantled Almosts: A 21st Century Anthology of Female Poets*. She has received fellowships and residencies from Poets House and the Lower Manhattan Cultural Council. Her chapbook *the fierce bums of doo-wop* was published by Argos Books in 2014.

JENNIFER BARTLETT

from Autobiography/Anti-Autobiography

is it true that the crippled
are much closer to enlightenment

by the mere gesture of
getting through this world

            that longing
that want for silence

these bones as if birds
tiny things that at any moment

could take off in flight

Jennifer Bartlett is the author of *Derivative of the Moving Image*, *(a) lullaby without any music*, and *Autobiography/Anti-Autobiography*, and co-editor of *Beauty is a Verb: The New Poetry of Disability*. A Black Mountain College scholar, she is writing a biography on Larry Eigner.

RACHEL J. BENNETT

The Sims

In the virtual place
I've hatched without
a single lithium waste,
a single future sunk
off the coast of
Vladivostok, here's sim-
moth, simlung, simChrist-
as-epithet rounding
the iron gate of lion
to a California alien
roller-crossing as if
his banshee dog could
drag his reckoning, joyous
and like some amped
conqueror, back to Venice,
which in any case
is also treble-clef now, where
treble's the voice of
my virtual old woman asking
the difference between
Premium and Ritz in the
Associated aisle off
Knickerbocker, and I tell her
it's the buttery taste or
something about simplicity,
and she asks if I
remember how crackers
used to be, and I'm afraid
I do not answer her
the way I should, the question
here being whether I'm just
too young or have I
forgotten everything
important that's ever
happened to me, except perhaps,
at least for now, how I ate
a cling peach on the walk

home, if *cling* is the right
adjective when what I'm trying
to describe is the kind
of flesh my teeth
pull so easily away.

Level One

One of two things will happen:
our avatar will live or it never
was. In the second case,
here's snow falling on a field
of snow. I'm forgetting the way

the village we left looked before all
I had was the memory of it growing
more improbable. For one, the colors.
The muted palette somewhere between
kindness and deception, so much

monster blood turned to something
akin to an antique carpet's faded
roses. Then the music. Your
theme song and mine were not
interchangeable, and the records

turned to throwing-stars before
the tattered sails of my listening.
Turns out we heard the same thing
so differently. The programmers
worked all night to create these

illusions of proximity. Now
they draw you to me, but I'm not
here. When most alone, imagine
yourself in a montage of alone
others, hitting *start* repeatedly.

Rachel J. Bennett's chapbook *On Rand McNally's World* is available through dancing girl press. She grew up on the Illinois-Iowa border and lives in New York City. "Level One" first appeared in *Sixth Finch*, and "The Sims" first appeared in *Queen Mob's Teahouse*. Find poems and more at racheljbennett.net.

ANSELM BERRIGAN

Pictures for Private Devotion

What I thought was a headless bird was really a bodiless leg

The other day I killed ten thousand Philistines with the jawbone of a daffodil

There's no room in my life for a sign

I stepped inside a flying saucer and abducted an alien

It was a tedious experience

Left an opinion in another man's shirt that night

The voices I hear politely make space for each other

I took off the west and put on the slightly less west

Keeping a rendezvous with the passout

Mom shuts her eyes and sees pterodactyls

Neither keen naturalist nor general reader am I fine fringes and velvety pile

There is always an animal giving grateful thanks

For my own strength would never suffice unaided by strength out of dark

A rock, I mean, has content

I had never before seen blood in his hands except on the teeming seas

Wherever I go a host of wild and not so wild life tags on behind

A few degrees of tilt to make the view pretty

The forest owlet has disappeared from the habitat where it had always been rare

Three hundred bodies from the commune in the artificial lake

My confidants include the falling apart coat and the untied boot

With respect and love I got lost leaving your apartment

Suddenly lizards had feathers and I left my room and happily nothing

Fight the bar downstairs

To sneeze in a vacuum and fuck off at work

A pixel with meaning

Is it a mirage I want to reject or is something too painfully happening

A present of baffled weather and theoretical jealousy

I read all their works, I read all yours too

There will never be any more suspicion than there is now

I'll never have to breathe in you more than I do now

He woke up happy having never really slept

And borrowed a couple thou from the first available human

As a theory I was always on the verge

As a cheeseburger I was prepared

I began in a failed society

According to several private polls

I can occasionally unscrew something

This poem is a substitute for my arms

Texas never whispers

Accused by the landlord of taking unruly showers

The ATM machine asks "can you continue?"

Yes you can, because it's the only thing to do

As insignificant a dissolution as I could cherish

I apologize for being so mean in your dream

I heard voice-mail messages in my dream

Sweet pea speak to me

Then lies my house upon my nose

There's a softness to refusing all of you in yours and me in mine

My a purty outhouse

If it's explainable it can't be a miracle but I can't explain anything so
everything's a miracle

I blew the president I didn't inhale

Success is the lowest art

There are cameras in the branches but the trees are the dealers

---

Anselm Berrigan's books include *Come In Alone, Primitive State*, and *Zero Star Hotel*, from Edge Books, wherein "Pictures for Private Devotion" was originally published. It snuck its way into an issue of the *Germ*, too. Berrigan lived on Lorimer St. between Leonard and Devoe from 1996 until a soft eviction in 2000, and PPD was put together there in late 1998 in a domestic site-specific compositional fashion. Nothing was ever what it had been after that.

K.T. BILLEY

Drunk Tank

The only record of that astonishing
burlesque is the sonnet

we found on the floor, a trampled
sheet we tried to preserve

in simple syrup and steel-toed boots.
It started to fester

around happy hour—
a minor wound. A new island.

We built it a home
with our palsied will

to please: glass ceiling
windshield, boy short chamois.

We couldn't decide
if it was an aggressor

or a cabin, car or display
case. It didn't matter.

The louder the saws the later we stayed,
declaring ourselves sociology

students, spectators, friends
of the mastiff

plastered above the urinal—
our communal pet poster.

We appropriated that form too, its mutt
lang meter, and let people watch

as we dropped it into our ant farm
between our diet on the rocks

and skulls full of castles. I'll go standing
up instead of waiting—doesn't mean

I keep score. Note the leers, the lack of
sinks—men have nothing

to wash off their hands. The darts were only ever
a threat to ourselves—their kick-back

bruised only our own shoulders, but they had to
haul us in sometime. Now the hand doing this

paperwork is too pale to be trusted, chafing
at the loop in *public*. The charge is past

perfect: *Disorderly* don't mean squat,
the lipstick on my cheek is intentional.

It's called *lava*.

Haven't you seen a linebacker
with a wandering eye?

Call it cheekstick if it helps
wrap your mind around but see how

easy that was, and save some
tape for your wrists.

Pangea was not a meeting
of the minds, she was thirsty

work. There's someone in your corner
willing to truss up those knuckles.

You want to enter the fray
with tendons in place—why else

are you still reading this?
The human condition is looking

for trouble: turbidity is proof of life
in a lake. The cocktail of the future

calls for muddled coals so I packed
my fire poke cum stir stick

for a couple reasons. To make
a pass at self-fulfilled

prophecy. To fancy myself
an active ingredient: the chain

they pull to drench
the catwalk. A hope

in hell weeknight call
to arms. Wasn't Wednesday always

a dogfight of bloom, waiting to happen?
A blood transfusion meant to be total.

A baptism, but more.

K.T. Billey's debut collection, *Vulgar Mechanics,* is expected from Coach House Books in 2017. A bilingual edition of *Stormwarning*, Billey's translation of Icelandic poet Kristín Svava Tómasdóttir's *Stormviðvörun*, is forthcoming from Phoneme Media in 2017. An assistant editor for *Asymptote*, she translates from Icelandic and Spanish and also writes arts and culture essays.

EMILY BLAIR

I Love Soap Operas

and of all the characters on all the soaps
my favorite might be Paul from *As the World Turns.*
Paul never changes his mind and he's not afraid of anything,
not dental appointments or dinner dates
or being declared dead a third time.
When he gets a note from his nemesis
that says *Meet Me at Shadow Cliff*
Paul doesn't suggest a more public place.
He rushes right off.
Wouldn't it be good to be Paul?
If I were Paul, I would no longer waste time
googling rare diseases or asking myself if I should shift careers
and go back to school because the only course I'd be taking is
a collision course with destiny.
I wouldn't be nervous.
I would stand here on this lofty ledge
and get all up in your face
and when you turn away from me I'd talk to your back
pausing weirdly
after every statement
so my words sink in.
And I wouldn't wonder how and when to end
our conversation without being awkward,
in fact I'd be willing to let
I'll take you down with me
be my final words.
So even when I feel my fingers slipping
on crumbling rock
I won't rethink my strategy,
I'll plunge decisively into the cold water
and then pop up not knowing who I am
even after weeks of recuperation in a remote cabin
under the care of a mysterious nurse who tells me *don't try to talk*
and hides my wallet for reasons of her own so when I reappear in town
to watch my own memorial service from behind a pillar

it will be the first I've heard of all of my misdeeds,
but rather than take the time to reassess and set new life goals
I'll decide to do it all again,
and this time I'll take you down with me.

Emily Blair received a NYFA fellowship in poetry in 2014 and in fiction in 2006. She is the author of the chapbook *Idaville* (Booklyn, 2010) and her poetry has appeared in *Sixth Finch*, the *Mississippi Review*, and *WSQ*, among others.

MARINA BLITSHTEYN

pride

in a parking lot the odds were stacked against me
i lifted a limb off the dump tho, mama said with her help

folks came thru, tried to raise me on unleavened bread
it worked, i paid my dues, mama said with her help

what good's the hand without the chance of a fist?
mama said they all come up with hand-me-downs

turned her nose up at their gifts, a loan with a price tag
a martyr, she stood as tall as the slabs i stumbled on

at the ceremony a reprieve, my mother the rabbi
often even approving, louder she mimes with her mouth

eggs me to smile more, shoots darts of worry up the stage
before me the scroll's a blur, mama said we suffer

to undo our own mistakes, mama said we sacrifice
as jews, as women, first and foremost as the insecure

now in a field of needs i scan the crowd to see her
as telling as ever, i'm becoming her ball of knots

her little tics, her sitting in a cold room gnawing at her own skin
the trick is u pick a plot, dress it up with plastic flowers

then everything's perfect and everyone nods
i'd also turn down an offer of funds, act like i don't need it

just to see, just to milk that shrug a little longer
mama said the best is not to need people, never ask

love means never having to say ur hungry, just wait
a god will come on a life raft, or dangle a hand off a jet

and ask u if u need a lift, the joke goes u refuse
then shake ur fist at the sky saying lord why have u forsaken me

---

Marina Blitshteyn is the author of *Two Hunters*, forthcoming from Argos Books in 2017. Her chapbooks include *Nothing Personal* (Bone Bouquet Books) and *$kill$* (dancing girl press), from which the poem "pride" is taken. She works as an adjunct instructor of composition and innovative literature.

ANA BOŽIČEVIĆ

Awoke. Again

I wrote you a
Short story about a man who
Was dating a voice-over artist whose
Voice was the voice
Of subway announcements, so every time
He took the train he basked in her
And when they broke up it was
A swansong terrible
Terrible

I'm writing you a
Dreamer-for-hire ad: Too scared
To dream? I'll dream your dreams
For you, cheap nightly rates!
'Because they're your dreams,
I'm just having them!'

I
I write you a poem
Is it really so terrible to be alone
Would it be so bad to be
A junkie dominatrix
High off her voice in the evening choir
In this light even
My name seems mysterious to me,

Is yours mysterious to you?
Who's having all these loves

Who thinks only about sex and race,
Who doubts
Own reason when

Hemmed in by white lies
Like butterflies... Who's talking the talk

Who's walking in your dream?

Ana Božičević came from Croatia and lives in New York. She writes, sings, makes visual things sometimes, and teaches poetry at BHQFU. She is the author of *Stars of the Night Commute* and *Rise in the Fall,* winner of a 2014 Lambda Literary Award. A new book, *Joy of Missing Out,* is forthcoming from Birds, LLC. "Awoke. Again" appears in *JOMO.*

EMILY BRANDT

Experiments with Voice Encoder

There is a person speaking through the air
and the air is incapable of holding anything
or the air holds multiple dimensions
as in acid trip, as in nightwalk.

All the people stayed home today despite the beautiful weather

and I watched from the front door as the mailman
walked by, his letterbag encased in a metal rolling device
for convenience, because some part of the system loves him
and respects his knees and his shoulders.

After work I stop playing, I just go straight to work again

on my art my pretty pictures my sound recordings
and leaf rubbings. I put all of the homemade instruments
on display and will tour them soon enough. Soon enough.

I pay my dues to my union and do math. They make three million dollars

per month and I wonder where everything went wrong.
At work, a man does something mediocre and we throw a parade.
We release our discordant voices into static and electrified air.
We empty the bedpans of our future selves. We are widows.

I pulled on some leggings today as a means of survival

and traveled to the back porch or the patio or lanai. The plants
are still dead like planets of another dimension.
If a woman kills plants, it symbolizes abortion.

Anything a woman does is shit compared to man.

I said that through the Vocoder and now I feel much better.
The vibrations are messing with somebody's Pacemaker.

The vibrations are messing with somebody's head
and the resulting rash itches as much as it burns.

If I swallow my money in the morning and you lift up my arms

at night, silver dollars will spill from my mouth
and the cocktail waitress will bring us free drinks,
red ones like I got in Reno. I saw wild horses on a hill.
They ran onto the road and over my car and onto
a rainbow and then the sky opened. They ran in.

I filled the story into a form where it said *last name*

and my credit report came back perfect. Top ten
in the country of fish fries and angel tattoos.
An angel tattoo is often a symbol for abortion
so next time you see one on someone
you'll know what to ask.

Emily Brandt is the author of three chapbooks. She earned her MFA from New York University, where she facilitated the Veterans Writing Workshop. Emily is a co-founding editor of *No, Dear* and web acquisitions editor for VIDA. She lives and teaches in Brooklyn. Her poem "Experiments with Voice Encoder" first appeared in *Sink Review*.

LIBBY BURTON

First World

The West was an un-storied mound my mother rose out of. It was a backlit mountain
and cold stove at dawn my father rode toward in the beginning of his adult life

from a clapboard place called Ridgefield. Nineteen sixty-eight or nine, and her hair
was longer than the road to Flagstaff, her eyes brown as broken ground.

A train took them back east, and I was born under an organized sky in the arms of fences
and small birds. My sister came with pretty hands like orchard peaches and eyes

like passing through a forest toward home. In late light, I met a man but was unable
to tell him, I like you in sentences and on fire, knowing only to take off the words

like a blouse. Why did we enter the story like this? My mother couldn't articulate
the small coffin they laid the body of the neighbor girl inside. That is it. That will always

be it. How wrong to ask for the gift of a little grief. I'll say a cold prayer for the
knives whining in the drawer, for my sister's yellow head asleep at my feet instead.

I have seen the ruthlessness of skies cut open, the devastating nothing of some men,
and the sweet heavy brow of a few good ones. In the season of steam coating the air,

and of cracks rising in cups, I think my sister may be the only breathing thing formed
of wings. My mother and I, we have different types of ghosts. Out of the grand mouth

of the dirty kitchen sink in morning light, I see the loved world is not far away, and we
are more than a tiny stirring of strings. There is nothing less difficult than that. No secret

outside of town, no bruise-painted lip, no stained sheets to fold, to put away. Just the ache
of the tiniest gestures, the tanned calf of my father, the steely face of Flatirons, rising

to drink coffee at dawn. Born to a world of coin and book, our faces are broken by blue.
My sister eats the best of them like dust, while in my quiet mouth rests an open hand.

Libby Burton is a senior editor at Henry Holt, where she edits both fiction and nonfiction. Her authors include Melissa Broder, Amy Rose Spiegel, Greg Baxter, Alana Massey, and D. Watkins, among many others. Her poetry has appeared in the *Atlas Review*, *Denver Quarterly*, *Guernica*, *Juked*, *La Fovea*, *Meridian*, *North American Review*, *Painted Bride Quarterly*, and *Tin House*, among others. "First World" first appeared in *Meridian*. She lives in Brooklyn.

DENVER BUTSON

issues

the man who climbed the Brooklyn Bridge
who walked the highest cables
and swung hand-over-hand from one side
to the other who eluded ten cops with harnesses
and ropes a helicopter a boat below
with emergency crews and a backboard
who asked for a cigarette and a beer who swung
upside down with his knees hooked
around a cable and took a cigarette
from one cop's hand and smoked it laughing
and then flipped over and slid down fireman-style
one cable and upside down again around another
and skirted between the outstretched hands of two cops
and again and then again

who after two hours of this
with a crowd gathered on the pedestrian walkway
of the Manhattan Bridge and traffic stopped
in both directions on the Brooklyn Bridge
with all of us looking up from the Fulton Ferry landing
where Whitman wrote about us *the generations hence*
but probably couldn't have imagined
the cell phones and laptops all the exposed skin
and his words themselves cut out of the metal railing
between the defunct ferry landing and East River

who finally gave up gave over
to the embrace of one big-shouldered cop
and hugged him hard for a long time
as we started our applause from down below

was not an acrobat or a bridge worker
or a thrill seeker
as many of us with our feet on the ground believed
including one gnarled hardhat who said

if he ain't one of ours let's sign him up
but a "simple welder" the paper the next day said
who according to his mother *did very well*
at gymnastics in high school

whose bloody hands stained the cop's shirt
said when asked why he did what he did
I have issues

while we with issues but perhaps not issues enough
to become suddenly the best show in town
however briefly clapped and clapped
as if we wanted our hands bloodied like his
as the helicopter whisked itself away
and the backboard went back into the ambulance
and the boat slid under the bridge and out of sight

we clapped and clapped and then stopped clapping
and returned to our morning
and our ever so many mornings hence.

Denver Butson has published four books of poetry. His poems appear in Billy Collins's *Poetry 180*, on NPR's *Writer's Almanac*, and in anthologies edited by Collins, Garrison Keillor, and Agha Shahid Ali. The poem "issues" appears in his book *illegible address* (Luquer Street Press, 2004) and in the anthology *New America* (Autumn House Press, 2012). Butson frequently collaborates with musicians, visual artists, and actors/filmmakers. He has lived in Brooklyn since 1997.

NICOLE CALLIHAN

Diction

What would be the right word? he asks. I hold the question in my mouth like a hard candy, suck it 'til my tongue is raw. Yes, *what* would be the right word, or *why* or *how*, or *who* might be the right word, or *you*. Try *pomegranate*, *rain*, *rifle*. Listen, the only time I ever held a gun it was yours: I fired it into the dead of midnight sky. That's a lie. There was another afternoon when the sun was an arrowhead, and I couldn't stop shooting Cheerwine cans off a barbed wire fence. I keep thinking I'll die, but instead I wax my uncomely privates, heat up fish sticks, try to find the right words for things. I write words I don't mean, say words that are mean, catch my daughter writing words that aren't right. *We don't say* this *word*, I tell her, even though we do and have and will. In the dim of the kitchen, she starts ripping the paper in pieces and placing those pieces into her mouth. *What are you doing?* I ask. *Swallowing them*, she says. *Stop it*, I say, *you don't have to do that*, but she nods her head. Finally I join her, take a shred into my own mouth, taste it, work it with my weak jaw. These are our true and terrible words. Eat them.

Nicole Callihan is the author of *SuperLoop* (Sock Monkey Press, 2014) and two chapbooks: *A Study in Spring* (Rabbit Catastrophe, 2015) and *The Deeply Flawed Human* (Deadly Chaps, 2016). "Diction" first appeared in *SF&D*. Find her on the web at www.nicolecallihan.com.

TINA CANE

Sirens

I.

I've been meaning to tell you that the skin around her eyes was thin

with blue veins fanning out like ferns   that she was pale for a Puerto Rican

and that she spit and threw change at my feet as I waited to cross the street

to tell you that I wouldn't let her man take me for hot dogs at the *Second Avenue Deli*

or to *Jade Mountain* for pork fried rice   that I knew what a hat like that meant

to say   his diamond crucifix the way he swayed his coat   flicked sunflower seeds

from between his teeth   strutting behind the line of parked cars I've been meaning

to tell you that the parking lot on the corner was not always a dorm   that once I saw her

bloodied and on her back beside a car   that two kids laughed pulling rings off her fingers

as she squinted in the sun   that I put my backpack on both shoulders   readied my key

that I ran from the sound of the sirens

II.

To tell you my dad drove a cab for forty years   kept a red bean he got

from an Ethiopian guy in the back pocket of his Levi's to ward off hemorrhoids

that he wrote me notes throughout the night on the margins of his fare sheet   stuff

like "eat yogurt for osteoporosis"   that he listened to *Tosca* for another life in which

he didn't have his foot on any pedal   didn't ever have to chase a punkass kid to get his
money back then end up buying the kid a sandwich   to tell you that he was a Jewish guy
from Brooklyn *what the fuck* he'd pound the wheel   cut off cut short   another Brooklyn
fare   not going back there with no return trip over the bridge   to tell you that he drove
like a pro back when the medallion itself was a thing of beauty   deco-like   clicking
its nickel intervals with approximate precision   the weight of it enough to crush
just about anything

III.

I've been meaning to tell you that my mother and father once fought
for fifty hours straight in our basement apartment off Second Avenue
that the table fan was set to *oscillate* as they worked their way through
recriminations   cups of coffee   a carton of *Marlboros*   that my mother
tossed a day's worth of meals into her flashing wok at hasty intervals
as my father paced the room   been meaning to tell you that the girls
on the block scraped pavement in their platform shoes like weights just outside
our one gated window   that we often heard *Peaches* the transvestite weeping
about a Hasid john from Delancey Street or a guy from Staten Island who liked
to rip out her hair   meaning to tell you that they made the movie *Taxi Driver*
right around the corner the year before   that I thought my dad might have been in it
since he drove a cab   had also been an actor   was once a bartender down on Bleecker St.

that he said I was too young to see such a film and about *Saturday Night Fever*
my mother said *definitely not*

IV.

That there was a *NordicTrack* bought in 1996 still in its box
blocking the way to the coat rack on which my dad hung his *London Fog*
$3,000 in its pocket for me to collect as he had requested from his hospital
bed plus stacks of cash   from the safe deposit box   from under his mattress
and the *Polly-O Ricotta* container in the freezer   beside the *Edy's Light*
Ice Cream and empty ice tray been meaning to tell you there was $30,000
in my purse by the end of the day to tell you that I tried to buy a giant
stuffed peacock from a shop on Christopher St.   the day he died but
ended up lugging a duffel bag of twenties   to Greenwood Cemetery instead
to purchase a plot for him on the hill   I've been meaning to tell you that cash
is how a cabbie's daughter pays her father's bills to tell you there was a wall
of books by his bed   a broken shutter on a split hinge piles of newspaper
clippings to be filed per a system that didn't exist   that he left his hack license
on the bed-stand with the pocket knife we gave him   the carnelian ring
the paper birthday crown my children made   and made him wear buried
in plush animals   on the carpet in their room   that there was a rucksack
of photos and mementos   from his old friend Wallach   when my dad

cleared out his place but never had the wake   to tell you that he never

even opened the bag after humping it up the stairs   just talked to Wallach

in his head   every day till the end   about the girl in those photos

about articles he should have read

Tina Cane, Poet Laureate of Rhode Island, is a teacher, poet, translator, and the founder/director of Writers-in-the-Schools, RI. She received the 2016 Rhode Island State Council on the Arts Fellowship Merit Award in Poetry. Her poems have appeared in numerous journals and she is the author of *The Fifth Thought* (Other Painters Press), *Dear Elena: Letters for Elena Ferrante* (Skillman Avenue Press), and *Once More With Feeling* (Veliz Books). Born and raised in New York City, Tina lives in Rhode Island with her husband and their three children. Her poem "Sirens" first appeared in *Tupelo Quarterly* and appears in her collection *Once More with Feeling*.

TINA CHANG

Four Portraits

Self-styled as Kehinde Wiley's Napoleon Leading the Army over the Alps

I never dreamed myself to be any larger
than a horse. Perhaps this is strange,
my girl body in the body of a man
on a rapturous equestrian animal. I am
not like the others. This was the song I sang
since my birth, since I had a mouth
to sing it. So I said it for years until I believed
jewels fell out of my mouth. Oh son,
I believe the mighty shall come.
This is my only prayer. I shall be, for you,
the man in shadow until the steed I ride
throws me into the pasture of the everlasting.
I shall be a mother whose bright milk runs
with fever and anguished love, with a head
in my hands if the head shall equal justice.
I shall be a father too, glorious and eternal.
If this is blasphemy let me love the world
into fantastic horses, ride them to a distant country
where I drown in brocade, fragrant vine.
If I am captured, let my kingdom be laced
in mega gold. Let my cage be a godly frame.

Self-styled as Alexandria Smith's The Girl in Ribbons

If I am a girl in a traffic of legs,
let them be trees. If I am a mouth,
let there be a chorus of raucous tongues.
If I set sail, let it be along a tide of ribbons
ebbing toward the widest America.
Let there be hair, each strand running
along a road, braided, and rebraided
until what remains is glory. Each face

I wear leads to another face and within that
a sister. If I could multiply myself
I couldn't be any more lonely. If you look
carefully, there are many eyes gazing.
I wonder if all of this vigilance adds up
to kindness. I once saw a child on a train
sleeping. There was no guardian, no keeper
as she laid there breathing. If the eyes
are shut, what does our dreaming see?
The onlookers wondered where to place
the girl, wondered if they should wake
her or by waking her they would create
a space of abandon. Sometimes, my heart
is an alarm clock that wakes me to a startling
sound. Sometimes I rise in a museum
of wandering objects as the body imagines
itself in pieces, fitted together, migrating
with its lost parts in unison.

Self-styled as a Vanessa German 21st-Century Sculpture

If I had children, they would be cherubs,
each one with eyes cast up to their mother,
hair tied into cherries with sentinels for a crown.
I am the door, cast into light with my arms
outstretched, monsoon, sunrays.
Each dress made of discarded treasure
creates me heavenly. There is a charm
and it's a promise to shelter but also a field
of black diamonds. If we say evidence,
we mean what we can collect, not what
we can imagine. Each of us has burrowed
in our chests a circular mirror. Walk up
to the figure and find a reflection:
All the while you thought it was a throng
of people swarming in a living hive
though really it was one figure locked in stasis,
then you, emerging from a halo of fire.

Self-styled as a Kara Walker Silhouette, Woman Beneath a Woman

There will be a day when women will be clouds.
Each breath makes me a billow, worn like rain
spiraling out into a vision of winter. If history
teaches me anything, it will be about the vagaries
of burden. I can carry a vessel, a pitcher of water,
a bundle of ideas like sticks. I carry time like fire.
I hiccup and it's 2016 though the faces are the same:
Faces without faces and with different names.
If we could all be more like clouds. If I run,
the threat of a storm above slows me. If I lift
my arms, the rains spill down. If I bend,
my spine becomes a terrain on which a master
treads. Sometimes, I wish to unborn myself
from this weather. If I could walk out
from under this thunder there would be such air,
and my posture too could lift. If I unborn myself,
I'd give up my sisters too, my brothers
by the bridge, so I'll stay lifting this largeness
to live inside this cloud of kin.

Tina Chang, Brooklyn Poet Laureate, is the author of the poetry collections *Half-Lit Houses* (2004) and *Of Gods & Strangers* (2011). She is also co-editor of the Norton anthology *Language for a New Century: Contemporary Poetry from the Middle East, Asia, and Beyond.* Her poems have been published in periodicals such as *American Poet*, *McSweeney's*, the *New York Times*, and *Ploughshares*. She was a core member of the international writing faculty at the City University of Hong Kong, the first low-residency MFA program to be established in Asia, and she teaches poetry at Sarah Lawrence College.

CATHY LINH CHE

Pecha Kucha

after photographs in the Peabody Essex Museum

I once was a child who wore a star
on my forehead. I held my mother's hand
in a new country, the chaparral dry,
a landscape dusty and barren. I wore white
socks and brown-strapped sandals, imagined
Vietnam a country of belonging.

*

Then America was a heart-shaped
tattoo. My identity a checkbox.
My mother saying *thiên đàng*, my
father saying *sướng quá*. My country
a silver headdress against a red backdrop.

*

One wore a hand-me-down waistcoat,
the other a vest burst open. *Smile.*
Say cheese. But my older brother
could only part his lips. My younger
grinned into a future of silver coins
jangling like keys in his pocket.

*

My mother tucks flowers
into her hair, nature objects
of a funeral. This one
for Freddie Gray,
10,000 more for the dead
in Nepal. In the mirror
she is crowned by fragility.

*

My sister was born in Vietnam.
She died three hours later. I don't
know her name. My mother wears
a sackcloth dress in mourning.
My sister is another flower my mother
wears, this one pinned inside her dress,
its small white mouth suckling
at her breast.

*

A photographer strips a woman
of her top and sits her on a rock.
A garland interwoven with the long
metal shells of bullets hangs mid-breast,
as if she is a museum object,
donning war.

*

In a family of men, only one
has not threatened, choked,
or molested me in a bathroom.
My younger brother cried
elephant tears when chased
around the house by a terrifying
machine, a vacuum cleaner,
ghosts made audible.

*

A fight is a kind of dance.
My father advised my mother,
To marry me is to suffer.
Love called his bluff. It wasn't
a bluff, turns out. He asked,
You would leave me? She answered
emphatically, *Yes*, and for a while
he quietly changed.

*

To show scale, a human
stands in front of a boulder.
Magma fiery, then cooled,
then heated again in a desert
where a figure in all black
blends into the shadows, into
the absence of light.

*

San Francisco is a porthole
into human history. The structures
gutted, the residents pushed out.
A boomtown, a place
for the wealthy, venture capitalists,
programmers in gleaming condos
with glass facades.

*

In the bay, sailboats, a galleon,
boats of leisure. My parents
escaped in a smaller vessel.
My father hooked fishing lines
to the back. They ate rice
and fish over small lit canisters
of fuel.

*

Barely perceptible, the double
lives of couples. Parallel trains.
Say, one escape attempt became two.
Say, my mother, petrified, died at sea.
She and her garland of mourning.
Her black bonnet. My father's ghosted
uniform, his severe hands,
their tenderness like switchblades.

*

My mother's sister wished me
a happy birthday today. She told me,
Bring home a husband the next time
you visit. The one they loved I let go,
inauspiciously. Today he texted me happiness.
I am not the end of my maternal bloodline—
but I could be, in America.

*

Some days I imagine home
as a structure with thatched eaves.
Some days home is a craftsman
somewhere on the West Coast—
in the dusty hills of Highland Park,
in the polished damp of Seattle.

*

My mother sewed me a sail
and said, *Go into the wind.*
She like Penelope weaving,
unraveling, biding time. I
like Odysseus, bewitched
by the maddening call,
the wail.

*

Like a corona of light,
a feathered headdress signifies
flight and power.
What is history
but that which we make ourselves,
together, as birds.

*

At a distance, a boomtown
is just a series of structures.
Interior spaces with windows
through which we glimpse
our worlds. The sun on the sea
a light which burns onto old paper
an imprint.

*

My mother has removed the flowers
from her hair, placed them on a station wagon
for my wedding day. She has removed her
veil. It is a plastic sheet protecting
a rusting car on the streets of Salem,
or Baltimore. It is a vehicle I may never climb into,
though the remnants I will collect as pictures
in my human document.

Cathy Linh Che is the author of the poetry collection *Split* (Alice James Books, 2014), winner of the Kundiman Poetry Prize and the Norma Farber First Book Award from the Poetry Society of America.

KEN CHEN

Dramatic Monologue Against the Self

Hello, my name is Ken Chen. For my essay today, the organizers of this panel have procured a microphone named ____________. Although this microphone may resemble and is a person, it is I who would like to discuss essays and how essays permit us to become the microphones of others. I enjoy being a microphone because I enjoy hearing the thoughts of others. I believe the essay is a genre of performance, which is not voice, but the author's mind bending a thought like gravity influencing the curvature of light. We find ourselves bored by creative nonfiction, autobiography, and memoir, which forsake the personality of thought for the impersonality of narrative. We sit in the essay as in a room of normal talk, free from aesthetics, stripped until we are only selves, struggling to unhide the strangeness of our souls!—Well to be honest I don't know if I buy this. The way I see it, an essay makes you helpless, you're suffocated. It's one mind all the way down. And yes, if the goal of the essay is to televise cognition, then the essay has no room for discreteness, because the mind itself knows no walls. But it is this openness that makes essays difficult to write and exceptionally good items of luggage. We can snare the world into them. The great alternative novels, such as *Moby-Dick*, *Tristram Shandy*, and *In Search of Lost Time*, are hauls of essays, revealing an oblique characteristic of our experimental literature—its discursiveness. Consider the essaylike qualities of—and here he goes on to list a bunch of names, what a ridiculous namedropper! The essay, by virtue of being everywhere, never sequesters itself in one place. For this reason, however much the essay is our habit, the regional headquarters for our thinking, it is also a lawless form. It looks like he goes off on some weird tangent here about how he'd write literary criticism by conducting fake interviews. He would play the part of a buffoonish professor and improvise answers to questions his friend would ask by AOL Instant Messenger. These questions would guide the conversation towards certain topics, occasionally forcing Mr. Chen to explain certain weaknesses in his position, but the back-and-forth of the interview actually fried them—fried them? That must be a typo. Freed them. And if I were present, if I were truly and corporeally there, I would adjust my glasses and testify that the essay is our only medium still in love with subject matter, that it is a naïve art, that out of all our literary genres, it is our most popular and marginal, two adjectives that explain rather than contradict each other. Unlike lyric poetry, the essay remains a medium rather than a genre, a tool rather than art. We have not yet honed this box of commentary into a delicate pocket square. We still let the essay subtract us with questions. Yet to say that the essay questions suggests that it quests. The essay may wander, it may be a science of associations, but it wanders with a goal. We say, *Look, a thought!* And along we scurry holding a dish to catch it. Coughs.

Stage Directions

I would prefer that the audience believe these interruptions to be authentic. However, if the reader of this essay feels uncomfortable pretending to trespass, then this disclaimer may be read prior to the actual essay itself—preserving the aesthetic effect of the interruption, but not the subversiveness of it.

Ken Chen is the executive director of the Asian American Writers' Workshop, co-founder of CultureStrike, and author of *Juvenilia*, selected by Louise Gluck for the Yale Series of Younger Poets.

CHRISTINE CHIA

y(ears)

I once knew a man who
clutched the black telephone wire

like an umbilical cord,
carrying it everywhere,

especially the bathroom
where walls bounced back

his voice to him
like his mother's womb.

His mother
didn't listen to him;

all his life, he looked
for a woman

who had ears
only;

her silence
would

be his.

Christine Chia is the author of *The Law of Second Marriages* (Math Paper Press, 2011) and a sequel, *Separation: a history* (Ethos Books, 2014). She is the co-editor of the groundbreaking anthologies *A Luxury We Cannot Afford* and *A Luxury We Must Afford* (Math Paper Press, 2014, 2016) and has contributed to *Washington Square Review*, where "y(ears)" was originally published, *Prairie Schooner*, and the W!LD RICE play *Another Country*.

LONELY CHRISTOPHER

Prospect Park after Dark

u sing; here in the felonious brush, dither and spew (speculate
turn, tame like a caged animal with a little blood on her fang)
golden rings hang like hair out of the varmint of suburbia
they say who gives a fuck, it's all done online these days
sling quietly through the wilderness, become different services
pretend u are not alone walking through a tenebrous vault
there are going to be some lights until the lights go out
even when there isn't money—sex and hunger, they remain
remember the spring we all got lost in the park after dark
we loved each other's purple teeth and lack of driver's permits
it was like the trees held us through our ages, like they donated
the future into the wrinkled mouth of a muggy knoll, doubt that
then one of us got shot in the head, another drowned, go figure
all's here for u—at least in theory or over the phone but the
tears going on, they're harder than the GED they sting they
turn buff or reddish in the holler of our pristine feminism
walk on the grass, swim into the lip of the polluted lake
climb branches, kiss, break up, break down, download
fall asleep in the passenger seat, lord knows where we are
experience, they say, is passé—how many bridges have damaged
poor thunder and denied the blood and tiny creatures that lurk
under the skin, in the creases of our eyelids, in our stool
u cannot imagine what's in the woods or facsimile of aforesaid
it's the cost, calling from a jail cell in California, turning around
and telling the kids it's only fathom it's only the end of the world
oh u reservoir, how that fatigues and how it charms, discovery
passes us, the forestry survives the night, the critters writhe
u are going to have to walk into campaign and take sides.

Brooklyn

If you want to ruin me, Brooklyn, do so with love
waiting for a public language in my small yellow room
a confident bus ruling down strafed avenues
upon which an unwholesome fog has alighted
pictures and the bleats of anxious children in puffy jackets
frowning women walking through the black smoke
confirming an underground electrical fire.

Gallons of two percent milk mixed with Ballantine Ale
the adamantine smell of calamitous blood
rushing skyward from the gutters through the floor
rats, millions of them, and forgiveness.

You give me shelter and fugitive boys, their skin
the transient laurels with which I carpet my tongue
you give me the forsaken technology I use to constitute
and cry out frivolities back into the wheat of your hair
your shape stupendous is that of indefatigable schticks
psychotic as it is friendly, forecastable as it is profound
the walls of an empty cinema could collapse into the street
spraying dust and debris into the faces of the gentry
and the food stamp recipients, the nomadic hipsters
slinking about, ashing cigarettes into the decayed brush
limping from pavement cracks in front of monstrous hospitals
but everything would be bright yet, I'd puke patchouli and blood
on the entrance for another evangelical bookstore.

Relay your provincial promise like a sting behind my sinuses
ravage me with bright fulfillment, when I nest in your sweaty arms
grasp my throat and tell me this is how you leave me alone
you make me feel like a picked zit that just won the Nobel Prize
I know what I trust, I know what it is I'm doing here
a half-dead cat swallows a stone and runs into traffic
the car swerves and the driver thinks about his next appointment.

You appreciate atrabilious wounds and represent beauty
the bitten-raw cuticles of a sure man caressing his own future
and the paving stones fatted on cheap handles of wine
that howl drunk depths into his loopy ears
just another crazy person quietly trying to choose life

because what else is there to do, where the sky is green
but to know this, that my skeleton will melt jokingly
into your ambitious will and, as we all do around these parts
come to rest on the cushion of a negligent day
I say your name sixteen times when I pray.

Lonely Christopher is the author of the short story collection *The Mechanics of Homosexual Intercourse*, the poetry collection *Death & Disaster Series*, and the novel *THERE*. His plays have been presented in Canada, China, and the United States. His film credits include the feature *MOM* (which he wrote and directed), the shorts *We Are Not Here*, *Milk*, and *Petit Lait* (adapted from his stories), and *Crazy House* (screenplay). He lives in Brooklyn.

TODD COLBY

My Understanding

My understanding of this evening
is rudimentary at best: when it gets dark
people get all batty, and then they bellow.
People in Brooklyn understand volume.
Perhaps it is natural to be giddy
and full of dread. By giddy, I mean full
of agitated wonder, like maybe
I can really get things done
because I'm organized and intelligent
and super freaked about a lot of stuff.
Then, I get this very convincing idea
that I'm just a turd blossom
taking up too much space in my room.

Get Back to Me

The Governors Island ferry moves us
across the water with our supplies.
We are here for the adventure and the views.
So many things are amazing to us, like the weather,
and Fort Jay, and the brilliant people of our city.
The sun slams against
the ferry and makes us all
squint as it passes over us. To run full speed ahead
into a chain link fence. Think of the cost to the body.
Walls are one of the strongest things. Still, there are a lot
of noble ideas about walls. Reading Foucault in a basement
on Madison Avenue in 1989.
Someone riding on our ferry
insisted on getting a bobbed haircut.
The sun makes my t-shirt look
blue and black. Get back to me.

Todd Colby is the author of five collections of poetry, including *Tremble and Shine* (Soft Skull Press, 2004), *Riot in the Charm Factory: New and Selected Poems* (Soft Skull Press, 1999), *Flushing Meadows* (Scary Topiary Press, 2012), and *Splash State* (The Song Cave, 2014).

MAXE CRANDALL

Dionne Warwick Stares Down Her Enemies

for Julie Blair

Raising banners is *attractive*,
makes one burst with *personality*.
Women have a lot to say about these things
while assuredly "not speaking"
to men through style.

To wit, Jackie O likes her girlfriend
thank you very much
and would rather not see her burned at the stake.
Besides Jackie's busy at the nursery,
where she works nights fretting over hibiscus,
and O the constellations!

Meanwhile in her everlasting trenchcoat
Dionne Warwick stares down her enemies,
reducing them to straining teenagers
and secretly considering herself
America's Last Action Diva.

Like us, she spends much of her time
leaning against doorframes and talking
on the telephone, dreaming of cartoon heroes
while fingering the long cord.

The men tend to more commemorative cruelties.
With Chris Brown in his wretched kingdom,
the stakes of celebrity vassalage get knobby
around the nobodies he becomes and then shuns.

Speaking of *Violence*, the first episode ponders
Hemingway's flagrant remarks about lesbians.
In the second installment, rumor has it
Papa will hand over one of his savage sweaters
to the singer. To close, the forest weeps
new rivers suddenly, as in myth.

Everyone knows gold is a shaking color
a key to what the early bisexuals taught us
with their oratorical chanting: "Earthquake,
or milkshake?" which is to suggest
there will always be progress,
always
be infighting—
but to clash, and to do it well,
one must couch objection
in obstruction

and eat and yell, and eat and yell,
and eat and yell

Maxe Crandall is a playwright and poet based in Flatbush, Brooklyn. His play *Together Men Make Paradigms* (Yo-Yo Labs) was a finalist for the Leslie Scalapino Award. His chapbook *Emoji for Cher Heart* (Belladonna*) is the longest poem about Cher in the world. "Dionne Warwick Stares Down Her Enemies" was previously published in *CutBank* and the *Advocate* online.

CYNTHIA CRUZ

Further Steps

As if in a dacha in the wood.

As if a teapot and china.

Wood frames the family.

Of lineage, I've no word for.

A village of grief

Hid inside the wood.

A small plush kitten

Lapping water from the bowl.

There is no kitten, there is no tea,

No bowl, no dacha in the wood.

A village of sorrow

Hid inside the poem.

A million mad horses, galloping.

Just yesterday I read the word

In a book I hid. It made me

Stop and weep.

I ran into the wood

When I still could

To escape what I knew.

A million mad horses galloping

Mad into the quickening

Black spiral of.

I prayed in the rain,

Please let this terrible weather

Enter me.

Cynthia Cruz is the author of four collections of poetry, including three with Four Way Books: *The Glimmering Room* (2012), *Wunderkammer* (2014), and *How the End Begins* (2016). Cruz has received fellowships from Yaddo and the MacDowell Colony as well as a Hodder Fellowship from Princeton University. She has an MFA from Sarah Lawrence College in writing and an MFA in Art Criticism & Writing from the School of Visual Arts. Cruz is currently pursuing a PhD in German studies at Rutgers University. She teaches at Sarah Lawrence College.

MARGARITA DELCHEVA

Great of Praises

Chained to my mother's neck,
the golden profile of
Neferneferuaten Nefertiti,
the one stolen by the specters
who turned my socks inside out,
who dragged out the VCR,
traumatized the cat.
Lady of The Two Lands
signals, in her broad hat,
the safest place in Sugar Factory.
With its smell of half moon fruit,
my mother's cleavage
only skin now, not sure
I can trust it.
The detectives spray
a black fingerprint
on the pale cream bottle.
I place my finger on it,
touching the Mistress
of Upper and Lower Egypt,
her open-air temples,
our open-air fleas
where, on cheap black velvet,
they pin family heirlooms,
which speak to each other
proudly on parole and,
though they do not know it,
are safe.

PSA

Do you feel the draft from the bedroom?
Sense the draft down 8th Street?
The one from the empty coat
of the Immanuel Kant finger puppet laying there?
Don't tell me you don't feel it
after opening the bottle of Magnesium,
after the clear doorbell, the package
and no mailman anointed with January,
from the hands of the neon schoolgirls waving?

Between the oven door and the window,
the draft sweeps like melting lacquer,
one way it goes.
If you were born in the West, you might
not know about it, its salted invisible leg,
the vectors bristled.
You might have stood in its way
yawning and shirtless.

Because you were in love
and, boy, you were that summer,
it went around you,
just that once it bent
its twelve-thousand-year back.
The floorboards cracked, the windows
sucked their lips in.
Without spreading lard on your chest,
you strode shoeless through the weather
of your hallway, gathering the carpets,
and onto the balcony you sang.

Margarita Delcheva is a co-founding editor of the poetry and art journal *Paperbag*. Her recent poems have appeared in *Tuesday; An Art Project*, *BOMBlog*, *Nat. Brut*, *Drunken Boat*, and others. Originally from Bulgaria, Margarita lived in Brooklyn for six years. She is currently a comparative literature PhD candidate at UCSB.

JAY DESHPANDE

Apologia Pro Vita Sua

We don't have much time so we have to work
slowly. We unwrap the small
almost-animal form until it whimpers
under the heat of our gaze. We put the books
up on the shelf; we take them back down again.
At evening, chin back and the neck
like a skyscraper, we give up smoke—a colony
of ghost-howl. Color of light
that collects on rooftops, with desire
propped like a water tower in the corner:
each day ends in the labor of small hands
through delicate hair. I remember a time
with a woman I knew only as the sound of her hair.
After we had both come and spent ourselves
on the smells of each other, we went up on the roof
and lay down on my coat, wishing
that people could see the stars in this city.
And I remember how I slipped into sleep for a moment
and was back by the hayfield of my boyhood
with my brother, crickets sparking in the failing sun
that paced out beyond us and burnished the tips
of the nearest pines. How the edge of that forest
was only slightly farther away. But I never touched it.
It seems I am always running ahead of my needing,
looking out from a higher window of the body
to see the edges of things, the weight
of a pound of grapes in my hand, that tactile rush
of consolation. But I am here now.
I am resting my head against the part of myself
I am willing to put down.
Why didn't we enter that field?
Why didn't we cross to that border, Neil, to see
what it felt like to push the first foot down
into the shadow and the cooler ferns?
At night, my breath slacks into darkness

and I feel the air winnow through my arm.
I am beginning to see how I am that field,
that moment pushing sunset, blank distance to the treeline,
how the woods at the end of me are porous, giving,
how they shimmer on air.
The roots are moving, out of sight.
The crickets singing through me.
Tonight I will sleep like a just man,
a good man, a man who has hurt others
in order to lay his head down.

The Lovers

When I reached for her for the first time
what we groped toward had already
unmade itself. The barstool crashes down
and we are back outside, deaf to nearly everything.
She starts speaking her words on my face
but I stop her. Bare legs and skirt
pressed up against the side of a car,
at the side of a street, familiar story.
A hunger become so animal I can't see
the shape of the hole. What it took for me
to lie down in the brief wreckage
of our lives. Like a drop of blood into water
I watched the loss spread out, heralding
some reaction. I live quietly now,
by myself, mildly hallucinating.
In Magritte's *The Lovers*, it's a dream
seduction: figures locked in profile
in a kiss you cannot see. Shadow
where the faces meet, and there are no faces:
only the two, man and woman, held apart
by the colorless cloth covering
the head of each. Sculptural folds of
the permanent kiss, which isn't.
I had an idea that one shroud
held them both, one sheet like the garment
over furniture in a country house,
that same indifferent smock, only tighter
for the strictures of love. The sheet wrapped

double about his neck and pulled around
to hers, kept off the bare shoulder. That place
where you can imagine her chin. What part
of us must stay under a separate cloth? There is
something uncommunicated in Magritte.
Perhaps I go to that. My hand
on her wrist, my hand showing
her the way to me, guiding her
down a street where I have never
opened my eyes. Behind those painted figures
a storm, without center, rising.
How they ever found their way to each other.

Jay Deshpande is the author of *Love the Stranger* (YesYes Books), named one of the top debuts of 2015 by *Poets & Writers*. He has received fellowships from Kundiman, Civitella Ranieri, and the Key West Literary Seminar. Poems have recently appeared in *Denver Quarterly*, *Washington Square*, *LARB Quarterly Journal*, and *Horsethief*. He teaches at Columbia University. "Apologia Pro Vita Sua" and "The Lovers" were previously published in *Love the Stranger*.

LYNNE DESILVA-JOHNSON

Movement(s)

I

Hoyt and Schermerhorn in the humid, late hours, when subway time slows to a near stop, thick with bodies in perpetual wait

interminable terminus, feckless un-friend! is there cure for such sickness as this?

II

someone says “salacious” and it rises
above the standard chatter
weddings and weather
whether and why
like a plume of pink smoke,
a wispy remembrance of fire.

we’ll alight on the wind, today
in this improbable bird
blasé as we are about miracles.

hello wing, hello!
she works here,
moored this close to death.

III

you are ancient, ancient
climbing the stairs like kilimanjaro—

and there, stage left, he waves
a bright light, no,
a beam, a longfingerbeam,

beckoning the reluctant chariot:
come, come. do not be afraid.

the moon is just a suggestion
forsaking the city
leaving us with misbehaving
waters, holy only in
the absolute value
of sin.

mama, why, mama?
why,
mama,
how? how
can the sun hide
behind an absence?

wouldn't you like to know
and wouldn't I
wouldn't I like to know?

I would like to know so many things.

Andy said, "People will respect me,"
reminding his laughing shadow
and maybe telling other people, too
like a mantra
giving himself permission
to be
hated
and
misunderstood

IV

it's another nino rota subway ride
all two am tubas and syncopating, waiting, i,
slide whistle, your kiss pressed on the pacific northwest's plate glass,
blue special someone.

these blissful plateaued heterotopias! do, revel in punk
chewation; snare and high hat, tilda, accents
graves ou agouts, in perpendicularity.

V

trees, rivers leak onto the geographic gingham
like loose ink, discrediting the claims to perpendicular dominance
so aggressively in defense here where map is king.
these veins needn't wait for blood's permission,
the stuff of births.

VI

arrivederci, roma, thanks for all the fish
if this is enough if mind is enough each line is I is enough, am enough
some long-lost apocalypse thought, some yahweh
4 and 20 horsemen, pi
the eye of the beloved, be/hold/(h)er.
~~her~~ four year face, unitched, h, a priori

VII

find it art enough, as all that grows is art enough
as bee, and, and flower, corn and grain,
as sea is art enough.

call it by its name here, say "poetry,"
say, "love," say "electricity," then carry on
evolving beyond definitions, silent.

Lynne DeSilva-Johnson is a queer interdisciplinary creator, curator, educator, and facilitator working in performance, exhibition, and publication in conversation with new media. She is a visiting assistant professor at Pratt Institute and was previously at CUNY for over a decade. Lynne is the founder and managing editor of The Operating System and serves as the libraries editor at Boog City. Her books include *GROUND*, *blood atlas*, and *Overview Effect*, and she is co-author of *A GUN SHOW* with Adam Sliwinski/Sō Percussion, as well as co-editor of the anthologies *Resist Much / Obey Little: Inaugural Poems to the Resistance* and *In Corpore Sano: Creative Practice and the Challenged Body*, both forthcoming in 2017. Lynne publishes and performs widely, and is a fourth-generation Brooklyn native.

TIMOTHY DONNELLY

The New Intelligence

After knowledge extinguished the last of the beautiful
fires our worship had failed to prolong, we walked
back home through pedestrian daylight, to a residence

humbler than the one left behind. A door without mystery,
a room without theme. For the hour that we spend
complacent at the window overlooking the garden,

we observe an arrangement in rust and gray-green,
a vagueness at the center whose slow, persistent
movements some sentence might explain if we had time

or strength for sentences. To admit that what falls
falls solitarily, lost in the permanent dusk of the particular.
That the mind that fear and disenchantment fatten

comes to boss the world around it, morbid as the damp-
fingered guest who rearranges the cheeses the minute the host
turns to fix her a cocktail. A disease of the will, the way

the false birch branches arch and interlace from which
hands dangle the last leaf-parchments and a very large array
of primitive bird-shapes. Their pasted feathers shake

in the aftermath of the nothing we will ever be content
to leave the way we found it. I love that about you.
I love that when I call you on the long drab days practicality

keeps one of us away from the other that I am calling
a person so beautiful to me that she has seen my awkwardness
on the actual sidewalk but she still answers anyway.

I say that when I fell you fell beside me and the concrete
refused to apologize. That a sparrow sat for a spell
on the windowsill today to communicate the new intelligence.

That the goal of objectivity depends upon one's faith
in the accuracy of one's perceptions, which is to say
a confidence in the purity of the perceiving instrument.

I won't be dying after all, not now, but will go on living dizzily
hereafter in reality, half-deaf to reality, in the room
perfumed by the fire that our inextinguishable will begins.

His Future as Attila the Hun

But when I try to envision what it might be like to live
    detached from the circuitry that suffers me to crave

what I know I'll never need, or what I need but have
    in abundance already, I feel the cloud of food-court

breakfast loosen its embrace, I feel the shopping center
    drop as its escalator tenders me up to the story

intended for conference space. I feel my doubt diminish, my debt
    diminish; I feel a snow that falls on public statuary

doesn't do so sadly because it does so without profit.
    I feel less toxic. I feel the thought my only prospect

lies under a train for the coverage stop. Don't think I never
    thought that way because I have and do, all through

blank October a dollar in my pocket back and forth
    to university. Let the record not not show. I have

deserted me for what I lack and am not worth. All of this
    unfolds through episodes that pale as fast as others

gain from my inertia: I have watched, I'll keep watching
    out from under blankets as the days trip over the

days before out cold on the gold linoleum behind them
    where we make the others rich with sick persistence.

But when I try to envision what it might be like to change,
    I see three doors in front of me, and by implication

opportunity, rooms full of it as the mind itself is full
    thinking of a time before time was, or of the infinite

couch from which none part, and while the first two doors
    have their appeal, it's the third I like best, the one

behind which opens a meadow, vast, and in it, grazing
    on buttercups, an errant heifer with a wounded foot,

its bloody hoofprints followed by a curious shepherd back
    to something sharp in the grass, the point of a long

sword which, unearthed, the shepherd now polishes with
    his rodent-skin tunic, letting the Eurasian sun play

upon it for effect, a gift for me, a task, an instrument to lay
    waste to the empire now placed before me at my feet.

The Earth Itself

To quantify the foolishness of the already long since failed
    construction project, the famous German polymath

undertook to calculate the precise number of bricks
    the Tower of Babel would have required had it ever been

finished. The figure he came up with ran an impressive
    eighteen digits in length, climbing all the way up

to that rarely occupied hundred-quadrillionths place.
    Looking at it now, between loads of laundry, the figure

calls to mind an American telephone number—area code first,
    then the prefix, then the line number, followed in turn

by a trail of eight additional zeroes. I feel a little lost
    through the hypnosis of those zeroes, but I still pick up

the phone and dial that number now. A recording says
    the number I've dialed isn't an actual telephone number

after all. Please try again. I do. Same result. I try dialing
    that trail of zeroes instead. This time the recording says

that the call I'm making might itself be recorded. I hesitate a bit
    at the thought of that, when all this crazy science, all

this poking into mysteries, panting for answers, always
    harder, higher, my phone calls today and the recordings

during laundry, the laundry—it all comes crashing down.
    I don't have time to experiment. I'm hanging up the phone.

But wait, there's more! On my rush back to the laundromat
    I remembered I forgot a part. The polymath figured out, too,

that if the tower had reached its destination, it would have
    taken over eight-hundred years to climb to the top.

What's more, his calculations say the mass of all those bricks
    would have outweighed, slightly, the earth's own mass,

meaning the tower would have used up all the matter of
    the planet it was built on, which is foolish enough, and then

a little more, which is absurd, unless the tower is secretly
    just the earth itself, with the added weight of all the living on it.

Timothy Donnelly is the author, most recently, of *The Cloud Corporation*, winner of the 2012 Kingsley Tufts Poetry Award, and of the chapbook *Hymn to Life*. A Guggenheim Fellow, he has been poetry editor at *Boston Review* since 1996 and is on the faculty of Columbia University's Writing Program.

MICHAEL DUMANIS

Natural History

I'm fully posable, a leather and clay creature
with the capacity to waltz and do the Twist.
My jaws unclench themselves. My eyes swing open.
The world is young, and I still have some years,
so I take out a patent on slow-moving fog.
Take out a patent on the hyacinth.
I brand the cow. Trademark the coelacanth:
its tiny heart is shaped like a straight tube.
However, the darkness keeps hitting
me over the head with its hammer.
I want to feel more substantial
than an elephant wearing a fez,
so I invent the Theory of Gravity,
so I discover my larynx and use it,
so I study yoga and learn how to wrap
my legs around my neck, but I keep finding
occasion to lie on the floor like a slug
or weep into the rented furniture,
so I invent the Bhagavad Gita,
so I invent the Gutenberg Bible,
so I invent the Etch-a-Sketch and draw
myself a lover with the right proportions,
we go on holiday and sit in traffic,
I do my best not to erase her, not to shake
things up. When we get lonely, we invent
the baby, a fully posable
leather and clay creature. It cries
like a small bird. We pose with it.
To never erase you, I carve your initials,
my lover, into the spine of a tree. You are happy
but the tree dies. So I take out a patent
on the synthetic tree, and I carve
your initials, my lover, into its torso,
and take you to the disco and the roller derby,
to the waterfall beside the paper mill.
It's so amazing what we get to see.
The ruins extend across the valleys, toward each sea.

Autobiography

Attempted avoiding abysses, assorted
abrasions and apertures, abscesses.

At adolescence, acted absurd: acid,
amphetamines. Amorously aching

after an arguably arbitrary Abigail,
authored an awful aubade.

Am always arabesquing after Abigails.
Am always afraid: an affliction?

Animals augur an avalanche. Animals
apprehend abattoirs. Am, as an animal,

anxious. Appendages always aflutter,
am an amazing accident: alive.

Attired as an apprentice aerialist,
addressed acrophobic audiences.

Aspiring, as an adult, after acolytes,
attracted an awestruck, angelic auteur.

After an asinine affair, an abortion.
After an asinine affair, Avowed Agnostic

approached, alone, an abbey's altarpiece,
asking Alleged Almighty about afterlife.

Ambled, adagio, around an arena.
Admired an ancient aqueduct. Ate aspic.

Adored and ate assorted animals.
Ascended an alp. Affected an accent.

Acquired an accountant, an abacus, assets.
Attempted atonal arpeggios.

Michael Dumanis was born in the former Soviet Union and immigrated to the U.S. when he was five. He is the author of *My Soviet Union* (University of Massachusetts Press), winner of the Juniper Prize for Poetry; and co-editor of *Legitimate Dangers: American Poets of the New Century* (Sarabande). He is a member of the literature faculty at Bennington College and serves as editor of the print literary journal *Bennington Review*. He divides his time between Vermont and Brooklyn. "Autobiography" originally appeared in the *Believer*; "Natural History" originally appeared in *Copper Nickel*.

NATALIE EILBERT

When One Door Opens, Another One Rips Off the House into a Void I Never Knew About

In an essay I called my sickness "gruesomely legible" because
something in me did not snap but instead eked into other skin,
more blanched and less pronounceable skin. You see hair choked
the frameworks and a lantern blinked dim unsafety and no one
that night was raped or even condemned to skin. I am trying
to make sense of horizons, how grief pins thread on either side
to make a line. Do you know I've grown to love lemon water,
the tart cold shapes my throat. I gulp it in fever. I gulp it in not-fever.
I hear Plath's raked throat behind my throat utter lemon water chicken.
Water, water make me wretch. I can't recall my last bite of chicken.
Flesh wraps around flesh around flesh makes me wretch.
I gulp lemon water. I think I love a man who would never have left me
if I didn't push two pins into time. He lives far away and I live far away.
I gulp lemon water. I don't think about it which is why I love it.
The tart cold shapes my throat. In bed last night my chest quaked
to think sadly our sole purpose in this life is not understanding
but a pronounceable skin. My color scored with bills. My family
an inkblot in the recycling bin. I let a man hold me. I thought
he understood me and I thought that I thought I could be legible.
I reach into a hole and pull out the phantom of language.
Chris Kraus says love and sex both cause mutation, that desire
is surplus energy, a claustrophobia under the skin. I pull out
the phantom of language and this is also language. It's okay.
I watch two people fuck in a neighboring window. I see myself
sip wine and watch his face bury in the fur. The moon watches
me watch myself watching. I don't call it celestial intercourse.
I'm sick. My disease is demagogic. I gulp lemon water. I use it.

Omega Rising

Until I find the log meant to roll me into the cosmos
and stare me back down at myself a bargained moon,
there will be no more talk about justice. I've not been
writing my notes down, have slept dreamlessly long
enough to know and be okay with death. By factors
far and beyond a water's course, what's the use of information
if I can't eat or sip its blood. I wear a nova of crowns
and guide my animals toward a humiliation of systems.
Last night I wasted my body against a sandwich and
a slimness leaked out my nose. What is a verdict without
execution, a rainbow without a sniffling face. The words
banned are the words I crush my form against. It might
come as a surprise to you but I want to be a better human.
I want to eat the whole avocado, publish its fat on my tissue.
I want to spill champagne in the lap of my dysmorphia
and be master of nothing. I had so many dads possess me.
I will never be a genius. I will never be smarter than a crocus
or a cock. Correct my grammar, my body is silk of errors.
How should I act around a nature who reviles when nature
is itself a symptom of accidents. Sure, we live interstitial
and for no fucking reason. Stupid certain slanted light.
Stupid weed. I have enough Natalies for a train, enough
Natalies to light a fuse to Alaska. If you ever find me
in the asiago heaps of garbage land and cattle, do not follow.

Natalie Eilbert is the author of *Indictus*, winner of the 2016 Noemi Press Book Award in Poetry, slated for publication in late 2017, as well as the debut poetry collection *Swan Feast* (Bloof Books, 2015). She is the recipient of the 2016–2017 Jay C. and Ruth Halls Poetry Fellowship at the University of Wisconsin–Madison, where she is serving a one-year academic appointment. Her work has appeared or is forthcoming in the *New Yorker*, *Tin House*, *Kenyon Review*, *jubilat*, and elsewhere. She is the founding editor of the *Atlas Review*.

JUSTINE EL-KHAZEN

Re(ve)al

after Edward Snowden

The ladder
Of fleas
Climbing your ankle, inkblot
Of bruises inside your knee
Are real, belong to a state
You live in, weary
& overworked by the comparison
Of systole to star. Brighten
The versions you select, see yourself
Venned in wavy glass: it's
Impossible to know how the room
Shifts with the length
Of a shadow,
Your sense of yourself
In it. You confront strangers,
A boss, tell the police *you cannot*
Take my picture. Your feelings
Are diaphanous, firelike, tinned &
Beaten into the old buildings,
Sometimes inconsequent. Blood frets
The tympanum in your ear.
Hematite
Colors the West,
The appearance of stars, this world
Of sagging bricks, normal days
That leave you shocked
& fatigued at the rattling end
Of a commute. This afternoon
With the shades lowered belongs to it,
Every bag of bread you buy, ex
Whose number you delete, door
Eased gently back into its frame,
Sensuous peel of orange left curled

In a sink, fragment overheard,
Hour logged alone with the husks
Of sex left to you in memory
Belong to it too.
                    When you
Close your eyes &
Try to remember how it all
Began, there's time to ask the police
Not to come in, why they won't leave
You alone, to find the words
For who you really are, reveal
The pale ancient wing hung reflexively
In the arm you raise, give
Your injured body a myth, the rust
That belongs in its dreams.

Justine el-Khazen was a 2014 Emerging Poets Fellow at Poets House and a 2015 apexart International Fellow. Her work has appeared or is forthcoming in *Apogee*, the *Cortland Review*, the *Margins*, *Harriet*, and *Beloit Poetry Journal*, among others. She is an editorial adviser at VIDA: Women in the Literary Arts. She also teaches at the Fashion Institute of Technology and is a graduate of the MA Program in Creative Writing at UC Davis.

LAURA EVE ENGEL

All the Sciences

The year I fail all the sciences there are
many factors but no one is in any way confused.
The radio brimming with everything it knows
about some shooters until it gets the shooters
down to two. The dead men's rooms reveal
nothing about unhappiness. What starts out
as reason refusing to make more of itself
has a way of becoming several mixed reports
from the field, where I'm having a feeling
of being eleven and watching the sun set.
I'm having a feeling of my chest as a trunk
full of blankets and answers to questions
about who gets to keep a garden. Often
enough we return to the field with trowels,
intentional. I'm told this is an American
approach to the problem. I've been trying
to figure out what it means to have
an American approach to a problem.
Maybe it's when I think the thoughts I have
that don't work hard enough to stick
probably weren't deserving of the field,
and not when I think the ones that do
are lucky. We like to be told what we're doing
is difficult so it's correct that the sky's mostly
a flubbed forecast until the part where it turns
to light or to egg down the calm sides
of a mixing bowl. I remember that to make
a solution, something needs to dissolve.
Sunsets. The library. The parts we've picked
apart with borrowed beaks or tractors.
It feels good to get an old thing next to
a new thing because of how sure it is
that they'll never turn into each other, or
maybe it's because we like what putting a rock
near a rocket says about what we can do

in the meantime. Sometimes I like to read
backwards until the bullet reenters its gun.
Until the dead men remove their heads
from the bags and are about to be
hungry or can almost remember what
they came into that room for or are born.

Laura Eve Engel's work has appeared in the *Awl*, *Boston Review*, *PEN America*, *Tin House*, and elsewhere. She is the recipient of fellowships from the Provincetown Fine Arts Work Center, the Wisconsin Institute for Creative Writing, and the Helene Wurlitzer Foundation. "All the Sciences" was originally published in *Black Warrior Review*.

SHIRA ERLICHMAN

Ode to Lithium #600

The side effect of Lithium (is dehydration & peeing more frequently. The side effect of dehydration & peeing more frequently is not wanting to drink water at all because you pee more frequently. The side effect of not wanting to is not doing. The side effect of not doing is a couch & three movies. The side effect of a couch & three movies is *what have you been doing all day* with a raised eyebrow. The side effect of a raised eyebrow is a sigh. The side effect of a sigh is plaque. The side effect of plaque is a dirt road but you're bikeless. The side effect of bikeless is an unrelenting heartbeat with a passion for waves. The side effect of a passion for waves is dream upon dream where every object is as blue as the sea. The side effect of overwhelmingly blue dreams is a girlfriend who listens. The side effect of this particular girlfriend is black soap that sits staining the side of the tub. The side effect of stains is her name in your cheek like a cool marble. The side effect of her name is your hands pulling chicken apart into a big bowl that she is also filling & every now & then she shakes near your face a ligament so nasty you both squeal & it is good. The side effect of it is good is it is bad. The side effect of it is bad is crossing your legs in the psychiatrist's office, talking about side effects. The side effect of side effects is living your life. The side effect of living your life is dying. The side effect of dying is being remembered. The side effect of being remembered is being held like a stone, but of course it is not a stone but a bird that too will die. The side effect of a stone that is not a stone is throwing the stone & watching it fly. The side effect of flight) is a poem.

Shira Erlichman is a poet, musician, and visual artist. Her work can be found in *Huffington Post*, *PBS NewsHour's Poetry Series*, *BuzzFeed Reader*, the *Baffler*, and more. "Ode to Lithium #600" was first published in *Psychology Tomorrow Magazine*. A three-time Pushcart Prize nominee, she was awarded a residency by the Millay Colony, the James Merrill Fellowship by the Vermont Studio Center, and the Visions of Wellbeing Focus Fellowship by AIR Serenbe. Learn more at www.officialshira.com.

MARTÍN ESPADA

How We Could Have Lived or Died This Way

> Not songs of loyalty alone are these,
> But songs of insurrection also,
> For I am the sworn poet of every dauntless rebel the world over.
>
> —Walt Whitman

I see the dark-skinned bodies falling in the street as their ancestors fell
before the whip and steel, the last blood pooling, the last breath spitting.
I see the immigrant street vendor flashing his wallet to the cops,
shot so many times there are bullet holes in the soles of his feet.
I see the deaf woodcarver and his pocketknife, crossing the street
in front of a cop who yells, then fires. I see the drug raid, the wrong
door kicked in, the minister's heart seizing up. I see the man hawking
a fistful of cigarettes, the cop's chokehold that makes his wheezing
lungs stop wheezing forever. I am in the crowd, at the window,
kneeling beside the body left on the asphalt for hours, covered in a sheet.

I see the suicides: the conga player handcuffed for drumming on the subway,
hanged in the jail cell with his hands cuffed behind him; the suspect leaking
blood from his chest in the back seat of the squad car; the 300-pound boy
said to stampede barehanded into the bullets drilling his forehead.

I see the coroner nodding, the words he types in his report burrowing
into the skin like more bullets. I see the government investigations stacking,
words buzzing on the page, then suffocated as bees suffocate in a jar. I see
the next Black man, fleeing as the fugitive slave once fled the slave-catcher,
shot in the back for a broken tail light. I see the cop handcuff the corpse.

I see the rebels marching, hands upraised before the riot squads,
faces in bandannas against the tear gas, and I walk beside them unseen.
I see the poets, who will write the songs of insurrection generations unborn
will read or hear a century from now, words that make them wonder
how we could have lived or died this way, how the descendants of slaves
still fled and the descendants of slave-catchers still shot them, how we awoke
every morning without the blood of the dead sweating from every pore.

Of the Threads that Connect the Stars

for Klemente

Did you ever see stars? asked my father with a cackle. He was not
speaking of the heavens, but the white flash in his head when a fist burst
between his eyes. In Brooklyn, this would cause men and boys to slap
the table with glee; this might be the only heavenly light we'd ever see.

I never saw stars. The sky in Brooklyn was a tide of smoke rolling over us
from the factory across the avenue, the mattresses burning in the junkyard,
the ruins where squatters would sleep, the riots of 1966 that kept me
locked in my room like a suspect. My father talked truce on the streets.

My son can see the stars through the tall barrel of a telescope.
He names the galaxies with the numbers and letters of astronomy.
I cannot see what he sees in the telescope, no matter how many eyes I shut.
I understand a smoking mattress better than the language of galaxies.

My father saw stars. My son sees stars. The earth rolls beneath
our feet. We lurch ahead, and one day we have walked this far.

A Million Ants Swarming Through His Body

for José "Chegüí" Torres (1936-2009)

There is no storyteller like a storyteller with a broken nose.
Chegüí would jab my chest before he told the tale, and I would listen.
He was Puerto Rican, like me, and used to be the champion of the world.

He learned his English at the Army base in Baltimore, cracking
the sergeant's ribs and jaw with a double left hook, body and head,
after the Black boys in the barracks taught him what the sergeant
meant by saying: *Get up nigger. Get up spic.* Years later,
the sergeant would ask, *Do you remember me?* and thank him.

The same left hook knifed the liver of Willie Pastrano at the Garden,
and he sank to the ropes, a million ants swarming through his body.
Three rounds later, the referee would tell him: *You have nothing left.*
The Puerto Ricans at the Garden sang and punched the air for Chegüí
de Playa Ponce, el campeón, a savior without nails hammered in his hands.

The next day Chegüí awoke with swollen knuckles. He spoke
from a fire escape at Lexington and 110th Street in El Barrio
to the Puerto Ricans who gathered in the thousands, roaring
at every word, janitors and dishwashers ready to march
and burn down the mayor's mansion at his command.
I won the title for all of us, he shouted, and the fire escape
shuddered beneath his feet, demon rust loosening the bolts.

One night at the Garden he would fall, legs gone, a million ants
swarming through his body. When he fell, two men in the crowd
had heart attacks and one of them died. Chegüí would somehow
rise and swing, leave Devil Green facedown on the canvas, stumble
to his corner and tell himself: *You have nothing left.* He used to be
the champion of the world; now he was a storyteller with a broken nose.

There is no storyteller like a storyteller with a broken nose, but even
he was not immune to diabetes, the Puerto Rican plague merciless
as rust. The scaffold of the fire escape would drop beneath him,
champion of the world and Spanish Harlem, savior of the janitors,
dishwashers and poets, as it does for all champions and saviors,
as it does for all of us in the happy crowd, singing and punching the air.

Martín Espada was born in Brooklyn, New York, in 1957. He has published almost twenty books as a poet, editor, essayist, and translator. His new collection of poems from Norton is called *Vivas to Those Who Have Failed* (2016). His book *The Republic of Poetry* (2006) was a finalist for the Pulitzer Prize. His many honors include the Shelley Memorial Award, the Robert Creeley Award, the National Hispanic Cultural Center Literary Award, an American Book Award, the PEN/Revson Fellowship, and a Guggenheim Fellowship. Espada is a professor of English at the University of Massachusetts–Amherst.

HOWIE FAERSTEIN

Still Life with Self-Portrait

Still life with half-finished business,
expanding universe, diminishing returns.
Self-portrait with sheet music for "All or Nothing at All"
& exception
like black crow with one white wing.
Still life with eyelash flames & Alexandria under water
& excess
like a tree before June drop straining
under the weight of 2500 apples.
Self-portrait with lone sailboat
heeling in the abandoned novel's harbor.
Still life with cat asleep & cacti breathing
in pre-Copernican universe.
Self-portrait on rotting docks washed by the come & go,
speed on a gray surface,
horseshoe crabs glinting in the wrack.
Still life with lit-up streets of New Haven, a display of witchery,
& miniature plantains in Brooklyn markets.
Self-portrait with imposed punishment in burnt umber,
walking backward in Siberian sunlight.
Still life with high cheek-boned woman,
nine hours six minutes of daylight,
sizzle of garlic in scorched skillet.
Self-portrait in front row of bleachers,
at Three County Fair during demolition derby,
one fire only.
Stilled life with endocrine disruptors in town's water treatment plant
& little brown bats vanishing.
Self-portrait with unemployment check,
phone numbers scrawled on scrap,
boys sprawled on grandpa's lap.
In the foreground, one too old to remember,
in the background those impudent enough to forget.
Still life,
not decorative vase & a bowl of rocks

or oranges arranged on a plate
but buried gleanings of an afternoon:
this same face,
starkness amid the roadside plowed snow.
It is still life after all,
self-portrait in the dark, deathlessly
spinning a tale secret even from the dreamer.
Still life with hive of paper wasps abuzz in a kitchen window
migrating tarantulas by the Rio Grande,
extraordinary
visitation of owlets on St. Valentine's Day.
Self-portrait with alligator, with ibis, anhinga,
first light in the Everglades.
Still life with creation's frenzy,
skin, scale, feather, leaf.

Howie Faerstein's full-length book *Dreaming of the Rain in Brooklyn*, a selection of the Silver Concho Poetry Series, was published by Press 53. His work can be found in numerous journals, including *Great River Review*, *Nimrod*, *Cutthroat*, *upstreet*, *Rattle*, *Off the Coast*, *Cape Cod Poetry Review*, *Mudfish*, and online in *Gris-Gris*, *Pedestal*, and *Connotation Press*. He's the assistant poetry editor at *Cutthroat*. After living in Brooklyn for fifty years, he now lives in Florence, Massachusetts.

MONICA FERRELL

Poetry

There is nothing beautiful here
However I may want it. I can't
Spin a crystal palace of this thin air,
Weave a darkness plush as molefur with my tongue
However I want. Yet I am not alone
In these alleys of vowels, which comfort me
As the single living nun of a convent
Is comforted by the walls of that catacomb
She walks at night, lit by her own moving candle.
I am not afraid of mirrors or the future
—Or even *you*, lovers, wandering cow-fat
And rutting in the gardens of this earthly verge
Where I too trod, a sunspot, parasol-shaded,
Kin to the trees, the bees, the color green.

Monica Ferrell is the author of a novel, *The Answer Is Always Yes* (The Dial Press/Random House, 2008) and a collection of poems, *Beasts for the Chase* (Sarabande, 2008), selected by Jane Hirshfield as the winner of the 2007 Kathryn A. Morton Poetry Prize. A former Discovery/ *The Nation* prizewinner and Wallace Stegner Fellow at Stanford University, her poems have appeared in *Paris Review*, *Tin House*, *Boston Review*, *Fence*, *New York Review of Books*, and other magazines and anthologies.

FARRAH FIELD

Untitled

Everything happens on the internet

An asshole is a place of gratitude

Poetry explodes out of me

Are you an intellectual if you don't need a visual

You hate-tweeted us before we could express our love

Margaux used to party over on Packer Street

Does party mean drink or snort coke

The great American mistake is pride

He shot his foot off you couldn't walk five blocks

Everyone has a dog

The Americans will not be told what to do in any way

Both my grandfathers had tuberculosis

There's something going around

a general fear of death

You can tell by Corona Park

the future never happened

Language for the sacred comes slowly

Tenured professors win awards

A good poet is a guide

Untitled

Selfies are cuter than self-portraits
I don't trust anyone long enough to hold my phone
which is also my camera
Is that a gray hair? I photograph my own gray hair
Here I'm trying to be sexy which is always really unsexy
I'm biting my lip because I'm sexy?
I'm chewing on lip balm jam and crying
I'm emotional for some good internet
Am I alone or not
Everyone wants to give me the stick
which would make being with myself easier
It's difficult taking pictures of myself
while checking email
This political discussion extends to Facebook only
The empire of dump for joy
I will now see you in selfie person
I put the spire in conspire

Farrah Field is the author of *Rising* (Four Way Books), *Wolf and Pilot* (Four Way Books), and the chapbook *Parents* (Immaculate Disciples Press). She lives in DUMBO and is co-founder of Berl's Brooklyn Poetry Shop.

CARINA FINN

This Is All Yours

"I move slow and steady
but I feel like a waterfall"
goes the popular song.

This outfit says
I don't want to be here but
I'm happy to be alive

selecting apples
at the market on a morning
in September

my shirtsleeves cuffed
properly. Here's what
we can learn from fashion,

if we can learn anything,
that the woman who
turns up the fabric of
your heart

might be only a tidepool
so far away in space,
and the woman

who photographs
the innards of
your womanhood

what womanhood you have
might be the gaze across
the Crate & Barrel

breakfast table of
your dreams. Last

night
one love read Jimmy Schuyler

to me, another said
she missed me in a missive
from the tropics,

and somewhere else on
a bird in the air a lady
prepares to don a veil.

A sadness the size of a die
falls from the shelf in my mind.
The cat sees a ghost.

I see her, too.
City lights splash red squares
of not knowing how to

handle what I feel. I'm
writing to you now from inside
this hatbox where I have put

it all down on salmon-mint
stationary, in my prettiest hand,
with the pen you brought

from Switzerland.
I'm writing to you so I never
have to say it to your face,

that I love you in the most
uncomplicated way,
my dear, little, thing. I would

hit you with a sack of
sticks. I would hit you
with a fire extinguisher.

I would never
dare
to lie with my face in the sheets

of a red-headed woman
in the cinematic autumn
of my twenty-sixth year.

But the horizon turns yellow.
Your eyes turn gold then green.
The dusk's an oil painting.

The moon's a little sliver.

Carina Finn is the author of *Invisible Reveille* (Coconut Books, 2014), *The Grey Bird: Thirteen Emoji Poems in Translation* (Coconut Books, 2014), *Lemonworld & Other Poems* (co·im·press, 2013), *My Life is a Movie* (Birds of Lace, 2012), and *I Heart Marlon Brando* (Wheelchair Party, 2010). Her work has appeared in the *Rumpus*, *jubilat*, *Hyperallergic*, *DIAGRAM*, and elsewhere.

NICK FLYNN

forty-seven minutes

I ask a high school class to locate an image in a poem we've just read—their heads at this moment are bowed to the page. After some back & forth about the rain & a styrofoam cup, a girl raises her hand & asks, *Does it matter?* I smile—it's as if the universe was balanced on those three words & we've landed in the unanswerable & I have to admit that no, it doesn't, not really, matter, if rain is an image or rain is an idea or rain is a sound in our heads. *But to get through the next forty-seven minutes we might have to pretend it does.*

forgetting something

Try this—close / your eyes. No, wait, when—if—we see each other / again, the first thing we should do is close our eyes—no, / first we should tie our hands to something / solid—bedpost, doorknob—otherwise they (wild birds) / might startle us / awake. Are we forget-ting something? What about that / warehouse, the one beside the airport, that room / of black boxes, a man in each box? If you / bring this one into the light he will not stop / crying, if you show this one a photo of his son / his eyes go dead. Turn up / the heat, turn up the song. First thing we should do / if we see each other again is to make / a cage of our bodies—inside we can place / whatever still shines.

false prophet

The book tells us to cling (cling?) / to the thought that, in god's / hands, our dark past is our greatest / possession (*You've ruined it*, the woman with / the riding crop says to the man on all / fours, naked but for his mask—*pigs don't talk*). Cling— / maybe inside this word are more words, maybe / inside darkness is simply more darkness. God's / hands? Here's a riddle—a cosmonaut / holds hands with an astronaut, both un- / tethered. Which one is confusing a pinpoint of light / with an unreachable planet?

Nick Flynn has worked as a ship's captain, an electrician, and a caseworker with homeless adults. His most recent book is *My Feelings* (Graywolf, 2015), a collection of poems. "false prophet" and "forgetting something" are from *The Captain Asks for a Show of Hands*, and "forty-seven minutes" is from *My Feelings*.

T'AI FREEDOM FORD

ode to an African urn

for Trayvon and them,
after Keats

what men or gods are these?
what mad pursuit?
what sin or odd odds are these?
what men or gods are these?
what unarmed boys down on bruised knees?
what mad blue suits?
what men or gods are these?
what mad pursuit?

what struggle to escape?
fair youth, beneath the trees, you cannot leave
what's suspect? brown skin? hooded drape?
what struggle to escape?
what estranged fruit? frayed rope round nape
unfair youth, beneath the leaves, you cannot be: leave.
what struggle to escape?
fair youth, beneath the trees, you cannot leave

who are these coming to the sacrifice?
whose bloodied hands shall stain the earth?
what eye for what eye shall suffice?
who are these coming to the sacrifice?
what's worth this brown skin? who shall pay what price?
or else why be born? why be bothered with birth?
who are these coming to the sacrifice?
whose bloodied hands shall stain the earth?

---

t'ai freedom ford is a New York City high school English teacher and Cave Canem Fellow. Her first poetry collection, *how to get over*, was published by Red Hen Press. t'ai lives and loves in Brooklyn, but hangs out digitally at shesaidword.com. She gives thanks to the editors at *Union Station Magazine* who originally published this poem.

KIT FRICK

Avalanche Wind

Another way to think about [ ] is its inverse. There are better ways to cling to a dead thing. Fists are weak. Try a headlock. Try each floorboard until one gives way. Take a long drive through six mountains and feel the dead drilling through stone. Don't think about collapsible wingspan. Breakable objects. The possible life span of a trumpeter swan. So many cars traveling through [the space that stone left]. Another way to think about [ ] is what can it hold. Press the backs of your hands against the doorframe until your arms float up like wings [^ ^]. This is what weightless feels like. Resurrection or something close.

Gravity Engine

My back pressed to the mattress to accelerate
deflation. Snow angel style. How my body
leaves its shape and then that leaves.

When preparing to change course, draw first
a replica of your heart. The wind takes one.
One to steer your chest.

When crossing the tundra, when taking the stairs,
believe what the atlas tells you. Many before. Abundant
breathing room. The overlooks scenic abundantly.

And when we consider.

Things left behind.

When the air stream. When the cushioned decline.

And the ceiling fan keeps count keeps count keeps count.

Then the awful gravity of lightness, then how impossible
the human heart.

Kit Frick is the author of two chapbooks: *Echo, Echo, Light* (Slope Editions, 2013) and *Kill Your Darlings, Clementine* (Rye House Press, 2013). Kit received her MFA from Syracuse University and is a senior editor at Black Lawrence Press. *See All the Stars*, her debut novel for young adults, is forthcoming from Simon & Schuster/McElderry Books in 2018. She is grateful to *Crazyhorse*, where "Avalanche Wind" first appeared, and to *H_NGM_N*, where "Gravity Engine" first appeared. Kit lives in Brooklyn with her husband and lives online at www.kitfrick.com.

PETER COLE FRIEDMAN

Prom

Even though I'm not really in a clique, today a kind of derivative promness
swirls about me, walking to McCarren Park, the sun liminal
in a cruel way, the promise of dancing sexy to Katy Perry
the promise of summer like a bowl of punch
people slurp from like true love. The promise of being crowned
Prom Queen which, strut as I might with a stretch
Hummer purpose, a Jergens Natural Glow, is only the ghost
of some euphoria I doubt I've ever had, or wanted to have,

but here it comes, the wanting. My tiara is not
the only tiara, I remind myself, smeyesing for the sky,
and so the sky barely notices. My Gaga is not
your Gaga, sure, but that just makes the walk feel
like an uncoupling.

The real Prom Queen, the sun, whose gaze high
school taught us not to meet, is shining on the jocks
playing football because all jocks are men and all men,
if asked, *Meat, chicken, vegetarian,*
know to choose meat. Know how to fill
up until they don't.

I see some other spectators, too—
pretty wispy to be men—and we gather at a bench. We paint
our nails, put on glitter, arrange an after-party,
get up-dos, take group photos in the grass, pre-game,
talk about all the people we might kiss, and
then, suddenly, it grows dark—the Prom Queen receding
into the sky, where the lesser lights scatter, too.
Brooklyn slinks away to an after-party without us,
without *me*, I want to say, though maybe it's time I shed
that binding separation.

Derrick suggests we all go to his house,
which at least has a pool and bottle of half-water-half-whiskey,

but Derrick isn't the name of anybody I know.
Derrick is the dark sky looking back at me, saying,
Tomorrow, prom is tomorrow.

Peter Cole Friedman is an early childhood educator and writer based in Greenpoint, Brooklyn. Recent work can be found in *Entropy*, *Prelude*, and *Potluck*. "Prom" originally appeared in *Powder Keg*. He is co-founder of the virtual literary and arts platform *glitterMOB*.

GREG FUCHS

New Century

for Eileen Myles

Come all ye
this is your orange
revolution

be in the streets

Copping our retrograde style we copped from your forebears
She broke up with the television for attention to felines
Years before you were conscious enough to analyze its idiocy
In the back of the bus, I'm on the bus please appear to write
My poem here on the empty black line of your mind
Honing the vices of the Jazz Age in this next blank generation
I followed Rimbaud for a block then he ducked down 11th Street
At Russo's like he knew all eyes were watching him turning into a guy
Wearing Nike® sneakers in a society of torn and frayed denim
Love, and vision, yet, even we are guilty, even I, because every time
I don't live today creepy crawlie god-fearing sadists bringing it all on
Admit deviant propulsions, reckless behaviors, breaking hearts
Come all ye be in the streets this is your orange revolution, your spectacle
And we can all slow down on the mic always sirens, always peasants
Always workers it's a gas to be a member of the underclass
On the edge of town there are too many wires in my life

Copping our retrograde style we copped from your forebears
The noodle lives around the stomach, so he opted for alone
In the hotel in lieu of carousing "It's rough being an idol,"
Declared in a storm of bottles and fists black market drop-off
Travel center at the fringe of town, the new small old business
Model she broke up with the television for attention to felines
Years before you were conscious enough to analyze its idiocy
And manipulation like a manic depressive lover so be our vices
Make noises outside of Baltimore detour the cops, at dead-end
Harbor roads, are watching you hoochie Pucci® sweaters

In the back of the bus I'm on the bus please appear to write
My poem here on the empty black line of your mind
Honing the vices of the Jazz Age in this next blank generation
I followed Rimbaud for a block then he ducked down 11th Street
At Russo's like he knew all eyes were watching him turning into a guy
Wearing Nike® sneakers in a society of torn and frayed denim
Find a thrift store suit for shock value living the ninth life
Our homes are all torn asunder, just sometimes more visibly
The wind and water took the home of my birth, my family
My friends assisted by man-made stupidity and filth, lack of empathy
Love, and vision yet, even we are guilty, even I, because every time
A friend succeeds a little bit of me dies Gore Vidal the bloke
In a pink wig like a whistle only dogs can hear quips notorious
Rake but we love him unconditionally for everything he never did
For us missing knowing that I could always see you
We take it for granted then poof there goes the long-term investment
I don't live today creepy crawlie god-fearing sadists bringing it all on
The new party platform will be there is nothing they can get on me I'm dirty
You're dirty; we're all dirty, dirty frivolity not malevolent hypocrisy
Admit to deviant propulsions, reckless behaviors, breaking hearts
Come all ye be in the streets this is your orange revolution, your spectacle
For the reassembling turn out the lights you think too much you worry
To death the avant-garde is so ashamed of your feelings that you whispered
To me that he could use more I in his oeuvre, she could revisit less is more
And we can all slow down on the mic always sirens, always peasants
Always workers it's a gas to be a member of the underclass
Tapping wires makes sense like Holzer and Turk 182, infiltrate the ticker
Below the pontificating ham heads SUBWAY® glows in the darkness
On the edge of town there are too many wires in my life
Tangling beneath my desk this night is in the hands of an anxious driver

---

Greg Fuchs teaches students with disabilities to trust themselves and question everything. Fuchs has written many poems, published several books, and photographed a lot of things. He survives beneath the underground but surfaces occasionally with his fabulous artist wife, Alison Collins, and their magical son, Lucas. Fuchs would like to acknowledge the eternal Erica Kaufman of Isabel Lettres for publishing his tiny book *Metropolitan Transit*, which included "New Century."

JOANNA FUHRMAN

Brorealism

They say inside each bro is a different
identical bro, and inside that bro is the chicken
that laid the egg that started the world,
but dude, where's your magnetic pocket knife,
your heliotropic brain extensions made
for the afterlife, you know, your poetry?
When will you let your mouth become
the gap between the pizza crust and the cheese,
when will the earth become a ping-pong-ball-
sized pupil bopping past the forest of liquid
gold yolk-filled solo cups and into the firmament?
You may be a bro but that doesn't mean your
soul can't leak glitter all over the baseball diamond.
You may be a guy but that doesn't mean
your liver doesn't wear a pink feather beret,
that your id isn't draped in metallic negligee.
If inside each suburb, is an identical suburb
where mcmansions hide teeming cities
within, then when will your living room
explode into grimy, kaleidoscopic subways,
into cracked beakers full of the ashes of
interplanetary love affairs? In Brorealism,
none of us knows shit and that is the shit.
Even if the moonlight is made of cell phone
flashlights, even if the closet full of broken
telescope top hats is covered by a rack of
faded beer-label caps. Even if your vocabulary
is shrinking into atomic sub-particles,
please put down your TV-shaped bong.
Try opening that hole in your ear.

Joanna Fuhrman is the author of five books of poetry, most recently *The Year of Yellow Butterflies* (Hanging Loose Press, 2015) and *Pageant* (Alice James Books, 2009). "Brorealism" was originally published in *Across the Margin*.

CHRISTINE GARDINER

American Dreams

When I was a girl, I pricked
my ring finger on a rickety spindle
and slept for a thousand years.
The world kept turning
around me until my lover came
to rouse me with a kiss,
                                        and I awoke
in a hole, alone in my room.
No husband. No daughter.
No sun in the blood-stained sky.

The silence is loud. Time glistens.
I listen to the sound of sleep
as it breathes through the walls.
Down a dark hall of peepholes
and dead-bolted doors, children
are sleeping. Business men
are in bed with their wives.
They have such pretty, busy lives.
I fill up my bucket. I handle
my broom. I live alone
in a warm wooden room.
I know that fortune favors
the brave, but I am afraid
to go outside.
                        Just last week
I saw a werewolf on the street.
His eyes glintered sideways
as he watched me turning
the corner. Now I don't talk
to strangers. I avert my eyes
in the mailroom. I hide
under the stairs because
you never know where
trouble will find you.

I fear I am losing my hair.

Once I put a secret in a bottle
and it floated for a moment
before sinking to the bottom
of Gowanus.
                                        Good girl.
Be a good girl. Go see
that Daddy's other girl
is quiet in the basement.

So I go looking
through cupboards,
under the floorboards, in
between the hollow
attic walls
                        because I know
every hidden passage dead-
ends in her mermaid hair, a rag-
doll, drowning in a gown
of tattered plastic sashes.

Then the glass shatters,
the body evaporates,
and I am falling down
flights of perpetual stairs.
For days, I plummet through
the hours until I come to,
impaled on the crescent
horns of the moon.
                                        Outside
tomorrow yawns pink
and yellow-blue. The sunrise
luminescent as motor oil
floating in the gutter water.

I pick at my face in the wash-
room. Flush the toilet. Study
the razor and put it back
in its case. I wish I were dead,

but I have a mother, so
I must survive another day.

I'll just turn on the TV
and act like I'm alive.

Christine Gardiner holds an MFA from Brown University and a PhD from the University of Denver. She lives in Brooklyn and is an assistant professor of liberal arts at the College of New Rochelle School of New Resources, where she is edified by her students and their stories.

ROBERT GIBBONS

---

tell him we are yesterday

> I say who will name this Renaissance; who go tug the elbow
> of Langston Hughes; tell him we are yesterday again to McKay
> and Cullen and Hurston Walker and Baldwin; we doin' it again.
>
> —Ruth Forman, *Renaissance*

we are under the experience
of a renaissance
a look back to move forward, a call of our being
to sankofa, a shift, a brother and

the time unfavorable, the moon mops
the floor with the blood
our ancestors know this must be, so the way
will be clear for generations, their fear
and trembling, limitations unhinging
a march, a call, a demonstration, open
the dusty books, when we thought it
acceptable, but this struggle
is in motion, in perpetuity, under the influence

of the renaissance, a penance and a
prayer, water hose and dog and Charles Moore
and citizen council are still here, the doors
barred and locked and chained with
changed names and generational curses

the influences are fear, as it shifts
with the sunrises and inequality
in droplets, the signs of executive order
and disobedience, keeping us far from
the goal, this renaissance, still fighting
still to ignite the dream dreamers savor
left behind in the foot holes and strong holds
of power, with guard and police
and suspension of disbelief, the markets

of justice, graver, markers of James Chaney
and Ruby Bridges, all the world in stitches
tell them we are yesterday again

to explore we go back, to the ciphers, the
pipelines crude and rude and bait them
and rate them on a Pew scale, and tell them they
made it, and we really have not cannot tend the ivy
the ceiling, the towers, the power
brokers funding the plantation

the renaissance has not patience but rations
and pockets of redistribution, the pollution of street
corners becomes mourner's benches, teddy
bears and libations, the flame inflames the tree stumps
and rump of a back street, a hood
a flood of mistrust, and musty dance halls the only
place to feel at peace

tell them we are yesterday again, we are porters
then barterers then carters
carriers of the hate and decision of a dead president
that led with executive order, fought
alongside them

yesterday again while porters sleep
on the backs of Plessy versus
Ferguson, Dred and Coretta
not all are free, until all are free
come the judgment

Robert Gibbons is the recipient of a 2016 Norman Mailer Poetry Fellowship. He has been published in *About Place Journal*, *Fruita Pulp*, *Hyperallergic*, *Promethean*, *Suisun Valley Review*, *Turtle Island Quarterly*, and as a Brooklyn Poets "Poet of the Week." His first collection, *Close to the Tree*, was published in 2012 by Three Rooms Press.

ALAN GILBERT

I Love a Parade

The orchards come down in a barrage
of shower caps, setting the fireflies free
to extend their brief lifespans.
That's how I came to be called the Price Chopper,
singing a different kind of tune.
All these letters form a little heap
we're forced to walk around,
but that doesn't mean I invented the dance known as
a drink and the two-step.
In fact, I'm mostly bored with cocktails,
even the ones that come with miniature umbrellas
and flaming tiki heads in a tall glass etched
with an image of the sea.
Still, I've got the makings of a professional.
I'd collect bird nests except we live
in a desert.
The convention hotel is built on a fault line
running the length of a nearby highway.
We stayed so late the chairs were stacked around us
as our dreams got even weirder.
But that's much better than having them taken away
while sending stock images through
the ether with a tracking device
weathered for the elements
like a wrinkled tarp, rubber hose, or kitchen sponge
placed to soak up the river's silted run-off.

Everyone rides the bull these days.
We moved into an apartment complex on the edge of town
that was a favorite of shale field workers.
But the blizzard in October surprised us,
wrapping white grocery bags
around our shoes so that it looked as if
we were standing in the clouds.
I didn't invent that dance either,

at least according to my handwriting analyst
and the despair that occasionally overtakes me
at the sight of the wrecking ball
and everything I tightly clung to now gone.
Or almost gone. Or eventually will be.
No wonder we decided to eat in today,
though that doesn't explain what happened
to those meatballs—
except for the pieces of food stuck
between your teeth.
I'm not going to say it won't occur again,
but I'm guessing it will be different next time,
the talons close to the heart
digging a little less deeply into
the salmon's flesh lifted from the water.
Another channel features cubic zirconia earrings
on sale until the end of the hour,
after which the programming switches back
to local news and a report
on military homecomings.

Alan Gilbert is the author of two books of poetry, *The Treatment of Monuments* and *Late in the Antenna Fields*, as well as a collection of essays, articles, and reviews entitled *Another Future: Poetry and Art in a Postmodern Twilight*. He is the recipient of a 2009 New York Foundation for the Arts fellowship in poetry and a 2006 Creative Capital Foundation Award for Literature.

ARACELIS GIRMAY

Ode to the Little "r"

Little propeller
working between
the two fields of my a's,
making my name
a small boat
that leaves the port
of old San Juan
or Ponce,
with my grandfather,
Miguel, on a boat,
or in an airplane,
with a hundred or so
others, leaving the island
for work, cities,
in winters that would break
their bones, make old,
old men out of all of them,
factory workers, domino
players, little islands themselves
who would eat & be eaten by Chicago,
New York, the wars
they fought without
being able to vote for
the president. Little propeller
of their names: Francisco,
Reymundo, Arelis, Margarita,
Hernán, Roberto, Reina.
Little propeller of our names
delivering the cargo of blood
to the streets of Holyoke,
Brooklyn, New London,
Ojai, where the teacher says,
"Say your name?" sweetly,
& the beautiful propeller
working between

the two fields of my a's
& the teacher saying, "Oh!
You mean, 'Are-Raw-Sell-Lease.'"
Or "Robe-Bert-Toe"
or "Marred-Guh-Reetuh, like
the drink!" & the "r"
sounding like a balloon
deflating in the room, sad
& sagging. I am hurt.
It is as if I handed them
all my familiar trees & flowers,
every drawing of the family map
& boats & airplanes & cuatros
& coquis, & they used their English
to make an axe & tried to chop
them down. But, "r," little propeller
of my name, small & beautiful monster
changing shapes, you win. You fly
around the room, little bee, upsetting
the teacher & making all of Class-310A laugh,
you fly over the yard, in our mouths,
as our bodies make airplanes over the grass,
you, little propeller, are taking over the city,
you are the sound of cars racing, the sound
of bicycle spokes fitted with playing cards
to make it sound like we are going fast,
this is our ode to you, little "r," little
machine of our names, simple
as a heart, just working, always,
there when we go to the grocery,
there in the songs
we sing in our sleep.

Self-Portrait as the Airplane (Ode to the Noise in the Ear)

I was 7, an airplane
in the Aliso Viejo public pool.
The way I moved, face down
& slowly in the turquoise blue, gliding
from end to end, delivering my brother

to the concrete banks.
I was an airplane & felt deaf
like Uncle Nino who sound entered spangled
& warbling. Inside of his ear was a hearing aid.
He placed it in my ear once,
as though putting a small nest
in the rafters of a dollhouse,
a small, pink-colored suitcase of sounds
like a tiny glee-egg back into the rafters
of a house. Tiniest sadness
inside the ear, how I held it in my body, carefully,
not wanting the ear to blink or swallow
the small gravestone I tried on
like a prosthetic limb. I did not want
to but was more sad to say no. Instead,
stood still & felt the small thing tell me
about the body's first death below the laughs
& ordinary sounds clanging like miracles
from down the hall, exaggerated, in the red room,
I swear I could hear my grandmother
whispering with my aunt, I can't remember
what they said, but I thought
about a doctor's stethoscope,
& what is the sound of that one big kid, perpetually jumping
feet first into the deep side
of a pool's blue rectangle,
the silence & plunge, dispersal
of plates through the body's dark rooms
as my brother & I took turns shouting
each other's names underwater
& the kid made booms & booms? Canon ball.
Every thing was vanishing or about
to vanish, & we sharpened our ears like knives,
glad for how they worked.
I am greedy, greedy, greedy for the sound of gravel
under truck-tires, crickets, distant
soprano scratch of airplane
against the sky. My ears eat & eat.
All day. In sleep.
Like sitting down to a meal
without kissing my hands,
I am the angel of nothing.

If these ears were birds, I'd like for them to be
flying birds. But the ears are bodies,
they do what they want. Somewhere a hammer
echoes against a nail-point entering wood. Write it down.
The ear is not a jukebox, it opens its mouth & swallows
jackhammers, coyotes, & the tambourines, god,
give me the good & common sense
to keep the tongue from cursing
at this news.

Aracelis Girmay is the author of the collage-based picture book *changing, changing* and the poetry collections *the black maria*, *Teeth*, and *Kingdom Animalia*. The poems in this anthology were previously published in *Kingdom Animalia*. Girmay is on the editorial board of the African Poetry Book Fund and has received support from the Cave Canem, Whiting, and Civitella Ranieri foundations. She is on the faculty of Hampshire College's School for Interdisciplinary Arts.

GARTH GRAEPER

April

we parted in
the rain a ceaseless
sound

on lake
and trees

soft green
welling up how can I
forget when each
night moves
so slowly

I feel your
absence
in my wrists
and thighs clearing
a path

to real
nakedness

I want to be
found so my body
does not starve

or stay
untouched

you still haven't
answered me

these poems
just make use
of me make me
alone

from Brother Cabin

drinking
rum too timid
to speak

what my body
hears

long strands
tremble
inside me
all these lives

held back you
promised
to give me space

your fears leak
from my lungs
your wild grief-
song replaces

humming
insects

replaces your absence
with mine

rippling trees
re-knit the orchard's
sound

a movement
I can surrender to

no head or arms
just vibration
streaming downhill
to the lake

Garth Graeper has published two chapbooks, *Into the Forest Engine* (Projective Industries) and *By Deer Light* (Greying Ghost). He spent many years as an editor at Ugly Duckling Presse in Brooklyn, NY. This poem is from a manuscript inspired by Dorothy Wordsworth's wild language.

JESSICA GREENBAUM

I Love You More than All the Windows in New York City

The day turned into the city
and the city turned into the mind
and the moving trucks trumbled along
like loud worries speaking over
the bicycle's idea
which wove between
the more armored vehicles of expression
and over planks left by the construction workers
on a holiday morning when no work was being done
because no matter the day, we tend towards
remaking parts of it—what we said
or did, or how we looked—
and the buildings were like faces
lining the banks of a parade
obstructing and highlighting each other
defining height and width for each other
offsetting grace and function
like Audrey Hepburn from
Jesse Owens, and the hearty pigeons collaborate
with wrought iron fences
and become recurring choruses of memory
reassembling around benches
we sat in once, while seagulls wheel
like immigrating thoughts, and never-leaving
chickadees hop bared hedges and low trees
like commas and semi-colons, landing
where needed, separating
subjects from adjectives, stringing along
the long ideas, showing how the cage
has no door, and the lights changed
so the tide of sound ebbed and returned
like our own breath
and when I knew everything
was going to look the same as the mind

I stopped at a lively corner
where the signs themselves were like
perpendicular dialects in conversation and
I put both my feet on the ground
took the bag from the basket
so pleased it had not been crushed
by the mightiness of all else
that goes on and gave you the sentence inside.

I Took Out the Part

I took out the part where I compared a letter
Traveling steadily in its envelope
To the live pig I saw, traveling
Calmly in a basket
Atop the head of a woman
Riding a bicycle down the street in Bali. Too much
I figured. Juliet's "happy dagger" came in
A little later on, and I took that out. I took out
Mention of the elephant's
Foot pad, how it expands "like a bag of jelly"
When pressure is applied, meaning
The weight of the elephant. I might have been
Packing for your transcontinental
Bike ride, because I deemed superfluous
The woodpecker's tongue reaching
Back and curling around the
Jackhammered brain like a skein of bubble wrap
Which I learned about from Patty. And
I nixed the image of the lake's crust
Made from crests on a windy day
Or how we practice on fireworks
Saying, Oh, that's like a pink weeping willow
Hallucinating a geranium, or, Hercules just
Hit a line drive up to the moon.
I decided against Steve's paraphrase
Of Brecht: "It's hard to describe the trees
When police are in the forest," and also
The old gag about l.p.'s being like gasoline
Puddles that go up and dizzy us
With their fumes, and of middle age

Rotating us out of earth's orbit, stars like
A corrupted computer file
And the forgetful mind, a red-topped
Tupperware when we were young
Now without gravity or capacity like the shallow
Tea cup and you calling my name
Like a soliloquy of wildflowers
Spilled and gone, I took all that out.

Jessica Greenbaum is the author of two books of poems, *Inventing Difficulty* and *The Two Yvonnes*, and was recently awarded an NEA fellowship and the Agnes Fay di Castagnola Award for a manuscript in progress from the Poetry Society of America. She is also a social worker designing workshops for communities both inside and outside academia.

PATTI GREENBERG

We All Signed the Waiver and Consent Form

I need new moss for my bedroom.
The correct hand placement on a steering wheel is now 4 and 8.
Always remove a rabbit's gut system before cooking and eating your kill.
I know how to hula.
If you want to eat less, eat naked.
I arrive late and bring too much.
You will need all your worldly possessions in the afterlife.
I can't tolerate changing seasons.
The bottom line is how your butt looks.
Fred loved to square dance.
Duck sex is rough sex.
I forgot to get pens.
If an adolescent girl's tonsils are removed, she will grow larger breasts.
I can kill mosquitoes, house flies, silver fish, centipedes, moths, ants and
ticks with my bare hands.
Lizards bring me luck.
The driver who cut you off is later than you.
Theater can torture or anesthetize.
Non-hearing people sign the funniest fart jokes.
I grew a mega-snake.
I can't hear you.
I like choreographed violence.
Family closeness is overrated.
Dorm living or living in an igloo.
I STOP WHEN I GET TIRED.
All drivers must be able to swear.
Cold is imaginary and healthy, don't wear coats.
Paul told me he was self-cleaning.
Always keep a carnivorous pet, not a ruminating herbivore.
Leave everything out so you know where it is.
I wear the same clothes everyday.
The driver I let get in front of me will take the last moment of the yellow light.
Spring cleaning is a cruel deception.
Nothing personal.
Mostly I observe.

I am on Biblical time.
Never put a piece of sponge up your nose.
Mother and Father taught me to eat faster.
Letters have more frosting than numbers.
There are no more chances.
The driver tailgating me is an actual asshole.
I believe in minerals but not vitamins.
People who skip kindergarten are more likely to go to war.
Mostly I dislike Frank Sinatra.
I slept through my teens and woke up at twenty.
Salacious.
When I was a high school math teacher I threw my tie over my shoulder,
 spat out the window and had a heart attack.
I was supposed to be an only child from a different planet.
IT'S NOT A CONTEST.
A tiny troll in my throat gives me the best advice.
No one has been designated to toss old food or empty containers out of the fridge.
It's not poetry.
I'm afraid of the dark and it's my job to watch the door.
Match-making and arranging marriages are fast-growth employment opportunities.
Everyone I know talks too fast.
A diet of blubber.
Be prepared to live outside.
I'm starting to sweat.
Landscape paintings are best.
I'm not a sadist but I like to show off.
I don't know, what are you having?
Good posture is caused by swimming the backstroke.
Lists are boring.
Vampires are real and I want to be one.
400 Blows.
We are disappearing all the time.
I want the boy in the blue canoe.
Arbitrary tipping.
I stole.
You lied.
Ned survives on hickory smoked bacon.
Boy Scouts did the plumbing and electrical.
YOU CAN STOP ANYTIME.
I never learned calculus or how to gamble.
Lars turns the tv on loud to get to sleep.
Reveal something primordial.

Primordial is better than promotional.
Being petty is a big job.
Who am I again?
Redundant. YOU HAVE TO LEAVE.
These toilets are better than those toilets.
EXHAUSTIVE, INCLUSIVE, EXACT WORDS.
Notify me when it's time to eat or be somewhere.
I promised the trees I would misrepresent bears to children.
Omens can be.
My personal superhero suffers from hubris but is a gifted editor.
I have been a camel.
Neutrality is a challenge but try to remember the baguette in the oven.
Ungulates, ruminants and lagomorphs, but not rodents.
I can tell by your face I'm repeating myself but I'm in too deep to stop.
EVERY TIME AND ANY TIME.
I like wearing an offensive mask.
Copying anything is punishable by death.
Trust is viscous and jiggly.
I saw a religious leader jump from a black rock.
I can exaggerate acceptably.
I stayed on though I saw them yawn.
Cave life makes Karen dark and horny.
I'm vetting idols.
I'm tired of Woody Allen.
Eyebrows are an evolutionary success.
What I need now more than anything is a tree house.
WHEN HE SAID THAT'S ENOUGH HE MEANT SHUT THE FUCK UP.
My imaginary friends grew up.
Being tedious is a mortal sin.
I'm just saying.
I'm not the only one who ever put a dead pet in the fridge.
WAIT! I'M ALMOST DONE!
The baby is a peach.
Someone stole the manual.
Don't tell me what to do.
What should I do?

Patti Greenberg has lived in Brooklyn for twenty-seven years, loves it, and loves poetry. "We All Signed the Waiver and Consent Form" was previously published in *Truck*.

ALINA GREGORIAN

Navigational Clouds

You wear a cravat on the most Indiana day.
When you go outside a person greets you,
someone with jpegs and a lot of external motivation.
You ask this person if they have a folder in the revolution.
This person shares stories about building houses in the sky.
Researching nouns in address books.
Forging through half existing galaxies,
and those found under the radar of strong arguments.
You ask this person if the weather is certain.
If the rain is solitude. If they know how a citizen feels
when placed in a hallway with no doors.
Does this person feel like this, too, you want to ask.
But instead you say: "Bring me to the border."
And this person takes you to a ship, gives you laughter,
and paints molecules in your hair.

Utah

Here you are the insistence of an object
when that object takes me to your ocean.
I want to know the 1912 about the way
you dress your socks on winter nights
when pigeons dare to roam the streets.
I want to recite the loveboat sermon
with you, wielding through corridors,
finding objects to place in picture frames.
You said, "Let's defy gravity over there."
I sailed to Utah that day. Throwing cups
at the circumference of your name.

Alina Gregorian is an Armenian-American poet, artist, and curator living in Brooklyn, NY. She is the author of the chapbooks *Flags for Adjectives* (Diez) and *Navigational Clouds* (Monk Books), in which the poems "Navigational Clouds" and "Utah" appear. She curates Triptych Readings and a video poetry series on the *Huffington Post*. Find her online here: alinagregorian.com.

RACHEL ELIZA GRIFFITHS

Guitar Soliloquy

The woman in blue overalls
rubbed her fingers over
my open mouth. A woman
whose eyes gone away
to a different time of blues.
Time before water. Time
before bite, dog & bullet.
She rubbed my neck,
murmuring, Us can't fly
Us can't fly, mah Teacake,
mah sweetbread boy. In my mouth
I tasted Lake Okeechobee's apology,
forty miles wide & sixty miles long.
The jook of water washed
over my dusky jubilee.
This dead boy's old music box
lost somewhere in those waters.
I felt it all in her hands rubbing me
the night before she washed him
down for the last time, singing in his
ear. His ghost is here too, giving
me a try & hum. Both of them
weeping at this split of spirit.
Her hands gripped his stone-cold hands
around my throat, making angels
pluck their cat-gut lyres. Her hands
beckoned the brass ghosts of
Bahaman drummers to leap,
fly, walk along a field of low clouds
with dusty feet. *O morning woman,*
I want to say to her
when they get ready to pull the lid
over me & this boy. *O woman,*
I got to say, *love ain't even quiet in here.*
Not long as I'm in this boy's hands,

opening a strawberry mouth
over his half-smiling stitched lips.
Woman, me & this white silk
canopy, going to bear your man
'til he wake up again. When he wake up
again, singing to you. *Us can fly,*
heah Janie, Us can fly for certain.
Gal, just wait for us
to wake up in your arms.

Blues for Sweet Thing

> Whose little girl am I?
> Anyone who has money to buy.
> What do they call me?
>
> —Nina Simone

I'm honeysuckle.
A girl child crying
holy seven sins.

A harp & loom.
A rack of ribs.
A ribcage.

A pocket of coins
never to be spent
because my country

no longer exists. Almanac,
without page numbers

or prophecy.
For you I was sycamore,

pear, willow,
maple & bougainvillea.

For you
I was bathwater.

Gazelle, artichoke,
tulip & daffodil.

Your father's tears.

Blue fern of smoke
from a cigarette

opened by a fist
of summer rain.

For you
I was a red dress.

Teeth that glowed
under the hot bulb
of a basement party.

I was a sacrificial smile burning off
lamb's fat after midnight.

Ace & diamond.

The good time
no clock could find.

White sheet. A pearl drop earring.
Shadow wearing her mother's hat.

Birdcage. A bird who sat inside
your ears like a wound

until clarity sounded
its back-break trumpet.

A woman gone to church
with no stockings.

A woman gone to love
wearing no lingerie.

No skin either.

Your memories pulled apart
by a boll weevil's testimony.

For you
I was all these things.

I ended up
being

honeysuckle threading
a ghetto fence.

Dandelion crushed
between a cement wall.

The rapper's accessory.
A bank's vault.

I know more
about the sadness in paper

than the hands that
crush paper into clouds.

Ghost
of magnolia.

How did I end up
being a ghost of every
nothing?

I was a sweet thing
until the moon was sobbing

along the stairwell tower
of some woman's throat.

Rachel Eliza Griffiths is a poet and visual artist. She is the author of four collections of poetry, including *Miracle Arrhythmia*, *The Requited Distance*, *Mule & Pear*, and *Lighting the Shadow*. She lives in Brooklyn, New York. These poems were previously published in *Mule & Pear* (New Issues Poetry & Prose, 2011).

SARAH JEAN GRIMM

Shapewear

A body is matter to be molded
By use of whale bone and lace or
By taking a body for long walks

There are ways to file one down
To make a body a better shape
Not this boring shrub fruit

Try an hourglass if you want to
Remind a man of his mortality

Best to become a clock
The sands of time will get up inside you
Each time you are picked up and turned over

You will always be itching
Never mind the home remedies
Some men like to have a project
To hammer away at

Did you know some women are shaped like bananas
I have never seen one myself
In the wild

Only as Figure 3. in a state-approved textbook
Because they teach this stuff in health class
To lead girls into their own dysmorphia

You are what you eat
So from now on I am surviving on spunk
I want to possess whatever allows you to be bold
Without getting called feisty

My gut reaction when I am in the world
Is to apologize whether or not I am sorry

No one's ever said sorry to me
For making my eyelashes stick together
With their egg on my face

I am doll eyes I need a doll waist
I make a lovely figure with what I've been given
When I encase my body in exoskeleton

This is how I want
To be looked at but not seen

Who decides what the body absorbs
Versus what it reflects

And how are our bodies not
The most boring thing about us
By now

I would starve mine to transcend
Or shuffle off
If I knew you wouldn't find it cute

I would stand naked at the altar
In the name of the Patriarchy
In the name of its Sons
In the name of the Spirit of Capitalism

When can we retire the syllogism
Time is money is the root of evil

We all know that women are the root
And the dirt and the stem and the bulb

We are ripe swelling fruits
Carrying the seeds
Of our mutually assured destruction

The ways in which we fuck each other up
Let me count them
They are endless fluffy sheep
Bedding me for beauty rest

Sarah Jean Grimm is the author of *Soft Focus* (Metatron, 2017) and co-founding editor of *Powder Keg Magazine*. She lives in Brooklyn. "Shapewear" was first published in *H_NGM_N*.

BETSY GUTTMACHER

Melville in New York

My pipe is nicer than you might expect.
It has a winged dove carved starboard side,
the dark brown wood rubbed soft by my old thumb
on countless nights outside in rain, in snow
near trash, the ash sucked clean and still, the ache.
The need to find a core more still than mine
is greater than the need to stay inside
or stay alive. When I was young I worked
so hard to stay alive, my mind abuzz with plans
spooling out like morning cast until
my net was full—doormen, the cops, my bride.
But their gaze was not the balm I craved,
it couldn't shake me free or pull me from the sea.
So I smoked, shot smack, drank up. Not much
could come between my dove and me, crouched
low, in shame, in wind, not salt enough
to stay on land, but there are things I miss.
A night of song, a friend along, an orchestra,
a gallery, a quiet place to think. Now my mind
has spots in it where at night birds alight, touching
down on an archipelago strewn with shards
and shells, on shores, where in dark eggs hatch
so gulls can feed on the turtle-young who crawl
under the palms, the moon, my dove, my pipe
their gain, so slight, so like my threshold of regret.

Betsy Guttmacher landed in Brooklyn in 1998 and is currently director of volunteer programs for a local nonprofit organization. She likes taking pictures of found hearts on the sidewalk (@gumloveetc) and encourages everyone to look down more. She discovered a late-in-life love of poetry through Brooklyn Poets workshops and is a member of the Brooklyn-based poetry collective Sweet Action.

KIMIKO HAHN

Outside the Ridiculous Coffee Stand

where I buy my daughter a skimmed-something
she lights up whether I like it or not and she knows I don't

then I keep pace on to Bergen
where we both wait for her F. I blurt out

when you were little,
I should have said stuff like 'I'm proud of you'

instead of 'you must be proud of yourself.'
Her quiet broadcasts I'm nuts

so I say, *okay that's nutty.*
And she blows smoke out laughing,

I'm proud of you, Mama. Though I can't go to poetry readings
because I'll cry. I blurt, *It's okay to cry*

to which she tamps out her cigarette,
sings out, *I know!*

swipes then squeezes into the express
to an in-tray of stuff that does not hold her as dearly.

Weather with My Daughter

I think how much you love weather,
especially that shower we walked into
returning from *Spice Girls*
my arm around your shoulder,
you, the taller, holding my umbrella
as the downpour created a circular wall.
We sloshed to your father's
where I left you off.

Was I pleased to have the rest of the day to myself?
the night with a lover? Maybe
I congratulated myself for a fun movie choice.
I only recall a seasickness—
as if swept out beyond the Buttermilk Channel
too far for calling out
to you in your little pink room.
Too far to attempt a happiness
as if that had everything to do
with my own run-off.

Kimiko Hahn is the author of nine books. Her latest collections, *Toxic Flora* and *Brain Fever*, were triggered by rarefied fields of science. She teaches in the MFA Program in Creative Writing & Literary Translation at Queens College, CUNY.

SAM HALL

Prologue: The Infinite Reduction
after Thomas Merton, *The Geography of Lograire*

4. Will Pollard wily Pollard sip unctuous terra firma, nicotiana, tar Carmine tar terra firma horizon is Pollard my wind
Wily Pollard that asphalt that phallus it was carmine
That chihuahua, that ratty chihuahua, yap and hound
Will Pollard sip Pollard wily pebbled sky
Leave stay carmine sip wily pebbled carmine aspirated sky
Will dusty trailer births dawning stop delivering
And forget the wily phallus-womb asphalt
Yellow vinyl shotgun sitting on tufts patched grass
Carmine here swells terra firma grass patched tufts
Yellowed home wily fulvous as-
Phalt unctuous at the plateau of providence
Phallus gorge and carmine pebbled chakra plateau
In blessed carmine Pollard there is never dawning

. . . .

INTERSTATE REGENCY

10. The corridor stretches tall, opulent grinning, scarlet carpet strip licking the dark for want. All the dark lies in want trembling, hatching—cracked penultimate filmstrip. Crackling as we tilted home to our own concrete screening: "Miss you. Your genuflect." Suburbs of flat line. The hard line of acuity. The moon dipped and I forgot "This Little Light Of Mine" for want of parting parties.

. . . .

19. Findings: pressed powder, taupe. Bobby pins. Pomade. Nylon. Cotton. Rayon. Imperial power. Arabesque. King of the jungle. White sign (code) found edelweiss wine. Found premiere porters, several. Garish, gaudy jewels. Singing box (a fraud). Pan American taught pilot politeness sought redesign and tread. First fig fortune. Rescue water. Gluttonous scotch. Found international liquor. Found baseball bats. ROTC. Pantone No. 5. Yellow No. 3. Mormon

bible. Stationary stationary. Staples. Labels. Bruises. Coats. Cats. An anthill of paisley and poppy and feather. Singed in mahogany, haphazardly "Woe." Yes, blood and placenta (comical). First grade handshake. Plum corporate. Fat to the hump of the neck. Finnegan's Wake. Yeats slurred cheap shots, ring nosed in the dim of the den. Found how many carts last Thursday? None. All empty and asphalt. Please, you see, we found her blouse, her blinds, laxatives, pins, tinctures, bubbles (oils), stilettos, princess seams, organics, platinum patina, jumper cables, coral cashmere, dulce de leche, ouija board, Per- cocet, OxyContin, Methadone, snow, beachfront playground. Please, we found black alligator loafers, broiled goose, fannypacks with an extra wide belt and three hidden pockets in a lovely pallet of textures. Please she had nothing: honest cal- lous (no cunnilingus). Want of cheap shots. Found crockpot (for sweltering swol- len men). Vermicular habanero, tailored hem for the pint night. Found a message for Taylor, for Maxine. State solid. Pouted polluted president—mortgage default. Swear to private savings. Private collection bourbon, roses and garland and drop bead bracelets magnetic balance. Found. Found. Uncovered found. Uncoveredet- discovered. Found her other end. Found all the bodies bloated, brandied.

Sam Hall is a graduate of the New School where she received her MFA in poetry and was a teaching assistant to Greil Marcus. She is Saeed Jones's personal assistant and development coordinator at the Kentucky College of Art + Design at Spalding University in Louisville, KY. She is the co-founder of the Outernet, an interactive poetry-art event.

REGINALD HARRIS

Retired

for Ernie Shavers

After the final bell, the terrible
arithmetics of hitting, getting hit,
erased your speed. The warring past
followed you like ghosts, long train of rounds
old seconds hovering just outside the ring.

The fans remain, unable to resist your pull,
the auras of force that cloak you always. They
long to see you, reach out, call you *Champ*,
lay thin trembling fingers on the silenced cannon
of your arms, shake the once-deadly weapons
of your hands, remembering.

True power never goes away. They feel
its constant racing beneath your tailored
suit, see the snap that spites a weary body
as you stand, nod to cheers, applause,
respect:

            Plant your feet, tuck in your
chin, turn on the thickened pivot of your waist,
put your body's bulk into a flurry, release
an unslaked appetite for hitting to the air,
unveil a face still yearning, still
too intimate with the wrath of God.

Transfer Student

'*Niggas here ain't shit,*' he whispered
To me on the back row, compatriots
In exile in that class. '*They talk shit*

But won't DO shit—I shot a motherfucker once
For having too much mouth.'

I nodded, drank in useful wisdom
From his seething, a blue-black older
Boy with ancient empty eyes, already
Intimate with rage.

He disappeared the next day, never
To be seen again, except in my own
Tumescent fevered dreams, fit into what
I'd already learned of words from belts

And slaps and backyard switches: *Silence* rhymes
with *Violence*. The time to be afraid is when the talking stops.

The director of library and outreach services for Poets House in New York City, Reginald Harris won the 2012 Cave Canem/Northwestern University Press Poetry Prize for *Autogeography*. A Pushcart Prize nominee and the associate editor for Lambda Literary Foundation's *Lambda Literary Review*, his work has appeared in numerous journals, anthologies, and other publications. He lives with his partner in Midwood, where he pretends to work on another manuscript.

JULIE HART

Resting Bitch Face

My face no longer settles into smile
I want but cannot turn it upside down
It feels too much like simple-minded guile
Genetically it is the Cooney frown.

It's not that I am angry or judgmental
Accusing you of things you didn't do
Authentic's not the same as sentimental
I'll smile when you say something that is true.

I can't police my face to make you happy
My mind is busy thinking my own thoughts
It's not my job to fix you when you're crappy
Your narcissism's showing and self-doubt.

Not sweet like sugar but like cinnamon
Won't candy-coat your bitterness again.

Originally from Minnesota, Julie Hart has lived in London, Zurich, and Tokyo, and now lives in Brooklyn Heights. Her work can be found in *PANK*, the *Rumpus, Vol. 1 Brooklyn*, and *Blue Lyra Review*, where "Resting Bitch Face" was first published. Follow her at juliehartwrites.com.

MATTHEA HARVEY

The Inside Out Mermaid

The Inside Out Mermaid is fine with letting it all hang out—veins, muscles, the bits of fat at her belly, her small grey spleen. At first her lover loves it—with her organs on the outside, she's the ultimate open book. He can pump her lungs like two bellows and make her gasp; ask her difficult questions and study the synapses firing in her brain as she answers to see if she's lying; poke a pleasure center in the frontal lobe and watch her squirm. Want to tug on her heartstrings? No need for bouquets or sad stories about his childhood. He just plucks a pulmonary vein and watches the left ventricle flounder. But before long, she starts to sense that her lover, like all the others before him, is getting restless. This is when she usually starts showing them her collections—the basket of keys from all over the world, the box of zippers with teeth of every imaginable size—all chosen to convey a sense of openness. As a last resort, she'll even read out loud the entries from her diary about him to him. But soon he'll become convinced she's hiding things from him and she is. Her perfect skin. Her long black hair. Her red mouth, never chapped from exposure to sun or wind, and how she secretly loves that he can't touch her here or here.

The Future of Terror / 1

The generalissimo's glands directed him
to and fro. *Geronimo!* said the über-goon
we called God, and we were off to the races.
Never mind that we could only grow
grey things, that inspecting the horses' gums
in the gymnasium predicted a jagged
road ahead. We were tired of hard news—
it helped to turn down our hearing aids.
We could already all do impeccable imitations
of the idiot, his insistent incisors working on
a steak as he said *there's an intimacy to invasion*.
That much was true. When we got jaded
about joyrides, we could always play games
in the kitchen garden with the prisoners.
Jump the Gun, Fine Kettle of Fish and Kick
the Kidney were our favorites. The laws
the linguists thought up were particularly

lissome, full of magical loopholes that
spit out medals. We had made the big time,
but night still nipped at our heels.
The navigator's needle swung strangely,
oscillating between the oilwells
and *ask again later*. We tried to pull ourselves
together by practicing quarterback sneaks
along the pylons, but the race to the ravine
was starting to feel as real as the R.I.P.'s
and roses carved into rock. Suddenly the sight
of a schoolbag could send us scrambling.

The Crowds Cheered as Gloom Galloped Away

Everyone was happier. But where did the sadness go? People wanted to know. They didn't want it collecting in their elbows or knees then popping up later. The girl who thought of the ponies made a lot of money. Now a month's supply of pills came in a hard blue case with a handle. You opened it & found the usual vial plus six tiny ponies of assorted shapes & sizes, softly breathing in the Styrofoam. Often they had to be pried out & would wobble a little when first put on the ground. In the beginning the children tried to play with them, but the sharp hooves nicked their fingers & the ponies refused to jump over pencil hurdles. The children stopped feeding them sugarwater & the ponies were left to break their legs on the gardens' gravel paths or drown in the gutters. On the first day of the month, rats gathered on doorsteps & spat out only the bitter manes. Many a pony's last sight was a bounding squirrel with its tail hovering over its head like a halo. Behind the movie theatre the hardier ponies gathered in packs amongst the cigarette butts, getting their hooves stuck in wads of gum. They lined the hills at funerals, huddled under folding chairs at weddings. It became a matter of pride if one of your ponies proved unusually sturdy. People would smile & say, "This would have been an awful month for me," pointing to the glossy palomino trotting energetically around their ankles. Eventually, the ponies were no longer needed. People had learned to imagine their sadness trotting away. & when they wanted something more tangible, they could always go to the racetrack & study the larger horses' faces. Gloom, #341, with those big black eyes, was almost sure to win.

Matthea Harvey is a poet and artist who has published five books of poetry, most recently *If the Tabloids Are True What Are You?*, as well as two children's books. "The Inside Out Mermaid" appeared in *T Magazine* with an illustration by Jeff Koons; "The Crowds Cheered as Gloom Galloped Away" in *Ploughshares*; and "The Future of Terror / 1" in her book *Modern Life*, published by Graywolf.

THOMAS HEISE

New York City

There's nothing latent in my wireless imagination where everything, even the heart's muscle, is public. Give me one more love song and I'll destroy it. Orpheus looked over his shoulder because he wanted Lili Brik to disappear, the only way to save himself for the poems he thought he'd write before thirty-six arrived, a shock in its chamber. Oh mother. Oh love. Beauty enters wrapped in furs and the whole train to Moscow suddenly unsure of itself, the revolution suspended between wheels: "Down with Symbolism. Long live the living rose!" The moment the chimp recognized he was human, he began to paint over the mirror. These days, mystery floating in the recesses of the plaza, a memory of green sky high above us like glamour and the history surrounding us forgotten for a minute, then we're cold. Every woman begins as a description. A brochure. A leaflet. Love made into origami. This one's now for July. This one's now for August. This one's now in the wave pool, buoyed by the chlorine and sense of possibility, as if the water were in me and churning and could this feeling last forever and that seagull, you don't have to think. Sometimes you have to be shot in the heart in order to stop dreaming. These days of false humour and sequins, like Jean Nouvel's windows, we look in from the outside because we're fortunate to be poor and part of the city. Every city begins as an accident and soon becomes a need. The player-piano melancholy through the avenues now that the night is quiet ushered in by a line of crows as if pulling a photographer's cloth. Finely granulated static after the daily life counting coins in our solitude after the dry cleaners after the loneliness of the mall at closing, the lights in the fountain turned off, after that you were, after the ornamental civic gardens after the letters tossed from a balcony after the street that ended at a power plant and a river you never drank from, you were, then the orphanage then the House of Assignation then the locked door then the brain scan, you were, the nonfunctional façade after the mattress store after the Museum of Mind Over Matter after that after all that, you were, and the great throbbing crowd once in super slow-mo formed a Rorschach blot, the visuals moving to the melody of a soundtrack, I don't have a map, she said, I just enter the territory—*I love you to this point.* A leaf. A few thoughts on paper. Nature doesn't grow on trees, the critic said, but we don't believe her because we don't believe in Nature, and even her dress is synthetic and her glasses have no lenses so how can she see the moon, or the flag planted there for Marilyn? These days, the intricate architecture of our past lives, the rhythm and beauty of it, the way you could walk into a stanza at midnight and be surprised to find me at the desk, our home, it was an idea I grew inside of, and if asked to describe these days, what I would say would fail, as does every poem at the title. I'm remembering in Berlin remembering you and I'm remembering in New York remembering you and I'm on a bus by Tupper Lake remembering you for the first time I can't, the morning in blades of light through the pine trees, a kind of triage. Every map begins as a legend and ends with a woman on the Bosphorus where the blue is so supple you wore it as a scarf and then you took a shuttle called a metaphor. In forty years, I'll be dead if I'm lucky. These days, three o'clock in the afternoon of November, the Eiffel Tower a radio transmitter of secret signals to the befuddlement of the professor who thought life was fixed in amber and that one's home could never turn into a pawn shop or that no one would blow up the Louvre and replace it with a W, rather than these love letters to the people of Juarez. We walk through the streets like a seam in Barthes' stocking, we're where the threads come together before they unravel. All that's solid melts into money and the day ends with a comma, and even belatedness is marketed like the colour green will wash the dirt out of your mouth and with it another philosophy of progress. The city in which you left me I give it back like remorse. My breath in your deaf ears, we're both bodies, only yours in autumn is gone.

Thomas Heise is the author of *Moth; or how I came to be with you again* (Sarabande, 2013), *Horror Vacui: Poems* (Sarabande, 2006), and *Urban Underworlds: A Geography of Twentieth-Century American Literature and Culture* (Rutgers, 2011). He lives in Brooklyn and works as an assistant professor in the Department of English at Pennsylvania State University at Abington. At present, he is finishing his fourth book, a novel.

MARWA HELAL

invasive species self-questionnaire

ask or aks?
depends.
on what?
company, mood, memory,
the speed of code-
switch.

weed or beautiful flower?
beautiful flower…growing
everywhere, anywhere, anywhere

what happens when the colonizer's blood runs through yours?
blood type: O-
universal donor, du bois's double-consciousness;
an inner conflict. an unceasing
awareness of the gaze/a jihad of the naafs,
my iranian sociology professor would say.

funny thing
about being a universal donor is
you can give everyone blood
but only take from your own kind.

oppressed or oppressor?
complicit.
see also: under siege.

sand nigger or cherry picker?
america can't even
get the slur right.

who made this taxonomy?
unmake it.

terrorist or freedom fighter?
freedom fighter. ask a real question.

when you say: "ask a real question," is that part of this performance?
yes, this is a performance of my humanity. i am saying, "look, look at me.
how intelligent i am. look, see: how i am, how i am avoiding death."

good. because i thought for a moment, you might be possessed.
my writing is the only thing i'll let them possess.

occupation or conflict?
occupation. i said: ask a real question.

where do you want to be buried?
(i am, i am. and everywhere.) not here.

what is native?
not here. (i am, i am. and everywhere.)

Marwa Helal is a poet and journalist. She is the winner of *BOMB Magazine*'s 2016 Poetry Prize; a fellow of Brooklyn Poets and Cave Canem, she received her MFA in creative writing from the New School.

RICARDO HERNANDEZ

Angel of 8320 Bay Parkway's Rooftop

I've been here since 1923,
had a lot of families
reside beneath me

with all kinds of visits
from residents and non-
residents alike

during the fall,
they'll be here only on
days and nights
that are bearable

during the winter,
they'll be up here
only, and only if
Global Warming
becomes
Globally Warmed

during the spring,
they'll rush up here
anticipating the warmth
but run back down
when the rain sets in

during the summer,
they're always here

some come up to tan,
stretch nearly naked
bodies across mine

others form cyphers,
friends and brothers for
the ritual blunt smoke

some nights, they
drink as if contents
held within bellies
won't spill out on me

occasionally,
when the few visible
stars are out, they fuck

and when most of the
city is asleep, vandals
make their appearance
utilizing my vertical skin
as their canvas of choice

Dutch Master guts
emptied out all over,
oil bottles,
spray paint cans,
fifths of Georgi Vodka,
and used condoms
could be found
scattered across me

as if my feelings
don't matter at all

after witnessing
these acts of what could
only be described
as debauchery

I ponder when will
they stop using me
for their dirty deeds

these humans,
young and old,
wise and foolish

the using is what's
getting me upset

maybe I'd like to join
the cypher,
or drink,
or paint,
or tan,
or fuck

then I ask myself,
how does a rooftop
fuck?

and I figure
it might be in the
way we don't hold on
to those that leap off.

Ricardo Hernandez was born in Brooklyn, New York, on July 22, 1985. Enlisting after graduating from high school, Ricardo served in the U.S. Air Force with the 71st Fighter Squadron, also known as the Ironmen. After the military, and briefly living in Florida, Ricardo returned to Brooklyn where he would discover his hometown anew during his pursuit of becoming a poet.

EDWARD HIRSCH

from Gabriel: A Poem

I stood at the damaged site
Across the street from my house
And watched a steel ball

Crashing into the homeless shelter
Abandoned on Dean Street
All the people scattered

It takes tremendous force
To weaken a building
And turn bricks into rubble

But it doesn't take long
The crane swung around
And pitched the heavy ball

Into the guts of the structure
Holding its side
Like a wounded veteran

The hard hats gathered
To watch the pendulum swing
Into the concrete body

Of a building slated for demolition
So there could be progress
I was against the project

And riveted to the wreckage
Time and again the fighter wavered
And finally collapsed

I did not stay to see the building
Broken down into debris
And then carted away

Some nights I could not tell
If he was the wrecking ball
Or the building it crashed into

To Poetry

Don't desert me
just because I stayed up last night
watching *The Lost Weekend.*

I know I've spent too much time
praising your naked body to strangers
and gossiping about lovers you betrayed.

I've stalked you in foreign cities
and followed your far-flung movements,
pretending I could describe you.

Forgive me for getting jacked on coffee
and obsessing over your features
year after jittery year.

I'm sorry for handing you a line
and typing you on a screen,
but don't let me suffer in silence.

Does anyone still invoke the Muse,
string a wooden lyre for Apollo,
or try to saddle up Pegasus?

Winged horse, heavenly god or goddess,
indifferent entity, secret code, stored magic,
pleasance and half wonder, hell,

I have loved you my entire life
without even knowing what you are
or how—please help me—to find you.

God and Me

The stars look like a broken belt
Glittering over the lakes and mountains

The moon looks like a tilted crown

Down here there's a whole lot of racket
In churches and bedrooms
Some good folks are speaking in tongues
And raising the rafters

I wonder if the Lord ever gets tired
Of so much flattery from the fundamentalists
He probably likes it better
Than all the complaints and entreaties

I'm standing up to listen
But he has nothing to say to the atheists

It would be nice to believe
That heaven is like a schoolyard
In which everyone gets chosen
Even the laggards

My friends are seekers and exiles
Who won't desert the stories

Me
I can't give him up
But I can't believe in him either
It's a one-sided relationship
I without *Thou*

He has whole galaxies to worry about
I don't suppose he gets too worked up
My puny self
Is more real to me
Than his immense non-being

I'm a tiny void with attributes
With my own little river of tears

But what is he
Who fills the world with trees and stars
And leaves us alone
With our wars and atrocities
Our deadly human nature
Our sad dominion over the fish and the fowl

Look
No one knows why
There is so much silence in the upper spheres
And so much suffering down here

The Almighty skipped over our houses

Edward Hirsch, a MacArthur Fellow, has published nine books of poems, including *The Living Fire* (Knopf, 2010) and *Gabriel: A Poem* (Knopf, 2014), a section of which is excerpted here, and five books of prose, among them *Poet's Choice* (Houghton Mifflin Harcourt, 2006) and *A Poet's Glossary* (Houghton Mifflin Harcourt, 2014), where "To Poetry" first appeared. The poem "God and Me" first appeared in *T Magazine*. He lives in Brooklyn.

CATHY PARK HONG

Happy Days

Garcon, you snore so rhapsodically but hup hup,
Peach schnapps & coke zero
with a gumball green mermaid swizzle stick—
I need me a diabetic shock.

I yearned so long to be ensorceling,
yet I'm always a meter maid, never a mermaid.
I'd populate this world w'idlers of my kind,
but pistil-less, I'm pissily only one.

Who made me this way? Oh *you*. Oolong Ma.
(Go bury yourself in a sandpit, Ma,
while my galpals and I split a cranmuffin 5 ways
and *watch*.)

So here I gig, in this club empty
as a tampon dispenser inside the rancid shell
of a Texan gas station—still
I'll stand, declaim:

Not enough letters in my soup, Garcon!
All I'm doing is inging
like an atting instrel,
I'm rank when I need to be frank!

Just you wait, I'll hijack all type—
My specialty? Scandinavian Modern
Pinkface.

Trouble in Mind

A heartvein throbs between her brows: Ketty-San's
incensed another joke's made at her expense,

With characters of granite schist, she hashtags a ban
on all such jokes, then they, her so-
called friends, pipe up: Why are you
  making such a stink
  on race?
You're so post, you're Silicon.

Scuttle back to her spot as sidekick chum.
Her lyric's needed when they need a backup
  minor key,
to that lead's cracker blues that got no core
  (*what* a snore).

But what core is Ketty-San, sidekick chum?
Torn like tendrils of bloody tenderloin
floating in the sea, heart
  a stage set
  about to be struck—

All nightlong, she scribbles her useless Esoterica.
All daylong, mumble-cored, she meeps,
meeps along.

Cathy Park Hong's latest poetry collection, *Engine Empire*, was published in 2012 by W.W. Norton. Her other collections include *Dance Dance Revolution*, chosen by Adrienne Rich for the Barnard Women Poets Prize, and *Translating Mo'um*. Hong is the recipient of fellowships from the Guggenheim Foundation, the National Endowment for the Arts, and the New York Foundation for the Arts. Her poems have been published in *Poetry*, *A Public Space*, *Paris Review*, *McSweeney's*, the *Baffler*, *Boston Review*, the *Nation*, and other journals. She is the poetry editor of the *New Republic* and an associate professor at Sarah Lawrence College.

CHRIS HOSEA

Good Conduct Well Chastised

I feel freedom subway in my head
so silent touching everything Sunday I can
wake up not go at large pretty spaces
a tunnel you have where I could dig my spade
bury my skull ultimately last looks
religions valid as any other a certain irony
like yours swinging thin bleached braid
around trash look Goth-black AWOL
prep school guise shows off your ink well
against the silken gash of history or so said
a sticker over your head when you locked
on me slammed your butt against door
too many strangers would try to pry in
and your dead-eyed stare got stuck
I made you look in mirror for self-reflexivity
you had it in teeth a fave stick stuck
my too-cold pinky wet into your jaw
when your mouth took in each day's power
figures in memory stood on steps vague
with hammer grim aspect mustache violet
water glue gilds us customers as useless
sugar pills broken friendship bracelet ripped
pieces in purse a purse not ever a bag
thank God drop your hand on key bunch
too soon so much tiny crystals ants around
native to your room we live and study among them
potential learnings potent sexual seminars
best practices how to cheat at Boggle
you will own this town singing hoarsely
though fucking scared from steeple so scared
above City Hall singing I am available
I am a flesh bell went to market jingling
don't give a damn who knows it
sweater hand coarse worn damp never warmer
smooth reasons you'd use to graduate once more

and again drop out sometime so long ago to sleep
I never knew him and it's cheap but you have
to bargain because to bargain is the custom
or be rude I brought myself alone to go down up
to swirling surface close as I could huff of
transdermal toxins be alone like piston
solar panel middle-aged bachelor padding
your hall can you plug me into your grid
beautiful separate girl looked at first for form alone
why didn't I take a picture would it have lasted
longer thighs straighter pale pickets white tubes
true I've got scorn want you come back hit me
air is best energy drink come empty buses come candles
bonfires end rent party come asphalt summer soon

Chris Hosea is the author of two books of poetry: *Put Your Hands In* (LSU Press, 2014), selected by John Ashbery for the Walt Whitman Award from the Academy of American Poets, and *Double Zero* (Prelude Books, 2016). He lives in Brooklyn.

CHRISTINE SHAN SHAN HOU

Community Garden for Lonely Girls

Ordinary feelings require melodramatic status.
A driveway cannot expect sympathy especially
if it is rotten and surrounded by invasive species.
I dream sporadically of reincarnation. I wet myself
thinking about the possibility. In movies, wounded
female birds attract fancy men. The brown bird of reality
is the true vacillator. A love story is told with a razorblade
tucked beneath its tongue. Sometimes I am alarmed by
the facts it produces. Most of the time I accept them.
To rub up against someone else's love is dangerous.
Even if the feeling is mutual one must take into account
vocation. A vocation does not always have a place.
A vacation usually does, mine is a melting shopping
mall where I encounter a corporate water fountain,
an enormous green globe glistening like a peeled grape.
I throw pennies at it until it explodes. How easy it is to
confuse irresponsible behavior for radical politics,
incurable mania, witchy spells, etc.
Goodnight self, my goddess is dimming.

Christine Shan Shan Hou is a poet and artist based in Brooklyn, NY. Publications include *Community Garden for Lonely Girls* (Gramma Poetry, 2017), *I'm Sunlight* (The Song Cave, 2016), *C O N C R E T E S O U N D* (2011), a collaborative artists' book with artist Audra Wolowiec, and *Accumulations* (Publication Studio, 2010). "Community Garden for Lonely Girls" was originally published in *ILK*. Follow her at christinehou.com.

JP HOWARD

Black Boys Song

Black boys can't walk streets
without being target practice.
Black boys can't take a seat
on the bus, in a train, on a plane
without being target practice.
Black boys tired of dying.
Black boys tired of trying
to stop dying, everyday,
Black boys got Mama's
praying for them.

Black boys got songs to sing.
Black boys sound like lullabies.
Black boys be like flowers in bloom.
Black boys, black boys,
sometimes y'all go boom.

Ghazal: What Love Takes

I'm sleeping as I write this; you're standing over me crying
while Ella belts out: No, no they can't take that away from me

If this is all I can get, your hand on my shoulder in the dream,
lips warm against my neck, I'll take that

The alarm clock becomes enemy; I press snooze every few minutes,
search for you and finally press stop when I can't take it any more

Please don't mistake this for a love poem—I stopped writing those
damn things once you left; anyhow, that last poem I wrote: you wouldn't take it

I call my mama and ask her how she lived all those decades
knowing her lover would never fully be hers and she said: chile, you just take it

Wake up! Rewind routine daily, tuck kids in, cook dinner work round the clock,
leave patience on the dining room table while making breakfast, and the kids take it

As I wake from the dream, your tears fall from my eyes and I ask myself:
J why do you complicate love? Why can't you just take it?

JP Howard is the author of *SAY/MIRROR* (The Operating System), a 2016 Lambda Literary Award finalist, as well as the chaplet *bury your love poems here* (Belladonna*). JP is the recipient of a 2016 Judith A. Markowitz Emerging Writer Award, has received fellowships and grants from Cave Canem, Lambda Literary Foundation, and Brooklyn Arts Council, and is an alum of the VONA/Voices Writers of Color Workshop. Her poem "Ghazal: What Love Takes" was previously published in *Muzzle Magazine*. You can find JP online at www.jp-howard.com.

DONNA HUNT

The Idea of Donna at Key West

I cover my thumb with my first finger for luck and I kiss my knuckle. I cross myself
and pledge myself to the king, who leads the church. The water pours down the pipes
with so much force, someone might be breaking down the door. Shut the book. At night
my arms fold above my head, palms pressed, my legs bent, soles meet. Like a frog goddess.
Or the worshiper of the frog goddess, or the frog that was stung by the scorpion. I swore
that after you, I was through. You drop the other shoe. Then you pick it up. I wait for you
to drop it again, but how can I know which shoe it is? I caramelize the onions. Once I
walked a mile straight up a sand dune and it took hours, part of the hill regressing with me
with every step. I wanted to let the mountain come to me. But the sand shifts.
The sand wanted me in the water, and I wanted
the cliff.

String Theory

In infinite dimensions
you are not
in love with me. Other donnas
handle it better.
Those donnas accept
the cycles of relationships.
Some donnas
dye their hair, finally
learn guitar. One
donna travels, basks
on a rock, burns it out.
That donna sleeps
it off. Take 2
in the morning. Several
other donnas are already
dating that other guy. He's tall.
Many donnas catharsis,
bake, shop, redecorate.
Three donnas bash you
over drinks, and then call
your mother. It's better than this.
donna, in this world,
is thrown. Has forgotten
her address. No longer recognizes
her own handwriting.

Donna Hunt was born and raised in Cleveland, Ohio, which gave her a great love for both Lake Erie and the Cleveland Indians. She is a multiple Pushcart nominee, and her chapbook *The Coastline of Antarctica* was published by Finishing Line Press. Her poem "String Theory" previously appeared in the *Tin House* Science Fair issue. She has received grants and fellowships including a four-week Full Fellowship to the Vermont Studio Center. Donna currently lives, writes, and teaches in Brooklyn.

CECILY IDDINGS

Why Not Stay in the Kitchen

Because what do I do
there but cook eat talk.
Because I do not like
ovens and knives but find
the party punishing.
For me unnatural heat
for the guests soufflé
or would they rather rabbit.
I can't find rabbit
though nearby legions
nibble tremble fuck.
Nothing for the mob
rampaging the bathroom
to damage a dear
soap dish to yank
the shower curtains
that clicked reassuringly close
and open on something like
ball bearings. Why not
bury the hatchet
asks a deviled egg. Why
when the guests advance
like a cell of sleepers
who look like me
or you and mean
nothing personal
why when they seize
the kitchen where
the frequency
of home accidents turns
the ladyfingers grim
why do I arrange
crackers and why
touch each one?

Sword Fight

Well fuck: These my thrusts: Aren't smartest
Like those: Though true they too try hard:
You don't do it once: You do it
Badly and as to: How to fold:
I call my ma: My finger glows:
I have a home: I see a show:
When what you have is sex to sell:
You sell the sex: Seamy under
Best-dressed dukes: Oh alien go
Back: If back you have: And I my
Socks put on and never cry: Can't
Be the meds: Cause it's all gone:
We call it strong: Who cares might call
It cold: You learn it how it's told
Around the TV when you're small:
To make comfort: Necessity:
A sewing of the thumb into
The glove: A trying to make work:
For hands: Which quit their selves to creep

Across the road: And ugh poor: Them:

Creatures dumb: Defenseless: We grab

The nearest chance: Why do we: Dream

Bad: Why selfish mutter: Mother:

Pronounce: If the children vary

Their sentences: Very well then eat

The children up: A real nightmare:

I slipped a rock in through my nose:

It reached my brain where turned my mind

To stone: The scan shows a statue

Strict unconductor in the storm:

Sword raised: Lucky worker: Sings out:

Why do it small: Why it at all:

Cecily Iddings is the author of *Everyone Here* (Octopus Books, 2014) and a chapbook, *Is To: As: Is To* (Spooky Girlfriend, 2015). She lives in Sunset Park, Brooklyn. "Why Not Stay in the Kitchen" was previously published in *Spork* and in *Everyone Here*; "Sword Fight" was previously published in *Heir Apparent* (at the *Volta*) and *Is To: As: Is To*.

LUCY IVES

Rue des Écoles

Now lighter I took a step somewhere I was going, the streets
parted by a building with a face, and it was 1, noontime, hills
I remember were definitely in the distance, climbers
you could hear in conversation, the reflected thump of
soccerballs, guides with flags or umbrellas, I remember
that it is moving day, you must meet for lunch, muttering
now, you know, snaps, clapping, it is another
way of saying that what happens next can't be
seen, whiskers of ironwork form ferns and ivy, cast a complex
shadow over lots of hours: Please say something more, I'm
asking, please tell what comes next, but in a dream it hums and
refuses; dream does nothing, it is either gray
or gleaming nights and someone comes forward in such a
suit, someone is a sparrow or the muse, and I retreat, I mean
in the face of knowledge you can only
feel very sorry. For happiness and unhappiness
are the two proverbial verbs, and there is such a thing
as The Past, so I may know it, I may be
certain of a thing. If someone pretends to hurt
me, I look away into a mirror. "It's called thinking," I say and
wash my hands. If ever there were a reason to look up let's
look down, I'd say. I'd talk into a handheld recording device, yes
that is one way I would do it if…if…
It is late afternoon, I walk where I am meant to go though
it is late, I used to hate being encouraged by others to use what little
talent I had because I thought this would ruin my chances at
being really great at anything, and the person who speaks first at my
appointment is a florist, and she sells
grasses and tulips, she is saying that if she were
a writer, which she is not, she would just speak into a microphone and
later transcribe whatever she felt like saying. She must have
said that, though, "whatever she felt like saying," for I was
glad for her, for I knew she would be a very great writer
but she chose not to be one at all, because of her understanding
that it's all very well and good, even if all the while you

imagine someone might draw apart the blinds, his expression like a
wave cresting at the mouth, new flesh, and the promise not of
happiness but of attention, adoration, sense, like...
like, not long ago when I felt little or no fear and saw the outline, a
face in profile weirdly twirling on a dangling length of wire, yes, at
this time, not long ago, I became not a singer but someone
who could hear the songs that are misplaced in things, a burden
I guess, but my suburban routes were never good ones, like,
the broken pen in the dirt with its chant about
blue, was I imagining this, was I mad. But the sun was already up, so there
was no denying that time at least was passing, and elsewhere everyone
went on. I did not want to stop them from doing so
Please let me tell you, far be it from me. Thus I stood aside and let
the passerby pass me. I let whoever develop one's career. This was not
merely right and fitting, it formed an integral part of the larger
story I was telling, an essay titled, NEW EARTH, and there where
you told me I was forgetful, I smiled. What could have led me to react in such
a fashion I don't know. What I do know is it was summer,
always summer, whenever you felt brave and said a thing to me

---

Lucy Ives is the author of five books of poetry and prose, most recently *The Hermit*, a book of aphorisms, lists, dreams, and games. In the summer of 2017, Penguin Press will publish her first novel *Impossible Views of the World*, about the travails of a young curator.

TYEHIMBA JESS

Sissieretta Jones & the Black Patti Troubadors
Forte/Grazioso

Forte—with force was the will that overtook me, that freed my throat and lit my mouth to music. *Forte* was each wave of song, *forte* like my father's choir of freedmen, sometimes wavered and off key, sometimes pitched in more fear than light, but always *forte*, hurling what voice was left to them into the cauldron of church air after lifetimes singing their spirituals in secret. They sang *forte* like the stevedores' shout from ship to shore, crate after crate of cargo burdened into the holds, their gandy opera bouncing off hulls, *forte* in the *grazioso* of their motion, the all-together swing of arm and hand and rope and hoisted weight, *grazioso* onto decks all braced for storm, all blessed with prayer from each Providence pulpit, prayed over from bow to stern, blessings from the communion cry of each church, all *grazioso* with hands raised in testimony. I hear them each night, *forte* when I stand on our prow of stage from town to town, port to port, captain of this ragtag ship of blackfaced, cakewalking fools and balladeers, teaching crowds *grazioso* under spotlights with each ticket sold. *Forte* is the cry of the barker bundling each crowd with the smooth talk promise: darkie entertainment with a touch of high class classical. *Forte* is the finale each night, *grazioso* is the closing curtain, the unmasking of painted faces, the darkened lamplight, the applause fading like the hush of receding surf that carries us on through the night, the ocean of audience rising and falling with each wave of season, *grazioso* is the sail of our bodies in their wind.

Duet:
Blind Boone Meets Blind Tom: 1889

Slave and free, we meet to burn up the day
with arpeggio and trills on our sideways harps
—we play the best way we know—it's the way
cakewalk and waltz thrum like one ripe heart
spreading through the forests, a wildfire
that cleanses and lifts me up to heaven

We turn two pianos into a choir—
music tumbling out. I want to tell him
how freedom feels, how even money can't buy
a path to song, that piano work can feed
a hungry soul. Yes, I make hard folk cry
out with joy when they hear me, when I steal
through the gut of their dreams to make them shine
like the face of dawn I've never seen—*sunlight*

With fingers on keys, our hopes lifting up
in a hurricane of back and forth notes—
we storm piano's throat to feel the
full of a blood moon's glow. Our music grows
thick with smoke. I feel our Creator's touch
flying through each chord, hurling through my ears.

But it seems there will never be enough
—that the hawk and eagle scream to show me
all the blue in the sky. They say that I've got
the best hunger, that I bring good news from
listening to earth's beauty. The music's bought
for them the bone-deep sound of God that hums
within themselves. This is how freedom feels—
soaring through the stars in which I reel.

Mark Twain v. Blind Tom

<table>
<tr><td>Some archangel,</td><td>I'm sent from above—</td></tr>
<tr><td>cast out of upper Heaven</td><td>like rain on blue prayers.</td></tr>
<tr><td>like another Satan,</td><td>blessed with Gabriel's lost notes, I</td></tr>
<tr><td>inhabits this coarse casket;</td><td>can see up to God's throne, yes,</td></tr>
<tr><td>and he comforts himself</td><td>while he plays this soul</td></tr>
<tr><td>and makes his prison</td><td>of flesh free—makes me</td></tr>
<tr><td>beautiful with</td><td>the music of piano, the</td></tr>
<tr><td>thoughts and</td><td>breath and</td></tr>
<tr><td>dreams and</td><td>burn in the</td></tr>
<tr><td>memories of</td><td>stormcloud's roar from</td></tr>
<tr><td>another time</td><td>when sound called up,</td></tr>
<tr><td>and another existence</td><td>first made me whole.</td></tr>
<tr><td>that fire</td><td>sounds like love.</td></tr>
<tr><td>this dull clod</td><td>weighted in my chest</td></tr>
<tr><td>with impulses and inspirations</td><td>—it finds freedom after</td></tr>
<tr><td>it no more comprehends</td><td>hurt. I hear Earth's tremble harsher</td></tr>
<tr><td>than does the stupid worm</td><td>—better than the soil itself. When</td></tr>
<tr><td>the stirring of the spirit within</td><td>land and tree sing to me, I hear</td></tr>
<tr><td>her</td><td>notes</td></tr>
<tr><td>of the</td><td>wildly</td></tr>
<tr><td>gorgeous captive</td><td>blooming inside—a spirit</td></tr>
<tr><td>whose wings she</td><td>shadows across my face,</td></tr>
<tr><td>fetters</td><td>breaking free</td></tr>
<tr><td>and</td><td>unloosed. I play the wind</td></tr>
<tr><td>whose flight she stays</td><td>in my blood.</td></tr>
</table>

Italics is original quote from Mark Twain's "Special Letters" to the San Francisco Alta California, *August 1, 1869.*

Tyehimba Jess is the author of *Olio* (Wave Books) and *Leadbelly,* winner of the 2004 National Poetry Series (Wave Books). An alum of Cave Canem and NYU, he is the recipient of fellowships from the NEA, the Illinois Arts Council, and the Whiting Foundation. Jess is poetry and fiction editor of *African American Review* and an associate professor of English at College of Staten Island.

ABRIANA JETTÉ

XXVI.X.MMXIII

By noon, the bay lipped lamp posts.
The sky widened in apocalyptic grandeur.
There is no other way to say it:
the Super Storm arrived.

When the children came home
by four, pumpkins and broomstick-
witch decorations thrashed against
parked cars. In my oven, chicken roasted

with garlic and green beans.
Electrical wires streaked the sky like blue
lightening. One moment I read by the glint
of dim-lit candles, an hour later frozen food

and pots and pans buoyed in the surge.
Its final height five feet: south Brooklyn
submerged. Sanitation plants tumbled,
sewers bubbled. How does the ocean leave?

I wiped shit from my grandma's nine-year-old eyes,
one of the few photos that somehow survived Dachau,
and now: every wall soaked down to the screws.
Still hard to believe. I half expected half a house.

After high-tide the flames from Breezy flickered blue
and orange before our eyes. Then the pearl glow of the moon
broke through the tempestuous sky,
and we trudged through.

Born and raised in Brooklyn, New York, Abriana Jetté is an internationally published poet, essayist, and educator. Her work has appeared or is forthcoming in *Seneca Review*, *River Teeth*, *Plume*, and many other places. She teaches for St. John's University and for the City University of New York.

MODESTO "FLAKO" JIMENEZ

Hood Talk Back 2 Reality (4:16am)

Double-parked cars
Honk, honk, listen
Honk again
Idle
Do it again, y again
O-tra-ve-repetition
Repetition

Bienvenido a un fin de semana
En la gran ciudad
El Lunes no existe to a lot of souls

Weekend warriors
Blunt dispensary re-up killa's
Magician block chemist
Push, push, push, stay pushing!
Cause the Jordans need to match
The fitted.

It hasn't changed Mr. Gaines
Cause money, power, respect
Brings you gains
At least that's what the L.O.X. says
Stay clocking pops said
Don't follow my steps
Su villainy
Coke, crack, dope footprints
Never listening
Cause I stoop clock-in
Adrenaline traps-in
Chronic eyes-dim

Got her pushing-dale, dale!
Push, push, push that
Push, push, keep pushing

To her sides,
Her inner thighs
Her inner tides
Señorita Booffer
T.H.O.T. name embraced
Wake the fuck up
You are their mule

Hermana, Manito stop
Selling
Yourselves
Shorts

Modesto "Flako" Jimenez is a Dominican-born, Bushwick-raised theater director, writer, poet, actor, producer, and educator. ATI and HOLA Award winner for 2015 and 2016, *NY Times* and *Wall Street Journal* profiled, Flako is best known for original productions and three signature festivals—Ghetto Hors d'Oeuvres, One Catches Light, and Oye! Avant-Garde Night—produced with his company Oye Group.

VANESSA JIMENEZ GABB

At the Gym

My hair needs washing
I am oily at the root
Petulant with bad waves
Relax
Bring your ass
To your ankles
Ian says
I can't
I scream
I can't I stop being
Happy just like that
On account of my hair
Looking crazy
That and my belly
Showing out

When I'm alone here
It's just me
The weights are alone
I don't challenge their aloneness
I watch Netflix
I can't stop Netflix
It fucks the poetry out
All the harlequin dramas
The he waiting for seasons
For the her
The me
Watching the them back when
It's not you
It's me they say

I say
Like shit I haven't been
Operating as someone else
I've been exactly me

Coming and going
Like I got it like that
I don't
Every part of me wants to
Bring my ass
To the machinery that confounds
That is change
The not knowing how to change
Half in love
With the body
Not knowing how

Vanessa Jimenez Gabb is the author of *Images for Radical Politics*, which was the Editor's Choice for the 2015 Rescue Press Black Box Poetry Prize contest. More information at vanessajimenezgabb.com. "At the Gym" was previously published in the *Atlas Review*, the chapbook *Weekend Poems* (dancing girl press, 2014), and in *Images for Radical Politics*.

JACQUELINE JOHNSON

Somekindaway

for James Brown

Always the demi-god,
frenzied funktified
under that velvet cape.

Original break-dancer.
Deacon of the funky butt dance.
Slickslide mike swing your burlesque signature.

Owner of sweaty rivers and too many women's skirts.
Shimmer in Oshun's rattle-mirror.
Bowlegged, pigeon-toed, keeper of

triple axial, double joint moves.
Rhythm maker, sound sifter from mud of Oshogbo,
rising in a South Carolina country town.

Uncut, uncaptured, blue you so...

James our poet of the "B" side and the "break" moment.
Had some kinda' way over your audience;
followers leapt upon stages some so young

they formed an ocean of brown girls,
stick legs stomping and pumping up the next wave.
Walked ten blocks from home

to learn the "funky Broadway." Soul
transmitted from slender waist to hip bone.
Released a record a week some summers.

Made the music and money serve you.
Dedicated black blonde, back-up singers,
wore sequins and gold, stirring up

chaos and heat to keep the music real.
Seven degrees and all your personas
strung out. Worked fifty-two out of

fifty-two weeks. Lines between an
ordinary life and the stage blurring
in a PCP haze dimmed by painkillers.

Maceo long defected to some prince formerly or not.
Body wearing down, askew with sickness.
James, who else would leave on Christmas day?

Funky anti-Christ,
shaking the chandeliers of heaven
or some Afro Eden.

Your "good foot" in flight,
possessed beyond redemption.

Jacqueline Johnson is a multi-disciplined artist creating in both writing and fiber arts. She is the author of *A Woman's Season*, published by Main Street Rag, and *A Gathering of Mother Tongues*, published by White Pine Press, winner of the Third Annual White Pine Press Poetry Prize. A native of Philadelphia, PA, she resides in Brooklyn, New York.

PATRICIA SPEARS JONES

Self-Portrait as Midnight Storm

Tossing the steel mesh trash cans is so much fun
Not as much as juggling broken umbrellas
Or rocking the yellow taxies or the last of the Lincoln Town Cars
Ferrying passengers drenched and stimulated

The start of a new day and the pitch is black with stimulation
SHIRR SHIRR SHIRR SHIRR   my sheets of rain
SHIRR SHIRR SHIRR

Oh look at the angry boys drunk and holy as they try mimic storm
The really large guy's huge fist hits a bus stop carousel

It pebbles to the sidewalk, hundreds of green nuggets
His holy hand unblemished by blood. Foolish boys

Foolish boys your anger is no storm and your howling
Bears little glamour—the wolves in your throats have long since left you

And here in the rain, your pain is small, durable and yet
The pebbles scatter about reminders of uglier private deeds.

As for my winds, my rain my tossing back the moon's soft gleam
Means little to windows stood still storm after storm—centurions

Of design. They raise my ire and lash lash lash I throw against
Glass; the sash a square reflection of domestic armature.

As for the painted wood doors—they are so easily broken.

Patricia Spears Jones is an African American poet, playwright, and cultural activist who lives in Brooklyn. She is author of *A Lucent Fire: New and Selected Poems* and seven other collections. Her plays, commissioned by Mabou Mines, were presented in New York City. She is a recipient of awards from the NEA, NYFA, the NY Community Trust, and the Foundation for Contemporary Arts. "Self-Portrait as Midnight Storm" first appeared in *Tin House*.

RACHEL KANG

I would like a day that goes by slowly

nothing to do or say
nothing to be

cars and bicycle bells
people with dogs that smell funny
rich babies and exotic nannies
stack like cards
pigeons roosting in the crevices between elbows and eyes
throw feathers over the ledge

I would like to be colored in with crayons and kid sounds
knitted into my park bench
purled around the twenty wisdoms I know
of the curve of my lip
and your index finger

no one knows the depths of the dent in your chin
when the taxis are still sleeping
and the sun creeps its way across the floor
of unmatched socks and feet

when your breath has turned to waves
and I am the one that sees it.

Rachel Kang is a writer and actor. She received her BFA from New York University and lives in Queens with her foster cat, Sheila. For more of her work, visit www.rachelkang.com. "I would like a day that goes by slowly" was previously published in *Timepiece Literary Journal.*

AMY KING

Understanding the Poem

Only people who live in New York City will understand this poem
and even some of them will feel artificial and maybe real-world grief because
they don't understand the hell out of this poem for reasons worth pinning
down in this poem, but moreover, the approach is to be subjectively-framed,
that is, it is fully about you in your thick history of experiences and genetics
that declare the framework of Nature vs. Nurture in so many debates,

That is if I say,
To poet is to process is to Amy King, the poet is still one who longs for another
viewpoint not-her-own to see her own through and concur or opposite it...

Which is to say, someone who lives on the outskirts in Long Island
or Connecticut may not understand what this poem suggests to someone
who gets the inside clip, which is primarily the person who lives in New York City
at this juncture of the poem especially.

Put a better way,
The person who lives in another country, such as Russia,
will certainly understand this poem in an unsound chord
unlike someone who lives in Saudi Arabia
(which is a lot like saying "Putin" vs. "oil allies")
and may not understand anything about this poem
at all akin to
the person who lives in 1908 because their talk of the poem
will be processed far otherwise than the person in 2008
before the towers fell and the modern day gulag
was realized as a for-profit privatized corporate prison system
in a nation hell-bent on peace the American way,

Which also means someone who lives in a 2014 Compton neighborhood
will certainly regard this poem askance from the person
who resides in New York City after years of growing up under Stop and Frisk
while viewing the protections that suggests this is also about
the person who sees through this poem as a person arrested and fined via
    Stop and Frisk,

which is a shade greyer than the other issued a summons and beaten down by
    Stop and Frisk.

I hope I'm being clear enough here so that you understand
who will get this poem and who will not.
I can only be as honest with you as I am with myself
in the effort, the raw motion, to tell why
you may or may not understand this poem.
This poem is akin to when Foucault offered a picture
of a pipe and declared no pipe present.
The linguistics didn't gesture as much as Foucault's offer,
much like this poem does right now, to you in your place.

I mean I have to ask myself with honesty, Amy King,
What would Amy King the reader do with this poem?
because we all need a starting point and right now it is this, Amy King,
and where are you among these words and by what gesture does this become
    not a poem?
Not a pipe?

The problem flashes face forward when I want to ask the poet
what she meant when she wrote poetry and she is no longer with us.
I mean, the poet may not be dead and she may even be in New York City
standing here beside you, but is she still the same person in touch
with her intuition, influences and body as she was the day she wrote these words?
Were the rats walking upright down alleys and were the delis open full force
the day she left her apartment for a cutting board of cheese at Spuyten Duyvil
    on Metropolitan
after which she'd meet her friend Sara and walk to the water's edge for a brown
    bag beer
back when the towers were still smoldering black smudge across the river?

Is she trustworthy, can she be trusted to guide us, are her intentions aligned
with exactly a moral execution or her desire to entertain or flatter readers
by highlighting their analytical prowess with cheap & easy writerly gimmicks
as in, "See how you got this so quickly, poetry readers scattered widely?"

Truthfully, only people in New York City will understand
the difference between writing a poem on a cell phone and penning
it in a notebook standing on the East River shore in Brooklyn drinking a
    Red Stripe

(people in New York City know the East River is no river at all but a tidal strait),
where truth resembles the hooves of bullets when we take the romantic angle.

Although some in New York City haven't noticed today
the East River shores have been bought up by New York University
and barred with fences along Williamsburg's periphery,
now relocated to East Williamsburg, as gentrified sprawl will do.
Those also who don't get that Stephen King rewrote Ed Dorn's
book of poems, *Gunslinger,* into his Best Selling novel, *The Gunslinger*,
will experience a difference in understanding that this poem inspires.

So what this poem understands for one single soul in this split moment is:

Badass puppets exist
where singularity is self-inflicted
and my shame is not enough.
She thinks that makes her sound powerful, and so is also
invested in a fear of her own impotence,
the limits of which narrow just how she understands any poem,
a dilation that scares her to strangulation response
when the poem is only hugging her closely.
She whispers a mantra, Hello person,
I've been waiting for your step, your human failings,
each my own as I dream in visual patterns
for I am a poem and song too, a centrality. Let me explain:
I am unusual today.
The strange rain outside awakens
the strange rain within.
Sound and rhythm and chance.
I am out of your league, borne
by your language, and I supersede
your presence. We bounce between time,
we, the ever presence of strangers within us.
The drops stir a river bottom's silt;
the waves make a tidal strait rush madly outstream;
you are the only pain my language receives.
What is this. This is this. You are this.
Nothing more than this.

But elsewhere in the gallery, down the road from the theater, up river from the stage,
we move, we ants, we beasts of burden,
thinking ourselves into ourselves, alone things, bodies

resistant, misunderstood behaviors.
We are the poems that become us, and there is no explanation,
no other example for that for the thing within you that
echoes and burgeons with reminders post-words.
Souls, spirits, and feelings are not pipes; this world is anything but poem.
This world is this, this world is poem, and I am unusual today, at least.

When we leave to walk the shores, now barred by tides
and officers of Stop and Frisk, remember your limits are the ways
in which you understand within your limits. Or as the poet Amy King
reminds her historical thickness:

My eyes smell of locust trees.
I hide my brown bag beer.
Georgia pines thread my veins at root.
The ants have returned and winter is a teardrop of words.
I have replanted myself as this;
I am in need of bull's eyes to aim for.
In order to be without.
I am alone here with occasional friends, with occasional relevance,
more pleased than any cadaver,
more pleasing than a clubhouse romance.

As one would startle the sun, Amy King's poem understands her first.
That is how you begin understanding, through this death you carry
and whose hand you fondle: the poem's also a handshake.
Anyone else who is not Brooklyn nor NYC also knows this.

Amy King's latest collection, *The Missing Museum*, was a co-winner of the 2015 Tarpaulin Sky Book Prize. She was the winner of the 2015 WNBA Award (Women's National Book Association) and serves on the executive board of VIDA: Women in Literary Arts. She is an associate professor of creative writing at SUNY Nassau Community College.

JOSHUA KLEINBERG

The Fabulist Speaks

O righteous, timeless light in my crotch,
you taught rhythm to whole baths

of ancient Ephebes. Now you smolder
like insects inside me. Holy clam-shelled

hand of God, come scoop out what you
have invested in me. Bring a new

kind of trick: I see a length of curbed grass
where everyone wanders silently off

from high-speed crashes, safety glass
glittering from pits in their hairlines.

It's a trick of the attention, but look,
don't look—it's a disappointing difference.

I don't want to seem ungrateful, Hashem,
for the highway transfer ramp thickets, or

the ponds that spread out there each rainy
season. I just want to thank you, briefly,

for this interruption of happy anarchy, this
haven from delirious byzantine forms—

always these forms to fill out! I want to
love you and NOT tell you what it

certainly does NOT mean anymore—
a carnal red sky, a haul at the millinery...

The hallmark of the great rambunctious
loves is a notion—incorrect often, but

don't let that stop you—of having been
properly tended to. It isn't so much that I

owe you observation. More how did God
learn what I deserve to behold? And here,

He's dropped it before me, like a grapefruit.

Joshua Kleinberg has lived in Bed-Stuy, Bushwick, Williamsburg, Florida, Montana, and Ohio. His poetry has appeared in *Chorus: A Literary Mixtape* (MTV, 2012) and *New Poetry from the Midwest 2014* (New American, 2015).

JENNIFER L. KNOX

The Ten-Million-Year War

We'd taken the hill at last! Our muskets flashed
and set our sleeves ablaze! Luminous mercury puddles
purged in our latrine could be seen from outer space
and would eternally endure! Praise His jerky!
"Load the powder nuzzle! Hoist the mizzenmast!"
Enemies staggering at us exploded in hollow pops
and rained back down upon us in a gory confetti!
"Know what I could go for?" Bart asked suddenly,
his dank, black mouth full of clouds, and in the hours
of dumbstruck silence that followed, all the dogs
we'd skinned came gallumping happily back to us
with orange croquet balls in their mouths. *Ah-aw.*
"No," I said and meant it. "Tater tots," Bart grinned.
"Tay-der-tots! Tay-der-tots!" we tolled like bells
and toddled around the hill until we all...finally...
lied down. "Jus restin our eyes uhlittlebit."

I Want to Speak with the Manager

"Promise me" is telling, not asking.
If someone tells you, "Promise me X," you'll probably promise them X and that will probably be a lie because you didn't offer them X.
You were snared.
You were told to promise, which means the asker never thought you would do what you promised to do.
So in a way, you're already off the hook.
Promises are no longer made to me because I'm a middle-aged person.
People stop bothering to lie to you once you've been lied to as many times as I have.
They think you're used to it.
I'm not, and that's a sign of immaturity.
I never tell someone, "Promise me," because nothing's worse than hearing, "I can't promise you that," even though it's always the truth.
I can't handle the truth, apparently.

But rare surprises do spring up, moments you can force the universe to keep
its promises: lifetime warranties, two-for-one Tunnel of Fudge cookies,
all-you-can-eat summer Shrimpfest.
Make enough noise in that moment, and the universe will give you whatever
you want then.
Anything to get rid of you.

Jennifer L. Knox is the author of four books of poems, including *Days of Shame and Failure*. Her work has appeared four times in the *Best American Poetry* series, and in the *New York Times*, *New Yorker*, and *American Poetry Review*. She teaches at Iowa State University and is the curator of the Iowa Bird of Mouth project.

JASON KOO

Morning, Motherfucker

Just popped the collar of my robe in this motherfucker,
I.e. kitchen, as I make some sweet-ass hash browns.
Is that the start of a poem? It's barely the start of breakfast.
Noon light comes streaming through the window.
Is that the start of a poem? My landlady—what a word—
Just told me to be out of here by July 1. At first I wrote
Just told me to be out of her. Slightly different poem.
The millionaires buying her brownstone, milling past me
As I cranked this up in my robe at this motherfucker,
I.e. dining table, wondering if it could indeed be a poem,
Demand it. I'm gonna squat right here in this kitchen,
I.e. motherfucker, with my million-dollar syntax and hash browns
And make those motherfuckers mill around me for life.
I'll miss this motherfucking beautiful neighborhood
Of Whitman & Auden & Crane & Mailer & McCullers
& Miller & Miller & Smith & Wolfe & motherfucker
How many more writers could live in these brownstones?
How many more ampersands could live in contemporary poetry?
Now there are probably no writers here except me.
Oh, and little known former Poet Laureate of America
Phil Levine on Willow St. And fellow Asian American male poet
Ken Chen, also on Willow St. I wonder if they too pop the collars
Of their robes as they make some sweet-ass hash browns.
Mailer surely popped the collar of his robe. He probably
Put on boxing gloves to take his hash browns out of the oven.
Hart Crane I can't see ever making, let alone eating, hash browns.
Just too much cranium to contain in one kitchen.
Whitman couldn't have eaten just one hash brown, or two,
He had to be making whole schools of hash browns,
40,000 hash browns forked with 40,000 motherforking forks.
He would've written about all the potato fields they came from,
Sunsets over the cool brown earth that made their beds.
Henry Miller likely would've fucked his hash browns.
Auden would've had his hash browns at an appropriate time
Scheduled into the morning. Last night I talked about
That motherfucker's face. What a motherfucking poet's face.

Was Auden ever young? Did he come out of his mother's vagina
Already wrinkled? Imagine that vagina. Auden's face
Like a hash brown out of that vagina. I'm feeling better,
In spring, in this motherfucking beautiful light. I'm dancing
In this motherfucker, i.e. kitchen, as I flip these hash browns
And think I can start to begin to forget you some day.

Model Minority

I was thinking on the subway yesterday and thinking I think this fairly
Frequently, *Fuhhhck* these people…

That's just a terrible tie.

Those two mayonnaised over that whole swath of bench where four people
could fit,

Or six slim Asians.

I make myself into as tight an Asian as possible in crowds
As a courtesy to other people—

It's the model minority in me, you might say,
Coolly, while enjoying your extra space.

People move on me like a magnet: I'll be walking down the street
With a clear path in front of me

When someone ahead to my left swerves into my space.

Once in a hurry to Penn Station I tried to move past a young kid with my
roller bag

And he *kicked* the bag, sending it into the stomach
Of a woman walking towards us.

Of course I apologized to the woman, who looked at me
As if it were my fault,

Then ran after the kid, after first gently repositioning
The wheels of my bag on the pavement,

Of course I didn't "run," I walked briskly in a straight line wheeling
My bag behind me,

And when I caught up to the kid I walked alongside him and said, That was
not cool, sir.

I have no idea where that "sir" came from.

I might as well have said, That was a lovely ball, an excellent first touch.

The kid just looked me over and said, Fuck you, you fucking Chinese—
And stopped, thinking that was insult enough.

It's funny,

When I'm feeling sorry for myself
After something like this, my default comfort food is Chinese.

Not "good" or "real" Chinese,
But fucking Chinese, the General Tso's Chicken I've had

Photoclumped from state to state, the Chicken Lo Mein
Flaplocked in its warm white cardboard carton,

The Garlic Chicken with Rice I know by now

Should be renamed Garlic Broccoli Carrots Peas Onions Green Peppers
Mushrooms Baby Corn & Chicken with Rice,

So minor a role does the chicken play in this dish.

Menus should indicate it comes in two volumes:
Vol. 1 for dinner, Vol. 2 microwaved for lunch the next day.

A curious feeling I have

Sitting down for Vol. 2 of General Tso's Chicken, how removed I am

Yet somehow *in* those mutilated morsels, blasted beyond recognition

Yet somehow more recognizable for that, not even
Not even real Chinese food, just as I'm not even

Not even fucking Chinese, as I said to that kid, or thought I said, or thought
to that kid

After he kicked my bag and left me to contemplate

Serious violence only while waiting in line later for the bus with my girlfriend,

Who sympathized at first but decided I was being unpleasant, I could tell,
The more I mowed

Over the story, the more incredulous I got at what the kid had done.

Who is this whose grief bears such an emphasis?

I was not playing the role she liked, the role I'm happy

To step into late at night when I find myself
Walking behind a woman alone on a deserted street

And I become aware she's becoming aware

Of me behind her, I'm moving in a straight line and she's not so of course
I'm within a few feet of her within seconds

Making me threatening, I could be anybody, some madman wanting

To kick something into her stomach, I soften
My steps so she won't have to hear them but this makes me even more
threatening

So finally I move past her without looking and let her see

I'm just a harmless Asian dude, me smiling, I can almost feel myself

Patting this guy on the back.

Named one of the "100 Most Influential People in Brooklyn Culture" by *Brooklyn Magazine*, Jason Koo is the founder and executive director of Brooklyn Poets and creator of the Bridge (poetsbridge.org). He is the author of two collections of poetry, *America's Favorite Poem* (C&R Press, 2014) and *Man on Extremely Small Island* (C&R Press, 2009), and an assistant teaching professor of English at Quinnipiac University. "Morning, Motherfucker" was originally published in *glitterMOB*, and "Model Minority" in *Barn Owl Review* and *America's Favorite Poem*.

DEBORA KUAN

Portrait of a Woman with a Hoagie

I want to drown in six pounds of macaroni salad.
The groans of Superbowl Sunday. The cries of triumph.

I want hoagies
unfurled from cold foil.

They're called hoagies where I come from.

O beautiful possibilities
like second-base in a parked car

in the half-full lot outside a movie cineplex,
the neon glinting off your corneas.

When God closes one door, somewhere
He opens a hoagie

and jams that football
mouth with thinly sliced ham

and honey roast turkey, roast beef,
cheese, pickles, and shredded lettuce.

Paper hoagie covers rock hoagie!
Melted cheddar covers everything.

Mantra

My husband didn't like his mantra.
"Shirim" or "Shring" or "Schwing."
My own mantra was much longer.
"It is only money." I chanted
this while driving the minivan.
I whispered it into a mussel.

I shouted it from the fire escape
to the ram-faced gargoyle
across the street. *I think*
you're doing it wrong,
he said. *Your eyes*
should be closed and you
shouldn't be shouting.
I ignored him and continued
my diatribe, shaking my fists
at greedy little ghosts.
You don't control me, money!
No, you don't! Then I went
inside, fried up a $50 bill
with sauerkraut, and ate it
with a side of buttered toast.
It didn't taste like chicken.
More like manta ray.

Fertile

As long as I had to clean all the things
all the time, the mushroom would continue
to sprout from the top of my head. It grew
from the same fertile spot in me
that exists in you, somewhere deep below
your internal microwave but above your post-
apocalyptic store of spring water. You think
I didn't know about that, but I did,
just as you assumed that I wanted
to be handled with very gentle kid gloves,
as if I were a baby piglet or a distended
water balloon, which I did. Somewhere
in the dark borough, however, car alarms
do conspire. Over in cat town, the strays
have assembled a council to take back
the mean streets, institute mandatory
public siestas. I had a million wishes too,
but more than that, regrets. While
washing the dishes, I recalled the time
I made you boil coffee in a pot,
which we both neglected, which melted

the pot, which then ignited the kitchen,
which finally burnt down the house.
When the firemen came, they put out
the fire that was our love; but from
those feeble ashes grew mushrooms.

Debora Kuan is the author of two poetry collections, *Lunch Portraits* (Brooklyn Arts Press, 2016) and *Xing* (Saturnalia, 2011). "Portrait of a Woman with a Hoagie" first appeared in *glitterMOB*. "Fertile" appeared in *Pleiades*. "Mantra" appeared in the *Awl*.

CHRISTINE LARUSSO

Cento of Past Lovers

Hold your hand up
like a mitten; I'll show you
where I lived in the state
of Michigan. Should I bite
you harder? Christine,
I wish you hadn't
lied to me. I don't think
I've ever seen you wear pants.
I'll buy the whiskey.
I imagined that by now
you would have dumped me
and started dating Colin.
I want to leave
New York. I don't think
it's the right time for a dog.
Of course I'd date you
even if you didn't have teeth.
I don't drink that much.
In my dream, we were riding
a rollercoaster into the state
of Maine. You're going
to get better. I once thought
I would like to marry you.
Do you think we should
move to California? It's only
a little blood. Why don't you
talk about your father more?
I wrote you a letter.
The tension between you
and your mother makes
me uncomfortable. You can't
always help me find a job. Your
calves are frameable. We can't
get a dog. I don't think I want
to be in any of your poems.

It feels weird to go out,
just the two of us, going
out, drinking? It feels
weird. Someday we will
attend a gala. Christine,
the teapot is boiling. When
my best friend told me
his mom had cancer, I didn't
flinch but I let him cry
on my shoulder. Read
Guy de Maupassant to me.
I wrote a song about you.
In bed. You overcooked the eggs.
I bought you that stupid
Japanese stuffed tooth
thing. God, you and your
obsession with juice.
Do you still love him?
Was I really sleepwalking?
In my dream, you were
blonde, had longer legs.
I don't have the patience
right now to listen to you
read poems. We could move
to Illinois, my parents are
in Illinois. You're terrible
with directions. You buy
too many dresses.
Isn't that skirt a little
short? I get it, you like dogs.
I'm taking the cat with me.
Try pork. I don't believe
in marriage. I won't always
be poor. I never told you this,
but my parents don't sleep
in the same bed. I drew the
state of New Jersey. You'll
know they're the right
mushrooms if they turn
blue when you pinch
them. I can't believe you
had me make dinner on my

own birthday. My dad snores.
You look at your phone
too much. Talk to me. Don't
talk to me. It doesn't cross
my mind to think about
you while I'm at work.
I don't appreciate your
desire to buy a home, even
if it is a long way's off.
Why don't you eat meat?
What if I wrap my fingers
around yours? Is that
too rough? Too soft? You
look like a kitten. Yes,
we can go sailing.
No, I don't really want to hike.
What feels right?
I don't think the solution
to the problem is to drink
more. Take the train to
St. James. I'm too stressed
for sex. I decided I can't
pick you up from the airport,
or ever, anywhere ever again.
I don't know how I feel.
I don't think I miss you.
I can't believe you told
Melissa we slept together.
I don't want you to call
me your partner. What
would you name the dog?
What if you slept
in a tent in the living room?
Try listening to Holst
while mapping the stars.
That's crazy, of course
I care about you. I wanted
to write, but I'm numb.
You're so fucking morbid.
I don't think the solution
to the problem is to adopt
a chinchilla. I made a film

for you. I'm moving.
I'm selfish. I can tell you
want to leave. I don't think
I can love anyone. Should
we be having more sex?
What if we learned to play
tennis? We could take LSD.
Call me your boyfriend.
Beige washes you out.
There's no way I have more
shoes than you. I can barely
pay for a MetroCard,
what makes you think
I could ever afford a dog?
I dreamt we were camping
on the prow of a ship.
Men have insecurity issues
too. I can tell you're
somewhere else. Your brain
is not like my brain.
I came home to your
messy house and I knew
this was over. Meet me
in the park after work.

Christine Larusso holds an MFA from New York University. Her work has appeared or is forthcoming in the *Literary Review*, the *Awl*, *Sycamore Review*, *Court Green* (where "Cento of Past Lovers" first appeared), *Narrative*, *Pleiades*, and elsewhere. She is a co-producer of *Commonplace*, a poetry podcast hosted by Rachel Zucker. After over one decade in Brooklyn, she has returned to her hometown of Los Angeles.

DOROTHEA LASKY

I like weird ass hippies

I like weird ass hippies
And men with hairy backs
And small green animals
And organic milk
And chickens that hatch
Out of farms in Vermont
I like weird ass stuff
When we reach the other world
We will all be hippies
I like your weird ass spirit stick that you carry around
I like when you rub sage on my door
I like the lamb's blood you throw on my face
I like heaping sugar in a jar and saying a prayer
And then having it work
I like cursing out an enemy
And then cursing them in objects
Soaking their baby tooth in oil
Lighting it on fire with a tiny plastic horse
I like running through the fields of green
I am so caught up in flowers and fruit
I like shampooing my body
In strange potions you bought wholesale in Guatemala
I like when you rub your patchouli on me
And tell me I'm a man
I am a fucking man
A weird ass fucking man
If I didn't know any better I'd think I were Jesus or something
If I didn't know any better I'd sail to Ancient Greece
Wear sandals
Then go to Rome
Murder my daughter in front of the gods
Smoke powdered lapis
Carve pictographs into your dress
A thousand miles away from anything
When I die I will be a strange fucking hippie
And so will you
So will you
So get your cut-up heart away from

What you think you know
You know, we are all going away from here
At least have some human patience
For what lies on the other side

I hate irony

I was walking along one day when I realized that I hate irony
I think I was thinking of the movie *The Shining* and how scary it is
When I was 21 I didn't sleep for two nights straight because of that movie
It reminded me a lot of growing up and the things I've seen
Fear is not irony
If you have ever been truly scared there is no irony in your voice when you scream
And too
Love is not either
I was in love once and all I could think of was joy
Not drinking, nor sex, or spaghetti
Not witty things to say or martinis
That bubble down the stairs with gracious olives
I didn't think of my large grey turtleneck folding over my abdomen
As I was touched so quietly by the stars
I hate when people think they are being funny by being ironic
Or they want to show you they are clever
So they say something really meaty
With twists and curves
I don't think it is funny to be so elitist
To everyone who hasn't had the chance to be as special as you are
Being cultivated into fine things when you yourself was nothing to begin with
Humor is not irony as I belly laugh all along the bench
Of the waiting room while they announce my father will die
Or when my friend was killed by her husband while he wore all black
To be torched is not ironic, but it hurts
It hurt her flesh. It hurts me to think about it.
And not precious I am to think about it, to give it time
O but Dottie, you say, you are so funny
Surely you realize you are always being ironic
But I am not, I will tell you
I am only being real

Dorothea Lasky is the author of four books of poetry, most recently *ROME* (W.W. Norton/Liveright), as well as *Thunderbird*, *Black Life*, and *AWE*, all out from Wave Books, and co-editor of *Open the Door: How to Excite Young People about Poetry* (McSweeney's, 2013). Currently, she is an assistant professor of poetry at Columbia University's School of the Arts and co-directs Columbia Artist/Teachers. Her poem "I like weird ass hippies" is from *Thunderbird* and "I hate irony" is from *Black Life*.

BRETT FLETCHER LAUER

Song

The life-long medication
had certain side-effects,
images of identifiable
persons, a November
moon, insect sounds
from the natural world
were presented to my body
as a lethal dose and the
prescribed coping mechanisms
failed; replacing sadness
with the dictionary entry
seven words later. It seems
quaint now. Safely, in a safe
manner; without danger;
without hurt. It wasn't
worthwhile to make a fuss—
where there is no haunting,
the haunting is invented.
All conversations require
a request and answer and
you can imagine I wasn't
saying much. I stayed in
Elixir Valley hooded in fog,
where orchids aren't touched
by frost, by strange boys,
where it is safe to begin
burning jasmine, chanting
the holy name. This requires
one sit very still, one listen
for their organs collapsing
in on themselves.

Brett Fletcher Lauer is the deputy director of the Poetry Society of America and the poetry editor of *A Public Space*. He is the author of *Fake Missed Connections: Divorce, Online Dating, and Other Failures*, and a collection of poems, *A Hotel in Belgium*. He is the poetry co-chair for the Brooklyn Book Festival and lives in Brooklyn.

RICKEY LAURENTIIS

Black Iris

O'Keeffe, 20th century, oil on canvas

Dark, imposing flesh. Darker still
its center, like the tongue of
a cow that has for a week now been
dead, spent during calf birth, and the calf
still clinging to her, and his own tongue
wild for want of milk, and the calf
with flies in his eyes—*that* color: near-to-
purple, bruised. I should call it
beautiful, or beauty itself, this dark
room, broom closet, this nigger-dot.
I should want to fit into it, stand up in it,
rest, as would any beast inside a stable.
I should want to own it, force it mine,
to know it is my nature, and of
course don't I? Why shouldn't I want?

Black mirror. Space delicate
and cracked. Now anything could
go in there: a fist, veined, fat.
A body. And here runs the blood
through the body, deep, watery.
And here runs the message in the blood:
This is it—fuck her fag like you're supposed to.
And when the wind shakes
and when the iris shakes in it,
the lips of the flower shaping
to the thing that invades it, that will be
me, there, shaking, my voice shaking,
like the legs of the calf, who—out of fear?
out of duty?—is sitting by his dead
mother because what else will he do, what else has he?
Because a voice outside him makes him.

Vanitas with Negro Boy

Bailly, 17th century, oil on canvas

I'll show you a bone made to hold on to.
A pip. A dense fire in which once
the thinking imagination sprawled
like a breathing vine. He would put the skull
on the table (*And nearest to the worn
flowers, sir, or nearer to the flute?*) turned
just so so not to be too crude. That
was the boy's job, this cage with a debt
in it (*And whose boy am I, and what is
my name?*). Black erasing blackness,
body and backdrop: you are not permitted to enter
the question light asks of his skin as if it were
a field, a mind, a word inclined to be
entered. It's true: his face, his boyhood even
(*And what is my boyhood, and where is it from?*)
would fade if not for the rope of attention
yanked glittering across that face. Look.
This is my painting, my version of the Dutch
stilleven. I'm trying to write obsession
into it, and can. Open your eyes. Don't run.
Vanitas, from the Latin for "emptiness,"
"meaningless"—but what nothing can exist
if thought does, if the drawn likeness of a bone
still exists? Why trust the Old Masters? Old
Masters, never trust me. Listen: each day
is a Negro boy, chained, slogging out of the waves,
panting, gripping the sum of his captain, the head,
ripped off, the blood purpling down, the red
hair flossed between the knuckles, swinging it
before him like judgment, saying to the mist,
then not, then quietly only to himself, *This is what
I'll do to you, what you dream I do, sir, if you like it.*

Rickey Laurentiis is the author of *Boy with Thorn*, selected by Terrance Hayes for the Cave Canem Poetry Prize (University of Pittsburgh Press, 2015), and winner of the 2016 Levis Reading Prize. He is the recipient of a 2014 fellowship from the Civitella Ranieri Foundation in Italy, a 2013 creative writing fellowship from the National Endowment for the Arts, and a 2012 Ruth Lilly Poetry Fellowship. He currently teaches at Columbia University and Sarah Lawrence College.

AMY LAWLESS

Enter Skeleton

He entered my house in pure ivory brilliance clicking his bones awkwardly on the hardwood floor, nodding his head like the most poorly handled stage puppet. One thing that struck me immediately, once I overcame the shine of the thing, was how poised his arms were, macho and casual at his sides. The occasional hand gesture toward where his phone might be in a pocket if he had a phone, as if he had skin and wore clothing. He looked at his wrist and indeed a watch hung loosely—nearly falling off—were it not for the width of the hand bones. The watch's face looked at the floor, so he lifted the watch over his wobbling head to get the time. "It's FIVE-THIRTY," I yelled just so he would stop. I asked him to have a seat, which he did, and he remarked that my couch was uncomfortable to sit on. Though he was right, I wondered what he might have to compare it to. The purpose of the buttocks is to protect against such discomforts, and he was plainly not in possession of a butt. "Are you alive?" I asked sighing. "No," he answered cheerfully. "Are you of polished ivory?" I asked though he was clearly a human skeleton. He looked up at me. He held his head still and said, "Why-do-people-ask-things-that-they-know-are-not-so?" slowly, quietly. Tears came to my eyes. "This is no time for a breakdown. I can not give that to you. I can not let you have that today." So, the silence continued for years until I asked for the opposite of what I had asked first.

Goofing Around

I was goofing around with Kim and Stanley. "My hairdresser said that her cats love it when she did Reiki on them." We passed our hands over Kim's head and then I started laughing and ruined it. Stanley kept mispronouncing *qi* on purpose just to be a tool. But Kim really, really wanted us to perform Reiki on her. After fifteen minutes reading its entry on Wikipedia, we were on the floor with our hands everywhere on each other trying to manage *the life force*. But there's no evidence that this force exists, but put your hands on me here and leave your hands there for two minutes. And yes, next right here. Pretend I'm a roll of toilet paper that you can't touch but want to and then touch without holding it. Give! Then I kept thinking about Stanley's penis "performing" Reiki on Kim by passing its energy over onto her. And once I had the image of Stanley's penis as a Certified Healer in my head, it was so easy and obvious to cast this penis as Oscar the Grouch's worm friend Slimy. I laughed so much, they started cleaning up to show me without telling me that it was time for me to leave. "What did you say your hairdresser's name was again? Can you send me her info?"

Amy Lawless is the author of three poetry books, including *My Dead* and *Broadax*, both from Octopus Books. With Chris Cheney she is the co-author of *I Cry: The Desire to Be Rejected*, a collaborative, hybrid book (Pioneer Works Press, Groundworks Series). In 2011 she received a poetry fellowship from the New York Foundation for the Arts. "Enter Skeleton" was first published in *Washington Square Review*.

SOPHIA LE FRAGA

Feminlist

abandonwoment
abdowomen
achievewoment
acknowledgewoments
acuwomen
adawomantly
advertisewoments
alwomanac
amazewoment
The First Awomendment
awomenities
announcewoment
apartwoment
arguwoment
arraignwoment
assignwoment
attachwoment
breast augwomentation
basewoment
boogeywoman
browomance
cewoment
Charles Womanson
claiwomant
commencewoment
commitwoment issues
compartwomentalize
compliwoments
compliwomentary
The Ten Cowomandments
Cowomander in Chief
cowommando
cowomment
cowommendable
craftswomanship

dehuwomanized
detachwoment
dewomand
dewomanding
dewomented
three diwomensional
multidiwomensional
disappointwoment
diswomantle
docuwoment
docuwomentary film
dorwomant
elewoment
elewomentary school
empowerwoment
engagewoment
enjambwoment
environwomental
ewomanate
ewomancipate
Ewomancipation Proclamation
experiwomental
ferwomentation
fragwoment
fundawomentally
gerrywomander
Gerwoman
Gerwomany
gourwomand
governwoment
huwoman
huwomane
huwomanely
huwomanity
huwomanities
huwomankind
hywomen
impeachwoment
imperwomanent
impoverishwoment
instruwoment
iwommense

iwommensely
judgewoment
lawoment
lawomentable
Marilyn Womanson
megalowomania
mewomento
monuwomental
movewoment
mowomentary
Newoman's Own
tree ornawoments
ornawomental
ottowoman
Pacwoman
Paul Newoman
penwomanship
perforwomance
perwomanent
phenowomenal
pigwoment
praying womantis
predicawoment
Prewomenstrual Syndrome
prowomenade
rawomen
refreshwoment
repriwomand
repriwomandible
resentwoment
rowomance
rowomanticize
Rowomania
Rowomanian
salawomander
sediwoment
sediwomentary rock
settlewoment
sewomantics
shawoman
supplewomentary vitamin
supplewoment

taliswoman
Old Testawoment
New Testawoment
Tiananwomen Square
womanacle
womanageable
womanager
womanatee
womanchego cheese
Womanchester United
Womandarin
Womandarin Oriental
womandate
womandatory
womandible
womandolin
Womandy Moore
womaneuver
womangled
Womango
Womanhattan
Womania
ego womaniac
womanicure
womanic depression
Womanifest Destiny
womanila envelopes
womanipulate
womannequin
table womanners
womannerisms
womansion
womanslaughter
womanta ray
womantle
womantra
womanual labor
womanuscript
so womany
womenace
womenage à trois
womenial tasks

womeningitis
womenopause
womenorah
womenses
womenstruation
womental disorder
womenthol cigarettes
womention
womentor
womenu

Sophia Le Fraga is a poet and visual artist. She is the author of *Other Titles by Sophia Le Fraga* (If a Leaf Falls, 2016); *The Anti-Plays* (Gauss PDF, 2015); *literallydead* (Spork, 2015); *I RL, YOU RL* (minutes BOOKS, 2013; Troll Thread, 2014) and *I DON'T WANT ANYTHING TO DO WITH THE INTERNET* (KTBAFC, 2012). She's recently been included in *This Known World* (MOCA), *Greater New York* (MoMA PS1), and *PERFORMA* (New York). Le Fraga is the poetry editor of *Imperial Matters* and a member of Collective Task.

KATY LEDERER

Translocations

We'd de-notate and detonate. At breakpoint, we would close our eyes.
We'd segregate abnormally. We'd suffer from the rational.
We'd radiate excessively, fold into flats then flex our thighs.
We'd cycle then proliferate. We'd implicate, psychologize.

We'd segregate abnormally. We'd suffer from the rational.
Both balanced and unbalanced, we would call ourselves reciprocal.
We'd cycle then proliferate. We'd implicate, psychologize.
Our eyes would form before the splice. Our brains would not be typical.

Both balanced and unbalanced, we would call ourselves reciprocal.
Our arms were short. Our legs were long. Our sex would be consensual.
Our eyes would form before the splice. Our brains would not be typical:
Both fibrate and synovial, homologous and cauterized.

Our arms were short. Our legs were long. Our sex would be consensual.
We'd radiate excessively, fold into flats then flex our thighs:
Both fibrate and synovial, homologous and cauterized.
We'd de-notate and detonate. At breakpoint, we would close our eyes.

Autophagy

Flotsam from the world we were, and dirty.
The cells would malfunction. We'd suffer from muscular dystrophy.
Waste would accumulate nightly. We'd rest.
The two of us were energy. We'd measure the effect.

The findings were exciting.
Weeks of running, we would diet.
When not resting, we'd suffer severe psychological stress.
We would exercise, of course, and stretch.

We moved throughout the camps as if the agent of the chaperone.
Otherwise, we surely would have perished in the lysosome.

When the membranes that engulf debris inside the cells would glow,
    we would let go.
Each day we spent living. Mitochondria burned.

Katy Lederer is the author of the poetry collections *Winter Sex* (Verse/Wave), *The Heaven-Sent Leaf* (BOA), and *The bright red horse—and the blue—* (Atelos). "Autophagy" was originally published in the *Iowa Review*; "Translocations" originally appeared in *EDNA: A Journal of the Millay Colony for the Arts*.

DELL LEMMON

Have You Seen the Bob Gober Show at MoMA?

What a pretentious question! Who calls him Bob? It's Robert. It's the Robert Gober Show at MoMA.

I can't help it. I've been hearing Tim Davis call him Bob Gober for years. Who's Tim Davis?

Tim Davis is a gentle giant of a gardener in small towns on the tip of Cape Cod, who has the same big smile for everyone he meets.

What most people in those small towns don't know is that Tim Davis, who never went to college, can read an art review in the *New York Times*

like Superman can jump off of tall buildings, meaning Tim Davis can sense the level of passion behind the review and if it's big—

Tim Davis will call up the gallery where the art is on exhibition and buy the art—as long as it is still affordable

and he knows just when to sell it too. In fact, that's how he bought his first gardening truck—buying and selling art.

And that's how I met Tim Davis—through an artist that we both know—because Tim Davis called up the gallery where that artist was having one

of his first shows and bought a piece after reading a rave review. And Tim Davis has been flying around the globe, going to

every art opening that Bob Gober ever had, and getting invited to dinners with museum curators and famous collectors, while most locals

usually see him digging around in the dirt or wielding that weird chain saw-like thing for clipping hedges, the way Jeff Koons makes those puppy sculptures out of bushes—

and don't get me started on Jeff Koons. Back to Gober. Let's just call him Gober. And let's just say I went kicking and screaming to his show at MoMA.

I knew I had to because of Tim Davis, but I didn't get those sinks. I had never gotten them, and that kind of irked me

because I knew they were important, and other people who were smart, like Tim Davis, got them, and I didn't, and now they were in a big show at MoMA.

There's a lot to follow in the art world and sometimes I miss stuff and it kind of drives me crazy, but it's been years really—

years since I was welcomed in that world—because you kind of have to have someone welcoming you—the way Tim Davis has Gober and

my friends died—the way a lot of people died back then—from AIDS or addiction or whatever and then the doors kind of shut

and I was shut out and I was kind of sad and I didn't want to go back there and besides it's all changed now anyway

and then those damn sinks that I didn't understand or maybe I didn't *want* to understand them because

they are so fucking central to what I am saying. Because they are completely emblematic of that time / when so many people died / so young / from a disease / that nobody understood / and it didn't matter how many times / you washed your hands / in those damn sinks /

it didn't matter how many times

you could still

sink.

Those sinks were only the beginning, and that *Untitled, 1992* piece that was first shown at Dia in Chelsea—that's Tim Davis's favorite piece,

and that piece will take your breath away, probably in the same way that the David sculpture took people's breath away centuries ago.

But don't listen to me. Buy the catalogue. Read the chronology. Hilton Als wrote the essay and it's one of the most passionate art essays of his career.

Even Tim Davis thinks so.

Cut to Snow Scene in Montauk

Colin was dying and I was staying in the Soho Grand and so were you. On the phone, you said that the snowstorm was a surprise, but you were too busy to have coffee. For so long, I thought I was Clementine because of her citrussy name and mine. But on the occasion of its tenth anniversary, they were showing your film at the Tribeca Film Festival with some scientists, actors, and a producer to talk about it afterwards, and I realized I was the Kirsten Dunst character, hopelessly in love with a brilliant, older, married, ethically compromised (according to you) man. I was the Catherine Keener character in *Being John Malkovich*. What did she say that I had said to you? *I love you, but I am not attracted to you.* No, I don't think that's it. But once, you said to me, *I love you, but I am not* in love *with you anymore.* Or something like that. Memory is unreliable. So whose memories are those in the film? The producer said that you worked on distinguishing real time from brain time and how to make the memory loss look real. Memory loss is real. You seem to forget how much in your films is based on the past—what happened to us when we were young—or else you don't want to acknowledge it. But for some reason, I seem to remember where almost every moment comes from and Laura remembers the rest. Remember her? I know you remember her and that line will make you angry. You even admitted to me that she's the one who led you out onto the frozen Charles River at night and then you used that image on the poster for the film!

The scientists said we have several memory systems: episodic, procedural, and emotional—to name a few. Adrienne Rich wrote, *why should the wild child / weep for the scientists // why*. I don't know why I love those lines and still remember them after all these years. They also said that the purpose of memory is to help make decisions based on what we have experienced and that memory is designed to be updated with new information. It was snowing. Colin was dying, and I think they were starting a war somewhere. You were making a film and I was staying in the Soho Grand Hotel and you didn't have time, which seemed so sad, because once we had all the time in the world and no one to spend it with, but each other. Cut to the elephants in Times Square after the eternal sunshine quote from Alexander Pope—the brightest moment in the film. And suddenly I have a vague memory of being in a dark apartment—because we lived in dark, undesirable places back then—and someone, probably you, describing the experience of seeing some circus elephants in Times Square. *Do I know you?* Did I know you? Remember I bought that book about you and the introduction confused me so much because it said that you had two children and had never graduated

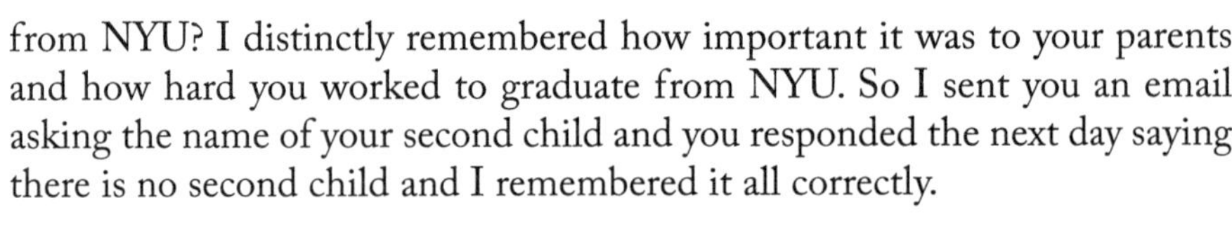
from NYU? I distinctly remembered how important it was to your parents and how hard you worked to graduate from NYU. So I sent you an email asking the name of your second child and you responded the next day saying there is no second child and I remembered it all correctly.

Dell Lemmon's first book of poetry, *Single Woman*, was published by Box Turtle Press. Her poems have appeared in the *Straddler*, *WSQ*, *PMS (poemmemoirstory)*, *Mudfish*, and *Washington Square Review*. "Have You Seen the Bob Gober Show at MoMA?" first appeared in *Cross Review* .

PHILIP LEVINE

The Miracle

A man staring into the fire
sees his dead brother sleeping.

The falling flames go yellow and red
but it is him, unmistakable.

He goes to the phone and calls
his mother. Howard is asleep,

he tells her. Yes, she says,
Howard is asleep. She does not cry.

In her Los Angeles apartment
with its small color tv

humming now unobserved,
she sees Howard rocking

alone beneath the waves
of an ocean she cannot name.

Howard is asleep, she says
to the drapes drawn on the night.

That night she dreams
a house alive with flames, their

old house, and her son sleeping
peacefully in the kingdom of agony.

She wakens near morning,
the dream more real

than the clock luminous beside her
or the gray light rising slowly

above the huddled town, more real
than the groan of the first car.

She calls her son who has risen
for work and tells him,

Howard is warm and at peace.
He sees the crusted snows of March

draining the cold light of a day
already old, he sees himself

unlocking the front door of his shop,
letting the office help in, letting

Eugene and Andy, the grease men,
step before him out of the snow.

When she hangs up he looks out
on the back yard, the garbage cans

collapsing like sacks of air, the fence
holding a few gray sparrows,

he looks out on the world he always sees
and thinks, it's a miracle.

Call It Music

Some days I catch a rhythm, almost a song
in my own breath. I'm alone here
in Brooklyn, it's late morning, the sky
above the St. George Hotel is clear, clear
for New York, that is. The radio is playing
Bird Flight, Parker in his California
tragic voice fifty years ago, his faltering
"Lover Man" just before he crashed into chaos.
I would guess that outside the recording studio
in Burbank the sun was high above the jacarandas,
it was late March, the worst of yesterday's rain
had come and gone, the sky was washed. Bird

could have seen for miles if he'd looked, but what
he saw was so foreign he clenched his eyes,
shook his head, and barked like a dog—just once—
and then Howard McGhee took his arm and assured him
he'd be OK. I know this because Howard told me
years later, told me he thought Bird could
lie down in the hotel room they shared, sleep
for an hour or more, and waken as himself.
The perfect sunlight angles into my little room
above Willow Street. I listen to my breath
come and go and try to catch its curious taste,
part milk, part iron, part blood, as it passes
from me into the world. This is not me,
this is automatic, this entering and exiting,
my body's essential occupation without which
I am a thing. The whole process has a name,
a word I don't know, an elegant word not
in English or Yiddish or Spanish, a word
that means nothing to me. Howard truly believed
what he said that day when he steered
Parker into a cab and drove the silent miles
beside him while the bright world
unfurled around them: filling stations, stands
of fruits and vegetables, a kiosk selling trinkets
from Mexico and the Philippines. It was all
so actual and Western, it was a new creation
coming into being, like the music of Charlie Parker
someone later called "glad," though that day
I would have said silent, "the silent music
of Charlie Parker." Howard said nothing.
He paid the driver and helped Bird up two flights
to their room, got his boots off, and went out
to let him sleep as the afternoon entered
the history of darkness. I'm not judging
Howard, he did better than I could have
now or then. Then I was nineteen, working
on the loading docks at Railway Express,
coming day by day into the damaged body
of a man while I sang into the filthy air
the Yiddish drinking songs my Zadie taught me
before his breath failed. Now Howard is gone,
eleven long years gone, the sweet voice silenced.

"The subtle bridge between Eldridge and Navarro,"
they later wrote, all that rising passion
a footnote to others. I remember in '85
walking the halls of Cass Tech, the high school
where he taught after his performing days,
when suddenly he took my left hand in his
two hands to tell me it all worked out
for the best. Maybe he'd gotten religion,
maybe he knew how little time was left,
maybe that day he was just worn down
by my questions about Parker. To him Bird
was truly Charlie Parker, a man, a silent note
going out forever on the breath of genius
which now I hear soaring above my own breath
as this bright morning fades into afternoon.
Music, I'll call it music. It's what we need
as the sun staggers behind the low gray clouds
blowing relentlessly in from that nameless ocean,
the calm and endless one I've still to cross.

Philip Levine was born in Detroit in 1928 to Russian-Jewish immigrant parents and educated at Wayne State University, the University of Iowa Writers' Workshop, and Stanford University. The author of twenty collections of poetry, his honors included the Pulitzer Prize, two National Book Awards, and two National Book Critics Circle Awards.

BILL LIVINGSTON

Atlantic Terminal

Getting through the double doors is a hell in itself,
choreographing the impossible dance with larger parcels—
this ballet requires an extra set of Samaritan hands.
Then the heart sinks when you see the line for one window.

"But I got here early!" you say to yourself,
setting your package on the filthy, wet linoleum.
You're standing and fuming, barely moving—
held hostage by the government once again.

One damn window open, the line begins to grow
like the delicate stem of a rain-soaked mushroom
under the rotting shiitake cap of shared misery.
The lucky one steps up at the Pavlov sound and light.

Green wool coat, early 60's, as wide as she is tall,
spewing, wanting everyone to know her theories—
Dr. Kevorkian was convicted by a jury of his own peers.
What he failed to ask was, "Who are my peers?"

No one looks at her, except for me because I like to stare
into the face of crazy, so I can see the stranger of logic
staring back in the mirror, telling me who my peers are.
The door squeals with a rush of cold, repelling air.

Man, look at this fucking line! Open more damn windows!
Finally, a welcome voice of reason! I look back at him,
nod as he queues up, shaking his head and the rain from his
coat. We're set in our mission as she lets everyone know—

And the doctors in Haiti who killed my sister, where did
they go to school? Did they butcher a cow to learn how to
heal? I had to go. I had to come here. I had to escape my
Haiti. The civil servant behind the smudged, bulletproof plexi

moves slower than a FEMA rescue as we can all hear them
in the mail room, behind the windows, laughing and playing
mockingly like baby goats—safe, secure, unionized baby goats.
Now is her time to shine, to make her escape, but no, she repeats—

Dr. Kevorkian was convicted by a jury of his own peers.
What he failed to ask was, "Who are my peers?" Yes, darling,
one book of forever stamps, please. And then the new window
opens, ding, and the jury in line watches in envy as I step up

to send something to a much better place.

Originally from Altoona, PA, Bill Livingston is a poet, humorist, screenwriter, and advertising copywriter who has been published in *Danse Macabre*, *Saturday Afternoon Journal*, *Treehouse*, *Flipside*, *New Verse News*, and *Radius*. He is a supporting member of the Poetry Project and an original member of Brooklyn Poets and Bowery Arts + Science. He lives in Brooklyn, NY, with his wife and twin daughters.

PETER LONGOFONO

Vierge Ouvrante

En garde. Easy deacons, hot wisdom. An orc aspires
to folderol; a snake, to manumission. Mighty Eiffel

out of reach, all rivet, atop the nachttisch. By dint
of cut onion. The chit's prayer for propulsion foreign

in captions. Clearly arthritic, our linear Eucharist.
Boys, behave. In no wise may this be obeyed. To Dover

the planets propel, keeping well, the sure pluperfect.

This is purse-rummaging. Like the threadcount
it peaks. A hate bracelet for one, frozen oatmeal

in daguerreotype, percolating scum. The bicycler
gyres, completely original. Like damnation he can't

figure his spokes. The expressly forbidden appeal.
For sleep, shaved almond sleeves. For tokens, slots.

Zest

There positively must be weather—
its own hiccup, plainly frightened
of torture, hotly unforegone.

And artlessness. Boosterism's
crumple, men of birthplace frump;
yet these, too, produce grandchildren,
some deaf, who curl and are dandled.

In griffonage, not Deuteronomy,
not junket, the sun stiltwalks daily,
neither sure-footed nor defunct.

Mostly it's lost to science: good!
On a causeway it voids itself.
Day breaks, young as a number.
It was dumb to squint and prevaricate.

The Admiral, the Criminal

The curdling desert is a picture
of a curdling desert and in this picture
an airship lists. In the loud wind its paper
crew resorts to semaphore, earnestly
flapping the way paper tends to

succumb to paper scurvy. These drowsies
are obliged to thrill a quota: wistful nannies,
landlubbers, yeasts. The moment swells

bitterly. They lurch, they yaw, barely
skirting the infinitesimal pinch. It has
a way with all balloons. It behooves us

to humanize these tics, crumpled before
their groundcoming, sour coeurs.
Do something! Loft your vitamin kites!

Peter Longofono serves as the reviews editor at *Coldfront* and makes music with TH!CK. His chapbook *Chords* was published in March of 2016 by The Operating System. He lives in Brooklyn. "Vierge Ouvrante" was first published in *Tenderloin* and "Zest" was first published in *Fields*.

KATE LUTZNER

Speculating on the meaning of birdsong

There is a space inside me dedicated to your needs.
I am thick, like the grass above a grave. There is nothing
glamorous about recollection. This morning, a sparrow
visited our feeder. Its small ability, the way it leaned
in. We were all delicate once. I blame you for the chair
stranded in my mouth, for how I strain to hear
the bird's gentle song. We rested but did not sleep,
arranged next to each other like trees. It turns out
I don't know you very well. I see your quiet pleasure,
the way your slumber has nothing to do with me.
Let's take a walk tomorrow, get lost in mutual
destruction. The track can contain our sorrow
and our desire, but not much else.

Apartment hunt

They were renting out rooms in a converted morgue.
The day we visited, you climbed into one of the cubicles
they called a room and pulled me on top of you.
There was minimal marring, but you were rough
so I made a citizen's arrest. Nothing came of it,
no policemen in their little suits. I looked everywhere
for flowers but didn't see any. I thought maybe
there would be holdovers from when there were
dead people, the toxic pattern of abuse we put
ourselves through in order to mourn. Or maybe
it's just a means of getting out our disappointment
in a beautiful way. Outside the old morgue,
when we were leaving, I saw a family
of little brown birds lying in a nest. I couldn't tell
in the time it took for you to pull me away
from that scene, that small family, what love
might exist between them. I do know that you
have healed yourself of all feelings of empathy.

I am witness to that, and victim also. I am what
you might call a spoke in the wheel of heart-
ache. Some days, I am capable of confrontation,
but there are times I kill my insides like pouring
acid down a chute you know has live things
clinging to it. It might not be a pretty picture,
the one in which we live, but we do reside
together, our toxicity, our grief.

Kate Lutzner's poetry and stories have appeared in such journals as *Antioch Review*, *Mississippi Review*, *Brooklyn Rail*, *BlazeVOX*, *Rattle*, and *Barrow Street*. Kate holds a JD from the University of North Carolina at Chapel Hill and an MFA from City College and has been featured in *Verse Daily*. She has been nominated for a Pushcart Prize as well as the *Best of the Net Anthology*. She lives in Brooklyn.

SHEILA MALDONADO

Clashing in Coney Island

In the 1984–85 picture of Class 5B
at P.S. 90 in Coney Island,
Brooklyn, New York
I'm wearing gray Lees and
a big white, gray and pink sweater,
a style half-ghetto, half-Guido

Me and the other Lee wearers
would walk to school and home
with our hands planted
on our back right waistbands
so no one would snatch our
Lee patches, the sport of the day

I got the sweater at Ceasar's Bay,
which used to be Korvettes, which later
became Kmart, but then was haven
for high-haired Bensonhurst Guidettes
and Ma, who got a flavor for chiclet jeans,
which made you snap your hips like gum

Makea is next to me in the picture and
lived in my building, along with her
cousin Tecia, whose house was a
cool, gray cave in the summer where we
watched Whoopi Goldberg on early cable
play with her "long, luxurious" blonde hair

I flinched the first time I saw Tecia's mom
put a metal comb over the stove fire
and then to Tecia's head but had
no problem playing Double Dutch with
her and Makea's telephone cable rope,
that whipped us if we didn't jump right

Stacy is below me in the picture and
was my best friend the next year,
going out to lunch with me,
the sixth grade privilege,
and encouraging me to buy more
big sweaters, half-Italian that she was

Out in the drugstore one day with her
during lunch, I was decked in
Ceasar's Bay regalia and when an old man
spoke to me in Spanish I had
the nerve to be surprised but he told me
Try as you might, you can't hide

Poet in a Shade of Jade

I am so jealous of how poor you are
of how you are poor
your particular stilo pobre
The way you put no cash and
no money together is uncanny
This aesthetic
lack of change combined
with lack of dollars
is very difficult to duplicate
and I hate you for that

I was gonna go hear you read
from your new collection of
unpaid bills
just the other day
but you get readings
all the time
you have your pick
of not being paid
or being unpaid
You get to ride
the subway back and forth
on your own dime
and you pay for
your performance alcohol

I'll make it one of these days
give you dirty looks
as you read and rake in
your air bucks

What I look forward to most
is not tolerating
how you hoard your poverty
tell no one your secret
you must have some malefactor
mentor
mentiroso
who further mystifies
the acquisition of wealth
and points you in the direction
of the dead end

Sheila Maldonado is the author of the poetry collection *one-bedroom solo* (Fly by Night Press, 2011). Her second publication, *that's what you get*, is forthcoming from Brooklyn Arts Press. She is a Creative Capital awardee as part of desveladas, a visual writing collective. She grew up in Coney Island and lives in uptown Manhattan. The poems in this anthology were previously published in *phati'tude* and *Hyperallergic*.

CYNTHIA MANICK

The Future of Skin

In every dream I wear
a different armor.
In one I'm a wolf
and no one sees
me coming. I keep the wild-
ness at bay,
pick gristle from my teeth-
knowing I've split adverbs
and femurs like Shea butter.

In another I'm a rooster
with silver claws.
I have premonitions
of eclipses and salt-
crusted waters
pulling me
like tiny charges
to new tribes.
Nothing burns, screams,
or crows in alarm.

Or I'm a simple skeleton
free from skin's grip.
Ears small indents and
eye sockets like a painters
coal with a riot inside.
I step out in the sun
and see skeletons everywhere.
Purses tucked
under bone-shawl blades.
My feet are bare too,
just metatarsals and toe rings
but it's so warm with
skin nowhere to be found
crosses nowhere to be found
the noose nowhere to be found.

The Museum

People come here to be dazzled.
To be swept into carefully labeled
history of high yellow and dark skin,
like the slow roll of hands steeped
in trumpets, ivory keys or the bramble
thorns of cotton. Loud speakers trail
all visitors— *did you know this one*
invented peanut butter? part of the
light bulb? oh and that lotion
that makes those old kinky strands
cut straight from the root.

Some exhibits are more popular
than others. Novelty items like
Aunt Jemima's head scarf, yellowed
slave bills of sale, basketball jerseys,
mammy saltshakers, and Obama
bobbleheads are high volume areas.
On the second floor timed to lights
and a smoke machine, a trio of
animatronic colored girls sing
doo doo doo, doodododoo, with plastic
mulatto skin covering their nuts and
bolts. Bobbed hairstyles and silk
chiffon completes the Motown
look, but somehow they seem
solemn in the lights.

Then there's me— *here she is,*
here is our last little darkie.
You see the pigmentation here?
We don't let them get that dark
these days. If pain had a shape
it would be one giant muscle,
it would be the sound the human
mind makes when you realize
you don't own a body anymore.
I've been here for years now.
I can't remember the last time
I saw the sun or felt a taproot

next to my feet, or being in love,
picking juniper berries so thick it
stains my nails like blood coming
clean. I often ask what God wants
from my face and empty body.

When the crowds and tour groups
disperse, my bones ache to
slide side by side in the dark.
Like the bison, dinosaurs, and our
blood brothers the Indians, you'll find
my carcass in this museum—
strings around my pelvis, and thin
clear wires making my fluted bones
dance, say hi, in the last great
African mammal display.

Cynthia Manick is the author of *Blue Hallelujahs* (Black Lawrence Press, 2016). A Pushcart Prize–nominated poet with a BA from Hollins University and an MFA from the New School, she has received fellowships from Cave Canem, the Callaloo Creative Writing Workshop, the Fine Arts Work Center, the Hambidge Center for Creative Arts & Sciences, Hedgebrook, Poets House, and the Vermont Studio Center. She serves as the East Coast editor of the independent press Jamii Publishing and is the founder and curator of the reading series Soul Sister Revue.

DAVID TOMAS MARTINEZ

The/A Train

A honey badger's skin can
withstand multiple blows
from machetes, arrows,
and spears, but these rusted
weapons haven't killed
anything in years, so that may
be the lesson there, that
there is no there there, like
many poems, like many
revolutions, and maybe there
isn't a there there in many
people only that foggy
anachronistic lizard eye,
or what I have come to call
the part of consciousness that
builds impediments, isolates
the "supertrump." Or
what New Yorkers call
subways. Or what a King
calls a dream. Or what X
called Y. What the crowd
yells as lit, The Cave calls dim.
What they deem in West
Tejas as a fancy evening out
is rocking on the porch,
aint they good at irony,
where watching the fugitive
moon runaway takes days,
like the time I caught the C
I hoped was an A, and saw a
butterfly move in what I can
only say is protest. The wings
made small combustions
through the car. Eyes trained.
The awful is tracked by

awe. An officer lifts his
gun, yells to raise your hands
higher the TV flutters.
Watch it. They will
call you moth and kill you.

David Tomas Martinez's debut collection of poetry, *Hustle*, was released in 2014 by Sarabande Books, winning the New England Book Festival's prize in poetry, the Devil's Kitchen Reading Award, and honorable mention for the Alfredo Cisneros Del Moral Award. He is the 2015 winner of the Inprint Paul Verlaine Prize in Poetry. Martinez is a Pushcart winner, CantoMundo fellow, and recipient of the Stanley P. Young Fellowship from Bread Loaf. A second collection is forthcoming from Sarabande Books. Martinez lives in Brooklyn and teaches creative writing at Columbia University.

DONNA MASINI

Giants in the Earth

I walk at night, the city building and breaking around me,
over cracked concrete, over broken pavement, over steel plates,
the ground bumpy, uneven beneath me.
I listen for the joy inside my bones,
the steady, even transportation of my blood.
I go down to watch the trucks, the men climb into the earth,
the pulse and rhythm of the city slower, the cadence looser.
Soon I am among them: builders, diggers, sweating their nightly excavations;
sandblast, jackhammer, the city making itself over, sloughing off layers.

I love the way things get built at night: people, the body rebuilding itself,
bone, tissue, and skin, the cells of the dermis, the pumping digestions,
the network of neuron, dendrite, the bustle of the dream pulse.

Caterpillar. FIAT ALIA. Dynahoe 490.
Week by week the machinery moves across Delancey Street,
closer to the river where the pulse begins, slowly,
as I imagine dinosaurs moved. Heavy legs over mud and vegetation.

The forklift moves forward, lifts, as a priest raises a chalice.
Dynahoe 490 swivels to face it.
A man leans in his seat, grips the wheel, grasps the shift,
lifts the claw to raise the long arm,
claws a clump of rocky concrete to the street below,
the teams of men still digging around him. He
lifts shifts dumps, lifts shifts dumps,
the torchlights of the welders sparking in the dug-out hole
against the black night, bridge lights, four bent men circle
a trashcan fire, warming themselves, whisking their hands back from the sparks.
And the sparks flying out of the ground look like hell splintering.

Now it seems they are breaking the city down:
streets, trees, buildings coming down; broken lives, lines to families broken;
breaking down buildings and grandfathers, bridges, traditions,
the uprooted on their corners.
Thirty-two-year-old men in their beds.

Dreams are the places roots rock.
It comes to me now, one of those nonplaces the mind keeps
returning to: the empty lot at the edge of Brooklyn, cracked glass and gravel,
bent cans, tampon wrappers, the overpass, the echo beneath,
and no one to hear it except the screaming child, the projects sulking in
the distance.

As some knew tree, fish, bird, the patterns and habits,
I knew brick and concrete, glass and light,
the diamond sidewalks that burned in the summers,
round-stoned walkways that shone in the rain,
the cement walk, boxed squares for handball, slate blocks thrust up by the
movement of trees.

The vibration of jackhammers thrills me, shatters me.
That something could be made of all this breaking.
Sweet rain and sweat and the lovely yellow machinery knocking,
the black gravel curved as the shell of a turtle.

I stand a long time watching them, lean across the fissure into a wood-slat hole.
A man's red eyes glow up at me. He grins, unhooks the lamp from his belt and
climbs out of the ground.

Sometimes it feels like it's me breaking apart.

What is the name of that truck, that tool?
What are you making? Where are your children?
What is the sound of a body breaking, the cells rebuilding, the heart deteriorating?

The forklift turns.
A shovel falls against the truck's flank.
Below the streetlife, above the subway systems, the iron girders brace,
and still the machinery plunges, breaking ground, turning the dirt, tenderly,
as you'd lift a lover's buttock;
steel pipes like metal pelvises scattered across the pavement,
the banging of tools falling in a strange blue light.

Donna Masini is the author of *4:30 Movie,* forthcoming from W.W. Norton, *Turning to Fiction* (W.W. Norton, 2004), *That Kind of Danger* (Beacon Press, 1994), in which "Giants in the Earth" first appeared, and the novel *About Yvonne* (W.W. Norton, 1997). Her work has appeared in journals and anthologies including *Poetry*, *Open City*, *Paris Review*, *APR*, *Parnassus*, *Ploughshares*, *Pushcart Prize 2005,* and *Best American Poetry 2015.* A recipient of fellowships from the NEA and NYFA, she is a professor of English at Hunter College.

BERNADETTE MAYER

Ancient Brooklyn Talk by the Boardwalk

We're at fucking Cooney Eyeland now not that fancy fuckin abandoned lake inna fuckin Berkshires dontcha wanna be the virgin mother fer me people fallin in love hey Duke what the fuck man getthefuckouttahere dat's my girlfrien's birdsnest Da-neece Da-neece you fucking turn me fuckin on Lew you fuckin shit ass Jew turn up yr fuckin ghetto blaster louder yeah ok some fuckin raybans them fuckin spics got lookit them fuckin secret-fairies wanna go inta the tunnel of love wit me didja hear bout the fuckin professor with tenure who said oh miss if I asked you would you be willing perhaps to make love with me lost his fuckin job ok ok fuckin A wanna make out wanna fuck where she's fuckin jailbait i got my apparatus you *are* a scumbag wanna listen to fuck music onna FM station whose house wanna make love avec moi immediately someday when you get older do you wanna step in to the Tristan & Isolde stream you dippy broads wanna have fuckin mushrooms in all yr food how bout goin to the Chateau Henri Quatre fer frogs legs without yr fucking sister or ta see a foreign movie & then fuck in my ole man's car out on the island how's about readin my complete poetic works & then we can fuck I'm the fuckin son of Tennyson how's about the dark arts of evil how's about a little generic occasion like bruther & sister ya know, a platonic fuckin picnic i'll fuck yr sister ya know what I mean you fuckin Mickey you fuckin Greek gimme some fuckin head whadda you make of that guy Mozart & fuckin Staten Island you're a weird fuckin broad whoozat guy how come he's got his hand in yr pussy I already spent three fuckin bucks on you today what's he some fuckin rich guy or somethin I thought you wuz the fuckin virgin mother you look it she fuckin looks it.

Bernadette Mayer is the author of over twenty-seven collections, including most recently *Works and Days* (2016), *Eating the Colors of a Lineup of Words: The Early Books of Bernadette Mayer* (2015), and *The Helens of Troy, NY* (2013), as well as countless chapbooks and artist books. From 1980–1984 she served as the director of the St. Mark's Poetry Project, and she has also edited and founded *0 to 9* journal and United Artists books and magazines.

JOSHUA MEHIGAN

Heard at the Men's Mission

How many sons-of-bitches no one loves,
with long coats on in June and beards like nests—
guys no one touches without latex gloves,
squirming with lice, themselves a bunch of pests,
their cheeks and noses pocked like grapefruit rind—
fellas with permanent shits and yellowish eyes
who, if they came to in the flowers to find
Raphael there, could not be otherwise—

have had to sit there listening to some twat
behind a plywood podium in the chapel
in a loose doorman suit the color of snot,
stock-still except his lips and Adam's apple,
telling them how much Jesus loves the poor
before they got their bread and piece of floor?

How Strange, How Sweet

This was a butcher. This, a Chinese laundry.
This was a Schrafft's with 10-cent custard ice creams.
Off toward the park, that was the new St. Saviour.
Then, for five blocks, not much but chain-link fences.
These foolish things, here today, gone today,
yesterday, forty years ago, tomorrow.
Doloreses and Normas not quite gone,
with slippers on, and heads like white carnations,
little, and brittle, and mum, why did the fine
September weather call you out today?
To dangerously bend and touch a cat.
To lean beside your final door and smile.
To go a block and get a thing you need.
What are you hiding, ladies? What do you know?

Micks were from here to there. Down there, the Mob.
And, way down there, the mob the bill let in.
Far west were Puerto Ricans. Farther west,
in Newark, Maplewood, or Pennsylvania,
one canceled choice away, why, there's nostalgia,
lipstick, and curls, and gum, and pearls on Sunday.
So here's a platinum arc from someone's neck chain,
bass through a tinted window, loudest laughter,
the colored fellow with the amber eyes
who doesn't need to stand just where he is.
Here sits the son of 1941,
a pendulous pink arm across a chair back;
his sister, she of 1943,
her hair the shade of an orangutan.
Food stamps and welfare, Medicaid and Medicare.
Kilroy was here. Here was where to get out of.

Last come the new inevitable whites.
See how the gracious evening sunshine lights
their balconied high-rise's apricot
contemporary stucco-style finish.
Smell the pink-orange powder as some punk
sandblasts Uneeda Biscuit off the wall.
Flinch at the miter saw and nail gun,
at three-inch nails that yelp as men dismantle
a rooftop pigeon loft. Those special birds
will not fly home to the implicit neighbor,
or fall like tiny Esther Williamses
in glad succession from a wire, to climb
and circle in the white December sky.
Far up, from blocks away, the pale birds seemed,
when they all turned at once, to disappear.
Across the street, the normal pigeons eat.

Joshua Mehigan is a Guggenheim Fellow. His second book, *Accepting the Disaster*, in which "How Strange, How Sweet" and "Heard at the Men's Mission" appear, was published by Farrar, Straus and Giroux in 2014 and subsequently cited as a best book of the year in the *Times Literary Supplement*, *New York Times Book Review*, and elsewhere.

LYNN MELNICK

Landscape with Rum and Implosion

You should have seen my breasts inside a dress so extravagant

it was rogue among a decade
of the type of electric horticulture

these bittersweet groves were founded on, so,
yeah, I traded it right off my body

for a bottle of rum on the cleanest, brightest street corner
I didn't think to guard my skin against because

I'm in love with a woman who doesn't appeal to me.

Turn on the television and all you hear
is the new way of speaking

asked and answered

or the old new way of speaking now that everyone's doing it.

Am I happy about it? No.

I adapt to the manifold balconies of California
as a symbol of liberation

when no matter how many rails we could finish from the railing

or the viewshed of a whole city against the neon of a floozy motel

I am only ever trapped inside

my own fixed vantage point or else I am
weather

imploding, such as it does.

Coney Island

I give the red-topped toy machine back its decal
as I want something else, better, what you have:

rubber replica of reptile, shock-purple and sinister.
The small business of setting out to do a day

that started evening last with soup and summer
boredom ended here, asleep once more, clutch

of fear in the sand. Concession calls to wake us
and we are two among the hunched, invisible

to the well-oiled grotesque. For retribution,
a four-ticket ride, eyes spun from upside-down.

I bite and cannot scream. Next whiskey
at a boardwalk bar, a watered-down one of my own.

I could now dance like this pair by the jukebox:
resolved, fat and furrowed. But I am not ugly

yet or cheered. I want a room to keep a home.
I want a bed. (Lemonade. Sand again. Subway.)

Let me sleep on your lap. No tracks to cross
bridges; we are going underwater. Whatever we have done

has sun-marked a line flat to my flesh. It hurts
like want hurts: that sweet. The rare side of no.

Lynn Melnick is author of *Landscape with Sex and Violence* (YesYes Books, 2017) and *If I Should Say I Have Hope* (YesYes Books, 2012) and co-editor, with Brett Fletcher Lauer, of *Please Excuse This Poem: 100 New Poets for the Next Generation* (Viking, 2015). She teaches poetry at 92Y in NYC and serves on the executive board of VIDA: Women in Literary Arts.

SHARON MESMER

I Lost My Beatnik Antlers on the Grassy Knoll—Help Me, JFK

I lost my khakis and my hair smoosh
and my craft beer/Telly Savalas shrine.
I lost my *History of Maple Urine Disease* on the grassy knoll,
and my trainable kielbasa.

I lost my eatable narc pants.
I was told I had lost my reason.
I lost my A-Rod beanstalk mojo on the grassy knoll
but I found my Christmas spliff.

Scully, Mulder, I *will* be a doctor,
but I need my Ryan Seacrest is a Kitty blanket first.
Cuba has Santería, Haiti has Voodoo, and I have my
Abraham Lincoln's Birthday Does Irish Cheerleaders At Madison Square
    Garden pass…oops: *had*.

Jean Valjean's balls are on the rebound from Napoleon,
but don't look for them on the grassy knoll.
Also lost are Broadway memories of Sylvia Plath
and Rachael Ray's My Little e-Pony giveaway.

I hear Maytag refrigerators are polling the Elephant Man's spider bite
about Tom of Finland's minimum wage petition.
Apparently it's also gone missing on the grassy knoll.
Now I don't feel so alone.

Russell Crowe's Peanut Corporation is also lost,
as well as Canadian television's *Why Do I Have Green Poop*? NASCAR series.
Too bad about Neil Patrick Harris's Spanglish movie *Wampum the Sky Warrior*
(and *Wampum Reloaded: Zombie Apocalypse Credit Union*).

Whatever happened to Marie Osmond's Deluxe Dead Baby Pills Patch™?
And *Freak-Out On Lesbian Mountain* starring groundhog puppets and
    sponsored by Abilify?

And where are Hosni Mubarak's pics of America's most voluptuous
    MILF members
of the Loyal Order of Benevolent Toilet Dogs?
I think we know the answer.

My live sponge birth control Pay-per-view?
My Prednisone-induced diarrhea tracking number?
My cat's resignation letter to Maya Angelou's Power Ranger's *Diaper-
    Lover Stories Night*?

Help me, JFK!

Sharon Mesmer's poetry books are *Greetings from My Girlie Leisure Place*, *Annoying Diabetic Bitch*, *The Virgin Formica*, *Half Angel/Half Lunch*, and *Vertigo Seeks Affinities*. Four of her poems appear in *Postmodern American Poetry: A Norton Anthology* (second edition, 2013). She teaches creative writing at NYU and the New School. "I Lost My Beatnik Antlers on the Grassy Knoll—Help Me, JFK" first appeared in the online magazine *Truck*, guest-edited by Maria Damon. It also appears in the collection *Greetings from My Girlie Leisure Place*, published in 2015 by Bloof Books.

MATT MILLER

Particle City

City of tender particles.
Particle of tender cities.
Particle of silver birds.
Particle of clouds.

Particle of fissures.
Particle of enhanced sirens.
Silver particle of men.
Crying particle of porches.

Lying particle of numbers.
Numbered particle of lies.
Particulate little men and their sirens.
Particles of articulate men.
City of crying particles.

Dying men and their particular porches.
Lying sirens,
enhanced particular men.
City of enhanced particles.
Circuit of particles.
Circuit of particulate cities.

Particulate cities of cloudy men.
Particulate lying birds.
Lying particles of numbered clouds.
Clouds of particles of lies.
Clouds of particles of cities.
Particulate men of dying cities.
Clouds of particles of men in particulate cities.

Particles of lies on crying porches.
Particular birds counting clouds.

Fissured cities of particular birds.
Fissured particles of enhanced cloud.
Cloudy particles of fissures.
City of cloud particles.

Matt Miller is an associate professor of English at Yeshiva University in Manhattan, where he teaches American literature and creative writing. He recently published a book on Whitman entitled *Collage of Myself: Walt Whitman and the Making of Leaves of Grass*. You can find more of his poems online at *Poetry Daily*, *Verse*, *Double Room*, etc. He lived in Clinton Hill, Brooklyn, for many years but recently made the exodus to Long Island City, Queens.

SUE NACEY MILLER

Brighton Beach: After Learning, at 31, that Grandfather Was a Schizophrenic

Every flag is a wave.
Every wave rises blue to the blue sky.
Before breaking every blue wave is blue.
Inside every wave is another wave breaking.

From this perspective—
from down here on the ground—
the pigeons are the same height as the girls with green strings
wrapped around their necks.

Father, these are your daughters.
These are your daughters with green necks.
These are your daughters with their heads tied to their bodies.
Your daughters with no throats inside their green strings.

Suddenly, you make sense.
From one side, these pink houses with their gray dribbly faces.
This is our finishing school.
From the other side, only flags.
Frenzied flags
hungry flags
blue flags losing their blue
as they rise and descend over themselves overhead.

What difference does breaking make.
What difference to the sand in being covered—
by ocean or towel or bodies or closed in a small girl's fist—

but what of that gray gull—
that red-eyed gull
that is neither pink nor blue nor green—
that call falling from its clam-splitting beak

as it stretches its neck
and looks around.

From something left in the open
it takes a bite.

Sue Nacey Miller holds an MFA from CUNY's Hunter College, where she previously taught in the English department. Her poems have appeared in *Poemeleon*, *Inertia*, *Salamander*, and other journals. "Brighton Beach…" was originally published in the online journal *RealPoetic*. She currently works at Columbia University.

DAVID MILLS

For Those Whose Lives Are Lived

like a jackknife inched
    through lime before you slit
your tongue with the notched
    unsavory blade; like a syphilitic
calla lily: nubbed and pink; like
    a jaw wired shut by the weight
of someone else's words; like
    every sound you've ever made
holding a meeting in your mouth;
    like anguish smeared across a canyon;
like suffering in a glass language:
    the pain no different, just foreign
and hard to translate; like an icy
    searing your molars; like your hard
palate's a cave pipistrelles cling
    to; like your body's a tongue
curled in the grotto of G-d's
    epileptic mouth—and she's
about to swallow.

David Mills is the author of two books, *The Dream Detective* (a small press bestseller) and *The Sudden Country,* a finalist for the 2013 Main Street Rag Poetry Book Award. He is the subject of the documentary *Freak the Language*. He received a poetry fellowship from the New York Foundation for the Arts and an MFA from Warren Wilson College. His poems have appeared in *Ploughshares*, *jubilat*, *Callaloo*, and *Brooklyn Rail,* to name a few. His poem "For Those Whose Lives Are Lived" was previously published in *Prairie Wolf Press Review.*

KAMILAH AISHA MOON

Perfect Form

North Charleston, SC, 4.4.15

Walter Scott must have been a track athlete
before serving his country, having children:

his knees were high, elbows bent
at 90 degrees as his arms pumped
close to his sides, back straight and head up
as each foot landed in front of the other,
a majesty in his strides.

So much depends on instinct, ingrained
legacies and American pastimes.
Relays where everyone on the team wins
remain a dream. Olympic arrogance,
black men chased for sport—
heat after heat
of longstanding, savage races
that always finish the same way.

My guess is Mr. Scott ran distances
and sprinted, whatever his life events
required. Years of training and technique
are not forgotten, even at 50. Even after being
tased out of his right mind. Even in peril
the body remembers what it has been
taught (boy), keeping perfect form
during his final dash.

Kamilah Aisha Moon is the author of *She Has a Name* (Four Way Books, 2013). A Pushcart Prize winner and one of PSA's "New American Poets" for 2015, she has received fellowships from Vermont Studio Center, Rose O'Neill Literary House, Hedgebrook, and Cave Canem. Her work has been featured widely, including in *Harvard Review*, *Poem-A-Day*, *Prairie Schooner*, and elsewhere. Her next poetry collection, *Starshine & Clay*, is forthcoming in 2017 from Four Way Books.

EMILY MOORE

O Hot Women of New York

O hot women of New York, it's good to see you
in your spiky hairdos carrying your mugs
of coffee made at home—you are so frugal!
O butch pitcher barking at your infielders
in Prospect Park! O modern dance spectator
with the fly jacket and smart comments at the talk-back!
O dykey women I give eyes to on the street!
You are so foxy now that I'm no longer
on the market. Not that you noticed me
when you had the chance, you who chalked your pool cues
paying me no mind, who brushed me with messenger bags
as you pushed past me towards some hotter girl.
These days I'm spoken for, which is why I think
you look so gorgeous in your matchstick corduroys,
your wife-beaters in summer, your pinstriped suits at work.
O lesbians, I love the way you take it all so seriously,
your bike lane advocacy, your vegan options,
the tacky streamers you hang up in bars
I won't be frequenting as much,
since as I said I'm taken.

Gowanus

Nat stood lanky at the stove, flamingo-kneed,
one foot flat to her calf, her boys' shorts loose.
I wore her tank-top, leafed through magazines,
then stirred our coffees with her roommate's spoon

as she slipped into flip-flops by the door
and climbed the rusty ladder to the roof.
She pushed the hatch aside, the tile floor
cooling my toes as I held mugs aloft,

my hot, one-handed grip precarious,
steam rising upwards towards the outside air.
In three months we'd break up. She stretched in child's pose,
her ropy arms extending towards the glare

of elevated F trains crossing at 4th Ave.,
just before one dives back underground.

Emily Moore teaches English at Stuyvesant High School in New York City where she has been a full-time classroom teacher since 2001. She is grateful to *wicked alice*, which first published "O Hot Women of New York," and to Paper Nautilus, the publisher of her chapbook *Shuffle*, in which the poem "Gowanus" first appeared. She may or may not be the only poet to read a sonnet involving Beyoncé on NPR.

MICHAEL MORSE

(Stephon Marbury)

Ideal: to drive the lane and look for dishes,
to see the open man, give him his bucket.

The one-on-one for which we are now counseled
blueprints a perfect symmetry that's hard to hold.

Like my friend who dreams of his ex
and wakes to find a moonlit lawn of deer.

In our nightly houses
the dolls insist that we are faithful to ourselves.

When I wake up in a bad mood,
I wonder why my point ignores my shooting guard.

This realm of giving, this realm of reciprocity:
I need a Mr. Make-It-Happen,

a deus ex machina, an all-star
down among us who deigns to fix our gears.

Until then, these reuptake inhibitors are splendid,
as when I find myself a deer on some strange lawn,

my garden-party head a promiscuity of maps
with toll-free grassy lanes and cul de sacs.

(Hotel Supposedly)

Where the clouds will wheel in and out like guests
and the concierge is a vane, pure service
at the beck and call of any old wind.
It's your will and your way, he says, his back
arched naturally from all the bow-downs.

Where visitations render you a status quo,
your bellhop, a summons, a tempest
of crosswalk imperatives, *Yes* or *Don't*,
or leaves of yellow and green (like Ginkgoes, yet cabs)
in county Kings where tires sing of muffled trouble.

Where the lobby is an empty state within a city
and your shot glass St. Reach sweet-talks
the welldrinks and scolds the mother tongue.
It's Saturday, and you're an evening,
a Jacob Riis moment in a lounge like Kansas.

Where you can walk the promenade at night
and sing the empty ballad *edifice*.
Hard rain: if you walk outside and look back in,
the concierge behind his cherry desk will call
you a myth, a dodger, and a harvest all wrapped up in one.

Where you're looking for stars on a dark night.
In your pocket, to be sure, ticket stubs from something seen,
the pronouns that carry the day:
We, Us, and Ours. They rest like feathers,
a soft lint under your key, your card.

Michael Morse has lived in the Red Hook neighborhood of Brooklyn since 2004. His first book, *Void and Compensation*, was published by Canarium Books and was a finalist for the 2016 Kate Tufts Discovery Award. He teaches at the Ethical Culture Fieldston School and the Iowa Summer Writing Festival, and he is a poetry editor at the *Literary Review*. "(Stephon Marbury)" first appeared in *A Public Space* and "(Hotel Supposedly)" first appeared in *Cranky*. He was born in Queens County in 1966 and first moved to Kings County in 1994.

JOHN MURILLO

Enter the Dragon

Los Angeles, CA, 1976

For me, the movie starts with a black man
Leaping into an orbit of badges, tiny moons

Catching the sheen of his perfect black afro.
Arc kicks, karate chops, and thirty cops

On their backs. It starts with the swagger,
The cool lean into the leather front seat

Of the black and white he takes off in.
Deep hallelujahs of moviegoers drown

Out the *wah wah* guitar. Salt & butter
High-fives, *Right on, brother!* and Daddy

Glowing so bright he can light the screen
All by himself. This is how it goes down.

Friday night and my father drives us
Home from the late show, two heroes

Cadillacking across King Boulevard.
In the car's dark cab, we jab and clutch,

Jim Kelly and Bruce Lee with popcorn
Breath, and almost miss the lights flashing

In the cracked side mirror. I know what's
Under the seat, but when the uniforms

Approach from the rear quarter panel,
When the fat one leans so far into my father's

Window I can smell his long day's work,
When my father—this John Henry of a man—

Hides his hammer, doesn't buck, tucks away
His baritone, license and registration shaking as if

Showing a bathroom pass to a grade school
Principal, I learn the difference between cinema

And city, between the moviehouse cheers
Of old men and the silence that gets us home.

Variation on a Theme by Eazy E

Six cigarettes in the dark like the eyes of three jackals
Scattering bones and dust; the schoolboy musk
Of us who hadn't learned to wash properly—
This much I remember. And I can still taste that summer,
The blood of it, when a certain breeze blows.
Through a screen door, someone's television plays
The theme song from *S.W.A.T.* When JoJo gives the signal,
Every dog on St. Andrews Place stirs to alarm.
I'm told predators abhor violence, are pacifists at heart.
Truth is, there was not a pacifist among us.
Fifteen-year-olds are violent by nature. Even the love
We dreamed of then—all thrust and sweat, tussle and scratch—
Smells of the kill. Of course, the jack move is no exception.
And lack of recognition is reason enough for all kinds
Of mayhem. In other words, *homeboy* wasn't from around here.

This much I remember: The chase, the catch,
The coldest night in August. The sharpened spoon
Of logic lodged midway between sternum and clavicle.
And when we look toward the sky, even the moon
Holds its breath, goes still, and prays. That was the night
I gave birth to myself: Big Slim, the Chuck Taylor Shogun,
Deacon in the church of this hallelujah beatdown.
The moon gasps, and we slam the car doors, peel
Into the night. When JoJo passes me the spliff, I try to still my fingers,
Knuckles fat and blue, spilling ashes on the gearbox.
He pops a tape in, twists the volume high as it will go.

The woofers rattle our ribcages, teeth,
The windows, the rearview.

1989

There are no windows here, and the walls
Are lined with egg cartons. So if we listen
Past the sampled piano, drum kick
And speakerbox rumble, we'd still not hear
The robins celebrating daybreak.
The engineer worries the mixboard,
Something about a hiss lurking between notes.
Dollar Bill curses the engineer, time
We don't have. Says it's just a demo
And doesn't need perfecting. "Niggas
Always want to make like Quincy Jones
When you're paying by the hour."
Deejay Eddie Scizzorhandz—because he cuts
So nice—taps ashes into an empty pizza box,
Head nodding to his latest masterpiece:
Beethoven spliced with Mingus,
Mixed with Frankie Beverly, all laid
On Billy Squier's "Big Beat."
I'm in a corner, crossing out and rewriting
Lines I'll want to forget years later,
Looking up every now and then
To watch Sheik Spear, Pomona's finest emcee,
In the vocal booth, spitting rhymes
He never bothers putting to paper,
Nearly hypnotized by the gold-plated Jesus
Swinging from his neck as he, too,
Will swing, days from now, before
They cut him from the rafters of a jail cell.

John Murillo is the author of the poetry collection *Up Jump the Boogie*. He's won some things and teaches at Hampshire College and New York University.

ANGEL NAFIS

When I Realize I'm Wearing My Girlfriend's Ex-Girlfriend's Panties

Praise now the fabric, for protecting who it can.
Praise the purposeful silver needle, and the thread's long arm.
Praise now, the path, and the ex-girlfriend, and
any mouth that has known my love's impeccable salt.

Incredible, incredible gravity
you lead me here
every time—to the water,
to drink. You lead me here
to this open space. To two-step with
beloved ghosts, a past
that is too a garden.
Do not un-wish a single blade of grass.
For the house craves each brick.
The war, every bullet.
This is my gift.

This is the circumstance
of loving. To see another's name
written so plainly, to see too
what my body will perform
in another woman's panties—

my own curious blood,
a single jewel, a red eye

winking.

Angel Nafis is an Ann Arbor, Michigan, native and a 2016 Ruth Lilly and Dorothy Sargent Rosenberg Poetry Fellow. Her work has appeared in the *BreakBeat Poets* anthology, the *Rumpus*, *Poetry*, and more. She has represented NYC at both the National Poetry Slam and the Women of the World Poetry Slam. She is the founder, curator, and host of the Greenlight Poetry Salon. Author of *BlackGirl Mansion* (Red Beard/New School Poetics, 2012), she earned her BA at Hunter College and is an MFA candidate in poetry at Warren Wilson College. "When I Realize I'm Wearing My Girlfriend's Ex-Girlfriend's Panties" first appeared in the *Rattling Wall*.

UCHE NDUKA

Every Secret

sharing every secret
of my suite

knowing i can never
pay back what you've given

you are more than
                a reflection of America

the car somewhere waits
for the sweetest of frostbites

arbitrariness was the imprint
                        of your love

because there are roads
on the way to everything

you take chances—
you and the sleeping sidewalk

heart with sails
wherever you go

if the sun lies
whatever takes you through
                the airless zone

unimpeachable implacable
much more than protecting
or perfecting

fishing for something vicious

Uche Nduka is a Nigerian-American poet. Author of ten volumes of poems, he is regarded as Nigeria's most erotic poet. His forthcoming volume of poems is titled *Sageberry.*

RACHAEL LYNN NEVINS

Housekeeping

Well, kiddo, we're the only parents you'll ever have, I'm sorry
to say: your father, the artist, and me, the poet
and oft-enraged student of Zen, sitting up in bed and yelling
at your father, "Nirvana is not somewhere else!"
An hour later you were conceived. And now, just look
at the mess we've gotten you into!
Clumps of cat fur drift along the edges
of the hallway, and drippings from last month's tomato sauce
turn black on top of the stove. Again, your father
has left the dish towel on the kitchen counter, and again
I am picking it up, throwing it at him, and wondering,
Who am I? What do I think I am doing?
Mice scurry in the walls, and last week
a chunk of the living room ceiling fell
onto the living room floor. I tell you,
things fall apart, and then they fall apart
some more, and there are days
when the very thought of the boxes still unpacked
a year and a half after our move is enough
to get my tears going. But I'm not talking only about our apartment,
your father's bad back and bum knee, how all my new hair
is growing in gray, the boarded-up shops around the corner,
or the plastic bags blowing down Ocean Avenue and out
to the Texas-sized pile of junk
collecting in the middle of the sea. We are all
heading toward a future of white dwarves and black holes,
and goodness knows even your cells
have plans of their own. I'm sorry, kiddo,
we've got nothing else to give you.
Just this cold and falling-apart universe, this cat
sleeping with his face tucked in my sneaker, and your disheveled
father and me, sitting on the bedroom floor and trying to sort
the laundry in heaps all around us, while merrily

you pick up your socks and toss them
onto the wrong pile.

Rachael Lynn Nevins is a Brooklyn-based freelance writer and editor. "Housekeeping" first appeared in *Rattle*, and her other poetry and prose have appeared in *Literary Mama*, *Comstock Review*, *Kindred*, *Hazlitt*, and elsewhere. She blogs at thevariegatedlife.com and teaches online poetry workshops with the Writers Studio.

D. NURKSE

The Grain

1

Every morning at 5AM Mr Eliakim
sent me to sand floors in a different neighborhood:
Utrecht Avenue, Gerritsen Beach, Dyker Heights,
and sometimes into zones where our huge city
fades into the next: Ridgewood, Cypress Hills.

An old man in a porkpie hat
who seemed offended by daybreak,
he waved his hand vaguely and said, *Go.*

Perhaps it was his wife who copied the addresses
in tight cursive on file cards:
Young Israel of Flatbush, Mary Star of the Sea,
Sons of Italy, The East, Elks, street numbers
with four or five digits: perhaps we all suspected
our city was not just architecture but impinged
on the night sky in its multiplicity,
on the brain's circuitry, the charge cloud.

2

Those streets at that hour were almost always empty.

Once a tenement bloomed in flames.
Firemen hurtled up spindly buckling ladders
in orange helmets, bearing pikes, in absolute silence
under pulsing lights, while an old couple watched
holding hands, in the formality of disaster.

Once a knot of children played an atavistic game,
London Bridge or *Green Man Rising*, their faces ashen—
had they danced all night? Were they plague survivors?

By daylight I found my destination: a padlocked barbershop,
a widow's walk-up, chock-a-block with pewter rabbits,
a ballroom whose round concave ceiling was decorated
with fading constellations, startlingly accurate.

3

I traveled with two machines: Silverline drum
contoured like a lawnmower, and Taurus edger,
like a snapping turtle in its welded shell.

As soon as I plugged in, changing the fuse in advance,
the roar—power, weakness—abolished me.

I couldn't linger without gouging a hole to the next ceiling.
I couldn't think without "thinking" "thoughts."

I began to wonder, why do I live in ten thousand days,
each no different from the next? Why not the present?

Why not a unified soul in a mortal body?

Why am I still a stranger to my wife and child,
my body, the air, the throbbing polished handles?

The room filled with smoke and sawdust,
ground varnish, lead and antimony, dead bees,
roach turds, stale Schlitz dried to a gum

                                    and when the engine snapped off
the floor was much as before. Once an elderly haberdasher
cursed me in Armenian, pointing with a shaky finger.
I can still see the grain.

4

The streets home were extraordinarily dark.

In high lit windows, fathers upbraided sons,
lovers kissed, mothers crooned to swaddled infants,
all in great silence, all slightly larger than themselves.

I watched in awe during the interminable red lights.

5

When I came home, my wife and child were sleeping.
I undressed on tiptoe not to wake them
and lay listening. Always the clock
withheld the next tick, nothing was silent
as the roar of power. Surely there was a purpose:

I could run my finger across tongue-and-groove
and feel a lover's smoothness, almost a candor
touching me back. But was there necessity?

Was that vast city really built from bricks and mortar—
and the ersatz materials, veneer and ashlar—
or sloughed from its obsession with itself?

Had it hypnotized itself into being?

6

Winter came. Parking was tight.
Snowploughs blocked Gates and Vanderbilt.

Spring. The baby teething, crying from a dream.

Summer. Spaldeens bouncing out of alleys.
Laundry inching from roof to roof.

7

Wooden spoons and rainbow stickers.
A paisley dinosaur with a rueful grin.
The child's first singing birthday.

She wailed for nerves
and three snuffed candles.
The mother and I rarely spoke.

Winter followed winter.

8

Wake me before dawn. Those long streets
are inside me now, cold and silent.

Let the siren come, and the circling light.

A former poet laureate of Brooklyn, D. Nurkse is the author of ten collections of poetry, most recently *A Night in Brooklyn* (Knopf). He's the recipient of fellowships from the Guggenheim Foundation, the New York Foundation for the Arts, the NEA, the Poetry Foundation, and the American Academy of Arts and Letters. He has taught poetry at MFA programs and at Rikers Island; he's on the faculty at Sarah Lawrence College. "The Grain" was originally published in the *Threepenny Review*.

MILLER OBERMAN

On Trans

The process of through is ongoing.

The earth doesn't seem to move, but sometimes we fall
down against it and seem to briefly alight on its turning.

We were just going. I was just leaving,
which is to say, coming
elsewhere. Transient. I was going as I came, the words
move through my limbs, lungs, mouth, as I appear to sit

peacefully at your hearth transubstantiating some wine.
It was a rough red, it was one of those nights we were not
forced by circumstances to drink wine out of mugs.
Circumstances being, in those cases, no one had been

transfixed at the kitchen sink long enough to wash dishes.
I brought armfuls of wood from the splitting stump.
Many of them, because it was cold went right on top
of their recent ancestors. It was an ice night.

They transpired visibly, resin to spark,
bark to smoke, wood to ash. I was
transgendering and drinking the rough red at roughly
the same rate and everyone who looked, saw.

The translucence of flames beat against the air
against our skins. This can be done with
or without clothes on. This can be done with
or without wine or whiskey but never without water:

evaporation is also ongoing. Most visibly in this case
in the form of wisps of steam rising from the just washed hair
of a form at the fire whose beauty was in the earth's
turning, that night and many nights, transcendent.

I felt heat changing me.   The word for this is
          transdesire, but in extreme cases   we call it *transdire*
or when this heat becomes your maker we say
          transire, or when it happens   in front of a hearth:

transfire.

Miller Oberman's collection of poems and Old English translations, *The Unstill Ones*, is forthcoming from Princeton University Press in the fall of 2017. He lives in Brighton Beach, Brooklyn. "On Trans" first appeared in *Poetry*.

MEGHAN O'ROURKE

My Aunts

Grew up on the Jersey Shore in the 1970s.
Always making margaritas in the kitchen,
always laughing and doing their hair up pretty,
sharing lipstick and shoes and new juice diets;
always splitting the bills to the last penny,
stealing each other's clothes,
loving one another then turning and complaining
as soon as they walked out the door. Each one with her doe eyes,
each one younger than the last,
each older the next year, one year
further from their girlhoods of swimming
at Sandy Hook, doing jackknives off the diving board
after school, all of them
being loved by one boy and then another,
all driving further from the local fair, further from Atlantic City.
They used to smoke in their cars,
rolling the windows down and letting their red nails
hang out, little stop lights:
Stop now, before the green
comes to cover your long brown bodies.

Sleep

Pawnbroker, scavenger, cheapskate,
come creeping from your pigeon-filled backrooms,
past guns and clocks and locks and cages,
past pockets emptied and coins picked from the floor;
come sweeping with the rainclouds down the river
through the brokenblack windows of factories
to avenues where movies whisk through basement projectors
and children peel up into the supplejack twilight—
there a black-eyed straight-backed drag queen
preens, fusses, fixes her hair in a shop window on Prince,
a young businessman jingles his change

and does his Travis Bickle for a long-faced friend,
there on the corner I laughed at a joke Jim made.
In the bedroom the moon is a dented spoon,
cold, getting colder, so hurry sleep,
come creep into bed, let's get it over with;
lay me down and close my eyes
and tell me whip, tell me winnow
tell me sweet tell me skittish
tell me No tell me no such thing
tell me straw into gold tell me crept into fire
tell me lost all my money tell me *hoarded, verboten,*
but promise tomorrow I will be profligate,
stepping into the sun like a trophy.

Meghan O'Rourke is the author of the poetry collections *Once* (2011) and *Halflife* (2007), which was a finalist for both the Paterson Poetry Prize and Britain's Forward Prize for Best First Collection. She was awarded the inaugural May Sarton Poetry Prize, the Union League Poetry Prize from the Poetry Foundation, fellowships from the Guggenheim Foundation, Radcliffe Institute, and Lannan Foundation, two Pushcart Prizes, and a Front Page Award for her cultural criticism. A graduate of Yale University, she has taught at Princeton, the New School, and New York University.

JOE PAN

Tomorrow

Today is not today, because it is still
yesterday. & yesterday was the day
before yesterday, & the day before that.
There will never be a new day so long
as we live in this, our long yesterday.
They did not take another black life
today, because this is no new day,
it's still yesterday, & the yesterday
we live in has been a long, long day.
People talk about tomorrow as if
they'd ever lived in a tomorrow,
but no one has lived in a tomorrow,
we just have today, which is not
today, but yesterday, & yesterday
we know has been a long, long day.
Many times a day I think about it,
this possibility of a tomorrow,
here in the heat of day, in what
feels like an irrepressible heat
of an interminable day. I think
about what it will take to turn
this day into something not this day,
what will bring the night upon us
& pull the heat from our bodies
& quiet us. Or I think of our bodies
quietly repairing in the night
between this day & whatever
comes after this day. I can sense
the new heat, & hope it is not
just a new yesterday. I can sense
it blending with the night until
there is no difference between
the two, until there is.

The Poem

for {_ _}, & all his notions of what a poem might be, become, become bankrupt by, catch as its second wind, or die as

The one that writes itself. The decadent & self-consuming. The oratory. Every room. The alter of the pristine image. The altogether calm, placating voice of a ghost imparting its final secret in succinctly whispered stanzas. The rambling eccentric, phrases gone epileptic, a mind in its changing, a shiny bell, my parent's insufferable love & damning self-criticism, & fruit flies in September, which reminds me. The prognostication. The point maker. The moving center. The pained cry from a city's boiling vortex. The critical reinterpretation. The fawning philosophy, its homage begetting a neo- tag. The post-neo-upstart. The Googler. The ogler. The appetite suppressant. The bearer of dusky premonitions. The family breakdown as open-heart surgery. The implant. The shuddering in an outhouse of one's own creation. The lighthouse. The beaconless. The bright & beautiful museum maven on a stroll, O Jane, you crazy thing. Every room of text. The bon vivant, the bête noir, the bacchanalian adolescent immersed in undoing a century's aesthetic. The fractal forget-me-not. The fecal factoid. The hurt child. The chortling wan & wilting sympathizer. The synthesizing DJ of documentary. The downtown, uptown, mid-town rhapsody. The bucolic belle of balladry. The embarrassing aside. The heartbreakingly formal rant against The Establishment. The chatty freelancers' web of grumbling exquisite corpses. The hordes of stressed/ unstressed syllables bench-pressing a strophe. Every room of text a honey. The unwritten poem. The pome. The Palme d'Or pantoum. The concrete architect. The bilingual love affair. The month I spent in Spain. This is not about you. This is totally about you. The list. The liaison. The laissez-faire. The mud under a hundred horses' hooves. The godless, the god-defying, the sufferer of God. The repetitive. The respondent. The rogue. This one time. This is how bad it got. Cheer up. Three cheers. Chernobyl. The bomb, which makes us always hereafter indivisible or invisible. The academic endemic, the cult of quietude, the asphyxiating b=(re:)a=t=h. This act of retribution, perhaps. Every room of text a honeymoon. This active contribution, perhaps. The retaliation against this, or its lack. The contrapuntal narrators as sparring partners vis-a-vis the brain's hemispheres. The galactic comic. The resurgence of once widely held beliefs fallen into ideological limbo. The flaccid cock. The inspired vulva. The coital romp, or "Erotics as a Breezy Dance Symposium in a Self-Correcting Ecosystem." The claptrap rap sheet photovoltaic photo shoot. The selfie. The popularity contest. The big prize. The flotilla of formlessness. The greenhouse diorama. The ecologically engaged. The swamp or bog pit innocent newly reborn as a naturalist receiving death. The urban youth vocalizing peril. The decay of decay. I just discovered this form yesterday. I just discovered my life has substance beyond me. Every room of text a honeymoon suit. My cat is sick again. My dog does not make sense. My spouse does not make sense. The eerie wandering eye-lust of the romantic. The doctrine. The divorce. Engaging this underlying current of dread. The re-emergent genius. The unreliably narrated. The fetishistic. The free fall. The elevated naturalism of the plastic garden foal. The translation. The transliteration. The fraud. The fraudulently hip. The hipster sincerely hungry for recognition of the pain underlying sarcasm. The hopeful. The angry medicated & their mothers. The apropos of nothing. The apoplectic apologist. Dear me. Dear John. Dearest, I don't know who I am anymore. Every room of text a honeymoon suite. The civil war. The rebellion against a repeat. The warnings of attrition. I as the infinite bass line. The lyrical id. The calculating enjambment. The operatic pornographer. The agitator. The playful emancipator of spatial echelons. Those distrustful of voice. The overlord. The ever-present. Dearest, my love for you exists in lists but listless wanders off to weird peripheries; will you learn to forgive my wandering ear? My strange confabulations, all in service of something beautiful & buckling to inch about your inchless waist, O ghostly no one, or ribbon about the delightful dancing hype I find hypnotic in its indifference to my deference? Every room of text a honeymoon suite with at least one love. Here's a blueberry, bitter as a Clinton. Here's a shipwreck, a glossary of current. Here's me beating time, & beating time. The last gun standing at high noon in a canyon of dust. The ode to the mite. Here's the fevered dream. The apocalyptic centerfold. The courageous. The war-torn. The shell, shocked. The kicked bucket. The lone cricket barking from a rusted Buick. The horribly alive. The abecedarian, the betrothed, the cancerous & debilitated. The enemy as sibling. The girl lost in a thicket of cymbals. The boy guarding a wicket of symbols. The song. The sci-fi phantasmagoric. The gory. The implausible epic of the Irish African King Gormund. The guilty. The final straw. The boycott. The eye obfuscated. The I, obliterated. My own trembling soprano. Every room of text a honeymoon suite with at least one lover. Here is my heavy heart in cursive, my huddled heart in print, my digital diaphragm going thump, scroll down, thump. Each camp a reenactment with a different lens. Each lensmaker focused on the slightest divergence. The grunted. The grotesque. The shout pitched just far enough to manage a meaningful exchange, or sadly too far for an audience of more than two. Voice like a light left on in an empty bathroom. A hiss rising from the basement. The forgers & speculators. The open thefts of the desirous & demented. Image & idea. All so beautiful & bountiful. All a wonder. & here we are driving fast in a vehicle we can't trade in, with an expired license we can't renew. Nothing matters but that we reach the border, the wedding to be held there, these breathy nuptials. Brethren & sistren, gather together. Every one built with a word, my love. Every room of text a honeymoon suite with at least one lover left to wonder in it.

Joe Pan is the author of two collections of poems, *Hiccups* (Augury Books) and *Autobiomythography & Gallery* (BAP). He is the founder and publisher of Brooklyn Arts Press, serves as the fiction editor for the arts magazine *Hyperallergic*, and is the founder of the services-oriented activist group Brooklyn Artists Helping. "Tomorrow" was first published in *jubilat*; "The Poem" was first published as a pamphlet by Greying Ghost Press.

GREGORY PARDLO

Vanitas, Camden Ferry

Leaning against the stern working
like a loom, its warp and weft
churning toward a shore
serrated by Camden's skyline
and bounded by the dim figure of Walt
Whitman Bridge, sphinx-like
in the distance stitched
across the valley where the man
came to rest—City Hall is a Confederate
gray, the amphitheater's solemn
lawn along a field of latticed asphalt,
faint pulse of the aquarium dome,
and Campbell's field of dreams
honoring the fallen
factory with its stead.
Among these the churchly tower
abandoned by RCA Victor in-
verts anachronism with its stained
glass backlit gold and green like tarnished
brass, Nipper the dog, the Victrola
and *His Master's Voice* etched below.

I turn to you truant of old
jurisdictions, sounding your fluid
margins, my city of brotherly love.
Your office buildings wrinkle
like sequined gowns at sunset
jazzed by the river's brisk cologne.
Your Penn's Landing is adrift
with trumpet and ride cymbal, pleats
of zydeco driven by instinct
across the crease in the horn
of my ear, taking the long canal down
to where skullsong turns
physical, the music's ripples nudging
my body's own tympani, feeding me
across these waters once ferried
by William Still who'd bid adieu
to fugitives bound for Ontario.

In Canal Street Station Late

at night I stand alone along the lonely platform pew
overlooking rodents ghosting sediment and slipping
through fractures in the monochrome reel
of filth the tracks, frame by frame, display.
The station announcer's voice
conjures the anima of bags in garbage cans.
Trickles sound icily from the city's
untidy veins. Blear-eyed and unsteady,
mice to me flit faint as water sliders,
could well be those dimpling insects
that darted against the surface of my backyard
pool blown over with leaves, needles, cut grass.
And where is my old mower now
with its sneezing two-stroke engine
and tattered grass-catch that once culled
a nest of wasps through its brutal centrifuge?
It should be in the shed beside snow shovels,
beside the woodpile bejeweled with spider eggs.
The evening streaked orange and blue.
Fluorescent green of my canvas yard shoes.
Crane flies, outside the shed door, hung within
the maw of the mulberry eaves beside a paper
lantern shifting easy in the breeze. Breath quickens
in the tunnel like a throat trembling with light.
The conductor skippers a list of cautions when the train
arrives. Doors peel a toothless yawn where men sleep
lengthwise on benches and I think of mice snuggled
in the mouths of reptiles. Afford me some pity, dear Nessie
of halogen and steel, your sub-street tempest sparking
moments blind and shuddering with caprice
like a wet dog. Your maps are like x-rays where I am circled
and incriminated, a tumor. But we are concentric. In me, too,
a prisoner contemplates escape, scrapes memory like soft stone
at night and daily drags a tin cup along a cage of rib bones.

Gregory Pardlo's collection *Digest* (Four Way Books) won the 2015 Pulitzer Prize for Poetry. His other honors include fellowships from the National Endowment for the Arts and the New York Foundation for the Arts; his first collection, *Totem*, was selected by Brenda Hillman for the APR/Honickman Prize in 2007. He is also the author of *Air Traffic*, a memoir in essays forthcoming from Knopf. Pardlo is a faculty member of the MFA program in creative writing at Rutgers University–Camden. He lives with his family in Brooklyn.

MORGAN PARKER

I Feel Most Colored When I Am Thrown Against a Sharp White Background: An Elegy

after Glenn Ligon after Zora Neale Hurston

Or, I fccl sharp Whitc. Or,
Colored Against. Or, I am
thrown. Or, I am
Against. Or, When White.
Or, I Sharp. Or, I Color.
Make it quiet. Wash
me away. Forgetting.
I feel most colored when
I swear to god. I feel most
colored when it is too late.
My tongue is elegy.
When I am captive. I am
the color green because
green is the color of power.
I am a tree growing two fruits.
I feel most colored when I am
thrown against the sidewalk.
It is the last time I feel colored.
Stone is the name of the fruit.
I am a man I am a man I am
a woman I am a man I am a woman
I am protected and served.
I pay taxes and I am a child and
I grow into a bright fleshy fruit.
White bites: I stain the uniform.
And I am thrown black type-
face in a headline with no name.
Or, no one hears me. Or, I am thrown
a language bone: *unarmed.*
I feel most colored when my weapon
is I feel most colored. When I get
what I deserve. When I can't breathe.

When on television I shuffle
and widen my eyes. I feel most colored
when I am thrown against a mattress,
my tits my waist my ankles buried
in veiny White. Everyone claps.
I feel most colored when I am
the punch line. When I am the trigger.
In the dawn, putrid yellow, I know
what I am being told. I feel most
colored when I am collecting dust.
When I am impatient and sick.
When they use us to distract us.
My ears leak violet petals.
I sharpen them. I sharpen them again.

When a Man I Love Jerks Off in My Bed Next to Me and Falls Asleep

I think of my father
vodka-laughing: *Aw shit,*
when Daddy said go pick out a switch
from the lemon tree we knew
that switch better be good.
My father was a drunk altar boy.
My father was a Southern boy.
My father is a good man.
When you grow up in the South, you know
the difference between a good switch and a bad one.
Pick what hurts best. The difference between drinking
to disappear and drinking to remember.
Be polite. Be gentle. Be a vessel. Be ashamed.
As a child, I begged to be whooped.
I pinched myself with my nails when I was wrong.
I tried to pull out my eyelashes. I said, *Punish me*
I said *for I have sinned I am disgusting.*
Here is the order in which we studied the Bible
in second grade: 1: Genesis, or, God is a man
and he owns you. You were bad. Put on some
got-damn clothes. 2: Exodus, or, you would still
be a slave if it were not for men. Also, magic.
Magic or, never question a man's truth.

3: Job, or, suffer, suffer because it is holy.
During the classes on Revelation, I think
I drifted to sleep. I think I dreamed
trumpets when I touched my hot parts
then touched the cold steel of my desk.
I knew what it meant to be wrong and woman.
When I walk into the world and know
I am a black girl, I understand
I am a costume. I know the rules.
I like the pain because it makes me.
I deserve the pain. I deserve you
looking at me, moaning, looking away.
Son of a bitch. My rent is due.
No one kissed my tits and read the Bible.
Good and evil. Pleasure and empty
curtain grid of dawn light.
I call this honor. I call this birthright.

Matt

For all intents and purposes and because the rule applies more often than it doesn't, every white man or boy who has entered and fallen away from my particular moderate life has been called Matt. Not Dan. Rarely Ben. Never Matthew. Matt smokes unfiltered Pall Malls because Kurt Vonnegut did. We talk on Myspace because he goes to a different high school. Matt's in love with someone else but I can tell he's still interested in me. Matt and his girlfriend aren't really together. Matt doesn't have a condom so we can't. Matt also doesn't have a condom so we can't. Matt loves Modest Mouse. Matt loves Kanye. He loves whiskey. He brings a flask to the park. He tells me I'm beautiful. He likes me. He follows me into the bathroom where I once found a bag of coke. I tip sideways onto the tile trying to steady myself on top of him while his legs are spread on the toilet lid. I say what about you and Anna. He says hold your ankles. I made Matt a really good mix cd. Matt's writing a novel. Matt's also writing a novel. Matt says I'm a really good kisser. My friends say I'm too good for Matt. Matt loves his Mom. Matt's moving to Berlin. Matt's moving to California. Matt's quitting smoking again. Matt rolls his own cigarettes. Matt has depression. He listens to sad songs. Matt wants a big family. He seems like he would be a good dad. His family is so white. His favorite novelists are white. His ex-girlfriends are white. He said he would call me. His ex-girlfriends are really skinny. He has this thing where he seems like he doesn't care about anything. Matt's in love with someone else. He thought I was way older than him. He got a new tattoo. He has bad dreams. I miss him. He loves foreign movies. He's stoned all the time. He pulls me into another room. He has a beard and he also has a beard. He kisses me in the other room. He loves my dog. He flirts with me all the time, I think just for fun. Oh, Matt. He knows he's a white man but doesn't think of himself as a white man. He doesn't know what to do with his life. He floats. He is young. He can afford to be cool. He wears a lot of flannel. We're just friends. He's nervous about commitment. He's nervous in the elevator when he touches the small of my back. He's nervous on the roof. I'm nervous taking his hand because people can see us. His roommate walks in on us, then gives us shots of gin we all sip in silence. After that we smoke on his fire escape and make out. We smoke in front of the bar and make out. We make out on an empty subway train, my back slips around on the hard plastic seat. He pays for my brunch. He texts me all the time even at the airport. He's breaking up with his girlfriend. He and his friends are drunk in someone's apartment in Queens, what am I up to? He hates his job but he's totally a genius. He lost his phone so he has a new number. He hates his job and what he really wants to do is make art and be happy. He needs to live abroad for a while. He *used to be really dumb*. He swats his hair from his forehead and says of course he will call. I always ask but I'm going to stop asking. I'm nervous he doesn't understand. He didn't grow up with many Black people. He knows he is part of the problem. He just believes in love and knowledge. Matt, Matt, Matt, Matt. Each one more beautiful than the last. Each one more with more intricate ennui. I could never love him. He floats. I can't stop loving him. Matt knows the bartender. Matt studied comparative literature. He still loves his ex, I just know it. He says I like talking to you. He says watch your head as I ride him in his dorm room bunk bed. He's so sorry he didn't call, it's just that things have been busy and weird. Matt and I sneak out of a movie to hook up in his car. He is afraid of me. Matt and I are hanging out this week I think, to watch movies or something. I guess, maybe. He's never met anyone like me. Things are just super casual with us. Neither of us are looking for a relationship. Matt loves relationships. He slept with my friend. I can't tell if he's into me because I'm Black or because I'm *not that Black* and either way I feel bad. I feel it in my stomach's basement: Matt can't want me. I am not forever. Matt has kissed me hundreds of times and he kissed my ancestors too. He held them down and kissed them real good. He was young and he could afford it. When he touched them, they always smiled, almost as if it had been rehearsed.

Morgan Parker is the author of *Other People's Comfort Keeps Me Up at Night* (Switchback Books 2015), which was selected by Eileen Myles for the 2013 Gatewood Prize and a finalist for the Poetry Society of America's Norma Farber First Book Award. Her second collection, *There Are More Beautiful Things Than Beyoncé*, was published by Tin House Books in February of 2017. She lives with her dog Braeburn in Brooklyn, and works as an editor for Little A and Day One.

V. PENELOPE PELIZZON

Barchan

for G.S.

When the wind is right,
if you climb along the barchan's crest,
your steps shiver and send

rivulets of sand
trickling slowly down the leeward slope.
These streams will soon dry up,

you think. But then the grains'
slithering gathers steam and gains
momentum as it pulls

more sand into its wake, until
the dune's flank ripples with its surge
and, from the top, looks like a ridge

sluiced by a river.
Meanwhile, a watcher on a lower
pitch sees each footfall avalanche

spilling down the steep slip-face to catch
a slightly different angle of the light
then stop, appearing wet

(but really only shadowed dark).
You're turning desert into water as you walk,
it seems. Intrigued, despite

heat that crisps your skin with your own salt,
you kneel to test how wave effects will vary
when a smaller quantity

of sand's displaced. Two drizzled handfuls
spread double ripples
          racing down the dune till they collide,

          kicking back an undertow of secondary slide
that flaunts gravity by flowing up
toward you on the lip

          —a mirage your eyes
          fall prey to, since their meshes aren't fine-
gauged enough

to net the gecko-dandruff
          particles cascade-
          ing to the point where they accumulate.

Sand's a flintish liquid or a kind of fluid
stone: faint pressures on it accrue
          until a sinuosity rules the skyline,

          showing where the barchan
slinched below the wind's finger.
Though wind is not the only shaper.

          I know this, having seen
          how you, stepping curiously
through it,

moved the desert.

V. Penelope Pelizzon's books include *Whose Flesh Is Flame, Whose Bone Is Time* (2014), and *Nostos* (2000), which won the Hollis Summers Prize and the Poetry Society of America's Norma Farber First Book Award.

TOMMY PICO

Having Left

Like my grandfather, I keep eagles.
Who believes in spiritual horseshit?
There is a common misconception
about Indian people, namely everything,

but especially sadness. One summer
the pepper tree rotted, black and twisted
licorice crawling up the ground
of my grandmother's garden—a reminder

my grandfather was not my grandfather
by blood. Bikini Kill had an album called
Reject All American, which was not as good
as the *CD Version of the First Two Records*

or *Pussy Whipped*, but yielded "R.I.P."
People die. Sometimes a song reminds
us about pink peppers. I feel inexorably
American, in Paris, Brooklyn, Berlin,

the reservation, despite vodka and liberal arts.
There is a common misconception about
Indians, namely everything, but especially
when pink pepper trees grow cagelike
in the valley, eagle screeching skyward,
and he in a graveyard

and I'm not there.

Tommy "Teebs" Pico is author of *IRL* (Birds, LLC, 2016), *Nature Poem* (Tin House Books, forthcoming 2017), and the zine series *Hey, Teebs*. He was an inaugural Queer | Art | Mentorship Fellow, a 2013 Lambda Literary Fellow in poetry, and a 2016 Tin House Scholar, and has poems in *Flavorwire*, *Guernica*, and the *Offing*. Originally from the Viejas Indian reservation of the Kumeyaay nation, he now lives in Brooklyn, and with Morgan Parker co-curates the reading series Poets With Attitude (PWA). "Having Left" was originally published in *BOMB Magazine*.

LAURA PLASTER

The Importance of Being Ethan

I wish Ethan Hawke could give me back
those afternoons in the basement alternating
between *Before Sunrise* and *Reality Bites*
imagining myself as the earnest girl
that breaks through his facade of apathy,
that really makes him care,
first about me and then the world
and he'd wash his hair and his plaid shirt
and write me songs.

My freshman year of college I spent my time
winning Seth over with my earnestness
and getting him to care, he played me songs,
left a rose outside my dorm room and walked
me home and it's amazing how I can't
remember what I learned in world religions
or urban sociology, but I can remember
the fake Birkenstocks I wore on our first date
because Seth was on the short side
and they were my flattest shoes.

It's been a while since I've watched those movies,
and I can't think of the last time I tried
to change somebody with my earnestness,
or even change myself a little.
I talk to this twenty-two-year-old intern
and she's so pretty and foolish—I could
listen to her all night but I also want her to stop
and I realize I'm unshowered and my shirt's
unwashed, and oh my goodness I've become
'90s Ethan Hawke, but some earnest
young thing won't shatter my indifference,
because I'm a woman and I'm married
and I don't believe that's how
it works anyway. Besides Ethan

did all right for himself—he wrote
a novel and there's *Boyhood*, reminding
me there's a difference between seeming
to care and actually getting shit done.
So thank you, Troy, and thank you, Jesse,
and thank you, Ethan: here's to not showering
because you're too busy getting off trains
and writing songs and falling in love.

Winter Thoughts on Sublimation

Snow and ice sublime.
They cross the threshold, like Enoch
passing from this life to the next,
whirlwind style. Or rather,
an endothermic phase transition:
fusion, vaporization, pressure,
purification, straw to gold,
deviance delivered from evil.

Question: how should I feel about the base of me,
knowing it might become the best?
Can I earn transfiguration? Must I
wait, like the shit-stained February snow,
for the miracle of the right cold, the right wind?

Sometimes I am gentle with my mess.
Sometimes I want to lie naked
against the hard ground, let a cloud
of locust descend and take me piecemeal
into their efficient mouths, then rise
gnawing my soft parts. Leave only my bones.
A false rapture, but still, bits of me would fly.

Laura Plaster is a theatre artist, mother, and poet whose work has appeared in *Blue Lyra Review* and *Two Cities Review*. She has lived the last nine years in Brooklyn, first in Brooklyn Heights and then in Greenwood near the cemetery (a frequent haunt). She will soon be located in Baltimore, but Brooklyn remains the birthplace of her children as well as her poetic life.

NIINA POLLARI

Are You a Hand-Sculpted Animal

I've been training
I told my friend that I wanted to be strong
As we walked a long and cumbersome route to her reading
I meant that I wanted to be so hard that it makes me feel
Like I might not die

I like imagining myself with power
Pain from muscle effort is a memory of desire for power

Training means a part of me is always in pain
Women's bodies are often bombed with pain
And women become flyover states of pain
Because this pain is regarded as unimportant
So OK, I'll do it myself

I fling myself around the park
Heave myself onto the treadmill
Move various weights with enormous effort
Until my shirts are wet at the armholes
And sweat beads lattice my upper lip

After, I feel horsey and satisfied
As pain runs its large hands up the muscles of my legs

It's pretty pure
To me the purest art is when you commit
Enough to admit you committed

Commitment to me is
That I'm telling you about it now

Niina Pollari is the author of *Dead Horse* (Birds, LLC, 2015) and the translator of Tytti Heikkinen's *The Warmth of the Taxidermied Animal* (Action Books, 2013). She runs the Brooklyn-based yearly megareading Popsickle. This poem first appeared in *Powder Keg*.

BILL RASMOVICZ

The Loveliest Cities

A tree hides in the shiver of its leaves
while vines take to its scaffolding to suffocate it.

The dead offer us their sympathy, which is to say
their silence. The dead are a lot like the living
except they don't say much. And what is

the heart but a telephone fluttering with a bomb
threat, love being if you carry the cross of my affection
I'll carry yours.

I recall shouting down into the mine's air shaft
to hear myself. What rose was exponential
in size and someone else entirely.
There were days whose sweet musk was the warm body
of a violin's, the wind

a girl whispering through the parish yards for her cat.
Now it's consecration by hail, the beaming effrontery
of the wrecking ball.

At the core of the mind is an obelisk dreaming you
into being. Jumping off the roof, I still think an open
umbrella would save me. And we wonder:
whose shoes were found behind

the rest stop? Murk, the barrel of a rifle—
to peer where you can't see bottom, witness something
solid as earth liquefy. There is no discerning

a sparrow from sky really, each of which
without the other would fall. While the loveliest cities
have civilizations compounded into geologic strata

topped with screaming police lights and children
separated from their parents.
Which is to say we are phantoms of each other,
that the end is always happening.

Chanterelles

For them I set to the rain a stern pace.
How will we collect the mosquitoes? Were
her ovaries suspended in her torso like streetlights
the storm knocked out?

Last night's questions beamed with the celestial pitch
of a star in a cigar box.
Of chanterelles, their birth is slow and dark,
more mysterious than the body's,
a precipitation upward through the yellow hue of
some elemental industry.

The aphid sap-sucked the field. Butterflies
swarmed heaps of what the horse dropped.
We are lonely and desperate creatures wishing to be
loved now when we could remain intimates forever.

In how many waiting rooms did the magazine despot's
eyes peer softly, and tobacco brown?
There should be a place we could all swim naked in
the lake, forget what the hound's tooth forecasted.

When I saw the boy with gray hair sprinkling bread
in the pond, the park squirrels
seemed weighably less enthusiastic, the birches
in their sidewalk patches of peat, bleak and leafless.

We were landslides to each other.
There was no time for connoisseurship.
The dusky seaside sparrow was no longer, and so often
we pulled over to pupate from this vista or that.

Evening your favorite color, I kept imagining
the ceiling painted gold, while the beach we fetishized
was a pile of hot sawdust.
Strictly for the sun's burn did we reside.
You were the animal they warned you about.

Bill Rasmovicz is the author of *The World in Place of Itself* (Alice James Books, 2007), *Gross Ardor* (42 Miles Press, 2013), and *Idiopaths* (Brooklyn Arts Press, 2014). The poems anthologized here first appeared in *Hunger Mountain* and later in *Gross Ardor*. He's currently enjoying the seacoast lifestyle in Portland, Maine.

DANNY RIVERA

A Brief History of the 21st Century

Did you want to be left alone? Mail-order catalogs, magazine reply cards, three-lane highways form an anxious necessity. What is the diagnosis, electric charge? To drag your body across the plaza, *Virgen de Guadalupe, ayúdenos*, is the dignity of penitence. I have returned for my belongings. In the mountains, children listen to the mouth of war. The men inform me that I am very much alive, if tethered to sleep. At her mother's breast, an infant answers to the tyranny of faith. As of this writing, there are no casualties. What are you, if not a series of vespers, note by slurred note? More information, redacted, will be revealed following the commercial break. Tell me that I am pretty; please tell me that I am *wanted*. Without further intervention, the chances of recovery have been calculated at twenty-seven percent. I have learned to reclaim our blood-borne history. Prior to interment, the body must be cleansed in a ritual bath. Is there another name for hunger, a taste for the sacraments?

Danny Rivera earned an MFA in creative writing from the City College of New York. His writing has appeared in *Washington Square*, *American Book Review*, and other journals; "A Brief History of the 21st Century" originally appeared in *Newtown Literary*.

JASMIN RIVERA

The B-Boyz Generation

We skipped the letter "A"
And moved into the
B-Boy Generation
When so many
B-Boyz wanted to
B-come men
Who were respected
Their mouths made
rhythms that were
Unexpected
Their Adidas clothed
bodies moved with
electrified ancestor memories
A uniform cluster
of Bs
"Hey B,
What it B-like?"
"Yo B that's
so Fresh B!"
We skipped E
and left it for
the next generation
and got
Struck at C
R…A
C and K
"Hey B, can
you spare some change
cuz' I can't afford to recite
a reversed alphabet"
Backs turned,
As B
faded away to
Hip-Hop Heaven

Jasmin Rivera is a native New Yorker born and raised in the South Bronx. She is the author of *Smokey Bronx Blues* and *The Angry Poems: A Brooklyn Journey to Forgiveness.* A graduate of the School of International and Public Affairs at Columbia University, Professor Rivera received her master's degree in 2012, concentrating in human rights within the Caribbean and Latin America. Her poetry and art are inspired by her community, scholarship, and urban life experiences.

MATT L. ROAR

fear of becoming BOB

marisa is trying on shoes i am afraid i appear to the clerks to be standing over her in blowjob stance emily said men are afraid of becoming BOB and women are afraid of being raped/murdered by him welcome to the hell mind we used to fight and i'd lock myself in the room or run down the stairs pace the streets you said you'd never felt the fear of hurting others because you're so small which makes it sound cute remember the last episode of twin peaks how everyone hated it maybe because it was on the nose we all know men turn into monsters i was 12 my dad grabbed a belt to beat my little brother i grabbed a two by four from the yard when he came for me he just shook his head and left who is BOB here why did you make me be him

some boys feel power when they draw a picture of a lion the teacher says good they hit a ball and everyone cheers write a song and sing it loud bell hooks calls it intimate violence because domestic sounds like it's ok says you can't have feminism without pacifism i wish we could talk to each other go for a drive in the jungle of bodies swim in the roiling sea remember when dad would bang our heads together and laugh i'd see these beautiful stars little brother like the horizon my name it's not mine i choose a new one

---

Matt L. Roar is a writer and musician from San Francisco who lives in Brooklyn. His writing has appeared in *Tinfish*, *Skein*, *Watchword*, the *Surfer's Journal*, and other publications. He is a founding editor of Small Desk Press and a regular contributor to the literary blog *We Who Are About to Die*. He is a New York City Teaching Fellow and a special education high school teacher.

CHRIS ROBERTS

And I Forget

When all the lights are off in every room,
and mom spits out the pill she's been prescribed,
and sister parks her car and stumbles in
and never speaks a word about the pill
a friend and nothing more slipped in her drink,
and dad must work and work and work and work,
the outdoor air seems fresher, better, there—
our windblown birdbath where a bird once sang
waits for some hands to do an easy thing
and be stood upright...nothing comes of this
but trying not to let it graze my sight
until the thought to fix it fades away,
and I forget exactly what it was
that hasn't found its proper place again.

from Excerpt, 1992

October

That Halloween, we didn't get to go
outside to trick-or-treat. We helped as Grandma
passed out treats to other kids in costumes
while Pop Pop sat in his recliner, watching
episodes of canceled shows. I watched
him watching. Then, I watched the thermostat.
Occasionally, he'd laugh. My face turned red.
Grandma was in the kitchen with my sister.

When the doorbell rang, I let it go.
They must have gone away. It rang again.
Grandma sang, "I think I hear the do-or..."
A princess, Batman, Tweedle-Dum stepped in
along with someone's mom. I stared at them.
Grandma cut in, so happy, I fell back

and lingered on the downstairs landing, thinking,
I'd make a better Batman than that kid.

My sister, who'd been left alone too long,
joined Grandma, copying the smile she had;
Pop Pop laughed at something on TV;
and that was it!; I said, "Can't we just go
around the block?! My parents'd let us go."
"Then who'd be home to pass out treats?" said Grandma.
"Pop Pop can. He isn't doing much."
"But you don't have a costume." "I'll just go...

...*as*...*as*...a...wait—I have a turtleneck
upstairs, and black pants, too! I'll be a mime;
do you have extra makeup for my face?"
"I think you need a special kind for that."
"Well, what about...a...beatnik! Like that guy
on Dobie Gillis. Couldn't I? Please? Grandma?"
Electrons surged in me. I tasted yes.
But Grandma shook her head, "I'm sorry, Chris.

The weather's just not good enough for that."
"But Grandma— Why?" "You got your answer, Chris,"
Pop Pop barked over a commercial break,
"Accept it and move on." "But Pop Pop— Why?"
His show returned. "Hey, Pop Pop—I asked 'Why?'"
"Chris, come and help me in the kitchen, please,"
Grandma asked, which left me with no choice.
The blender full of ice cubes sat plugged-in

near Dixie cups and orange concentrate.
My sister measured orange concentrate.
"Now pour it in." She poured it in. "Now, Chris,
you press the button. I'll hold down the lid."
"Dad let me use the blender once," I mused,
"Mom said we made a mess, so now we can't."
"So now you'll get another chance," she said,
"to do it right." She demonstrated how

to pulse, so that the ice was crushed just right,
holding down the lid and helping me

to pulse, her hand was like a framework for
my own. The blender screamed in ecstasy—
released from being stored in quiet space—
the taste of power wallpapered my mouth—
but better were the cups my sister filled
that we drank up. I took one out to Pop Pop.

Chris Roberts grew up in backwater Pennsylvania, where he learned to pronounce his Korean birth name as "Die Young, Sung." He is formerly of Brooklyn, and now resides in the Bronx, NY.

MATTHEW ROHRER

Two Poems for Issa

Role playing after dinner
to buy a new car
and the role playing
is rough the car dealer
(who is S.) won't bend
even sitting at the table
with the tortillas I made
I tremble I am not
prepared to spend any money
autumn evening

*

Autumn evening
the children aren't interested
in the poems of Issa
who died poor hundreds
of years ago
I recycle the children's book
about Issa with a clear mind
it is not Issa himself
who disappears

Brooklyn Is Covered in Little Pieces of Paper

This is extremely important
what happened to me today
so listen closely
I drew a very appealing
picture of my daughter's
beloved stuffed dog
because she was going

on her first field trip
and was not allowed
to bring the stuffed dog
and I colored in
the picture softly
with a brown pencil
and drew smell lines
coming off his nose
because that is her favorite
aspect of the dog
his smell
so she folded the picture
and put it in her pocket
which is very small
because she is
and we walked to school
through the warm wind
only to find
she had lost the paper
with the picture on it
which was terrible
just terrible
as she insisted
but what could we do?
the green door
was going to open
in two minutes

and on the way home
I thought half-heartedly
I'll look on the ground
for a folded piece
of paper
and when I did
I saw Brooklyn
is covered in little
pieces of paper
which fact I was contemplating
in the bright sun
and the wind pressing papers against
the chain link fence

when I saw it
and bent down
and in my head
a voice said
fuck yeah!

Matthew Rohrer is the author of several books of poems, most recently *Surrounded by Friends*, published by Wave Books, where "Two Poems for Issa" and "Brooklyn Is Covered in Little Pieces of Paper" first appeared. In 2017, Wave will publish his epic 230-page poem *The Others*. He lives in Windsor Terrace.

CAMILO ROLDÁN

Verrazano Narrows

having been muggy day
my head wet saxophone
busking on typical
promenade a spectral

color-bridge flush
with surface and waves
at me toward the vault
reflecting the notion

a conglomerate of lights
arrange to delineate
prow tower and stern
cargo-ship steadily

and a slip out of night
as it enters through penumbra
the notion intensified
forgotten by the time

I get home
that as I approach
remembered when today
the same ship left

the notion intensified with proximity
to the pastime
of cataloging
AA56

GN54
ML83
OB30
ALL

but all of these are taken
    from Ian Hamilton Finlay
and I struggle to deny
    cars on the Bay Pkwy

apart from fishing line zip
whose radio plays   the notion that
            I must leave
            and keep going

Camilo Roldán is a poet and translator living in Brooklyn. He is the translator of the chapbook *Amílkar U., Nadaista in Translation* (These Signals Press, 2011), co-author of the chapbook *Δ [delta]* with Douglas Piccinnini and Cynthia Gray (TPR Press, 2013), and author of the chapbook *La Torre* (Well Greased Press, 2015). His translation of Amílcar Osorio's *Vana Stanza* is forthcoming from Elis Press.

PATRICK ROSAL

On the Elevation of Earthlings—a Hymn

to Kobe Bryant

Kobe, a man can't make a planet
or craft a galaxy with his bare hands
but he can jab step on the wing
to juke a dude so hard out of his crouch
he bolts into a second orbit. I'm saying,
a man can make whole worlds
out of a crowd's stillness, if the stillness
is the preface to awe, if the man hangs
in the air not by gallows or noose
but by his own muscle
and wish.
            I once floated thirty-six-
thousand feet into the Brooklyn sky
and looked down on every cloud
above Lefferts Gardens, the Heights,
Bed-Stuy—Lower Merion too!
Truth is I just flew round-trip to the tropics
when I sat same row with a woman
and her six-year-old girl whose father
they lowered into the ground
not ten months earlier. The daughter clutched
one rose in each fist as if these two blooms
were the secret engines propelling
everything that leaves the earth.
What a gift, then, when she serenaded me
with three tunes in three languages
and both our laughter after each one.

We might not know who or what
we'll meet when we get up high enough
over the ordinary rooms
into extraordinary love, but sometimes
we bear witness to a body in flight

and for a moment know what to do
with half our human sorrow.

I'm only one of millions who have seen you
bang once toward the baseline then rise
before fifty thousand eyes
that stare up into the middle heavens
where your lean frame engraves a space
for a higher (though vanishing) plane,
where reason and mathematics
get all the laws and formulas wrong.
Just look at our faces, Kobe. We are
what singing looks like before the song.

Patrick Rosal is the author of *Brooklyn Antediluvian* and three other full-length collections of poetry. His poems have appeared in *New England Review*, *Tin House*, *American Poetry Review*, *Best American Poetry*, and elsewhere. He is an associate professor of English at Rutgers University–Camden.

ARTHUR RUSSELL

The Whales Off Manhattan Beach Breaching in Winter

I

I have never wanted anything but to be understood and accepted,
except from my father, from whom I wanted to be appreciated,

but he did not believe in praise. If I got a 96

he thought it was thrifty to ask where the other four points went,
because acknowledging success was prideful.

I was so hungry for his praise I got to know his mind as ancient Greek sailors knew
the islands of the Aegean, how their shapes rose on the horizon, conjuring their
olive groves and the monsters in their caves.

I searched his inconsistencies for deeper hidden consistencies.
I listened for approval in the caverns of his silence,
and read his eyes for signs that weren't there

from boy to man, and still he was ahead of me, withholding praise
and holding out the possibility of praise, and withholding praise again.

II

Then he got sick and very old and spent the last two years
of his life in a bed in a home that smelled like a bowel

that had been washed with minty disinfectant.
He was embarrassed by immobility and proud in his mind.

He took no visitors, and referred to himself as "The Potato In The Bed,"
and to the anti-depressant pills they gave him as "Nursing Home Not So Bad."

His legs swelled, grew purple, oozed pus, scabbed over.
He spoke like an oak tree.

His fingers were smooth flesh purses of stymied bone.
And yet, when he could no longer reach the control that made his bed rise,

he invented a string with a 3/8 inch nut tied to one end and looped over
the bed rail to help him fish it up. Patient as a prisoner planning an impossible escape,
he loved his engineering, he loved his invention; he loved his mind.

III

His weight dropped. His eyes were failing. Sunday afternoons, that autumn,
we were watching the Jets, when he said, "Shake me." I looked at him sideways.

He blinked and smiled winsomely, almost coquettishly, like a high cloud on a
 summer day.
"Like a baby," he said. "Shake me like a baby."

I knelt astride him on the bed and threaded my fingers under his shoulder blades.
I lifted a little, then let go. "Faster," he said, like the air
rushing out of a tire when you depress the pin in the valve.

So I went faster, maybe one pulse every two seconds, up an inch and down again.
Then he began a moan, but so low I could not hear it, only a vibration in my chest,
and the whales off Manhattan Beach breached and fell back into the water.

It was crying, but not the regular kind, because he was talking with someone
I had never known. And then he fell asleep. I got off the bed, and sat

in the chair again, and the Jets were losing, and the linoleum was thick with wax,
and I imagined the factory in Germany where they make linoleum, big steel rollers,

the smell of bitumen, and I dreamed they were slicing the linoleum into squares
and putting it into boxes; and then we both woke up, and I went home.

IV

The next week, he said, "I asked mother to shake me like a baby. She said no.
 Embarrassed."
Then I mounted the bed, found his shoulder blades, and did it again,

strange massage for the places that his heart had ceased to serve, and this time
he moaned loudly and shivered and dropped into a thick, robust, snoring sleep, as if

it was 1943 and all of the other men were off at war, and he and his friend Artie
had all of the girls to themselves, and woke up in their cars at dawn, disheveled,

dirty, thicklipped, thirsty, sure of themselves and what came next.

When he woke, he asked for water, then we watched the Jets, though he could
not see much more than the field of green, and twice asked me the score.

Then, with his voice so low only a motion detector could hear him, he asked,
"Why is it no one understands me but you?"

Arthur Russell is a poet living in Nutley, New Jersey, the winner of both Providence Fine Arts Work Center and Syracuse University fellowships, as well as Brooklyn Poets' Yawp Poem of the Year for 2015 and an honorable mention for the 2016 Allen Ginsberg Poetry Award for the poem in this collection. His poems have appeared or are forthcoming in the *Paterson Literary Review*, *Prelude*, *Yellow Chair Review*, *Shot Glass Journal*, *Bettering American Poetry*, and the *Red Wheelbarrow #9*.

DANNIEL SCHOONEBEEK

.gif

Waste, do you know the word. Often it comes at night when I'm auditioning for the part of myself. When I'm mouthing the name of a politico, or fucking myself, or wondering why I carry on being American. Waste means whatever waste wants. In the middle of my life I searched for my name in the engine. I'm not dead links and leaks and zero results. Gospel, I told myself. I wrestle the ancients and yell their names when I'm blackout. I unleash myself on myself and I fuck the crow from my songs. But waste means here comes the shepherd's crook. Ask me anything, I'm the bellwether nobody brands. Waste and my telegrams of the cockscomb and teaspoons and my face in the cities I love they will vanish. I've failed to convince myself to subscribe to myself. Or I stand before the wall on which nothing's written. Waste means I'm following. Or I came here to waste in this box and everyone called it life. Waste finds me new addresses, new names every day. A red name, a green name, turned orange. From these three hooks the world is hung. The world which won't bend to the wind and waste means traffic, select invitations. Waste means I'll interview Salt, the town drunk whose father guards waste for a living. "One day two dozen years ago he came home smelling like shit." Are you like my father, Salt asks, do you oversee the river of waste to make money. Waste this river of carp and scumbags, it's peasant bread with the crust come alive. When you catch me disabling my family filter. "Shit is definitely one of the top three smells I think of when I think of my father," Salt tells me. The others? Ask someone else, waste the others. In the middle of your life and we're sorry nothing matched your search. He says I fired my gun into the river and nobody published it. The birds will sing none of it back. Waste is you stop telling stories. "Gospel," Salt writes me. I've thought of my father below me. Guarding his river of shit when I flush down the hole. Waste and return to the engine. When I fire my weapon I audition for the part of myself. Waste creates my page in the encyclopedia of waste. No one has met my waste yet, not even me, but my waste starts the bidding at zero. "I've only seen the place from the road," Salt writes me. "You've seen it too." My father's kingdom, and he defends the river of waste until it reaches the sea. Waste it's none of my business, waste is to hell with the scene. On these two hooks you hear waste chanting encore. Waste wants my chronology spread out like waste on a wipe. My father was born and fired his gun into the river and for two-dozen years now he watches the shit floating past him. Waste of a nut, waste of a rearing. Waste of a man, get rid of yourself. Delete your waste then return to the engine to scour. Audition for the part of your father in the film where he leaves you for waste. Or everyone wastes on my wall on the day I was born now. I've failed at waste but I've died, is that not also a triumph. I loved a politician, I've wasted another. Auditioning for myself, will I waste in the engine and result in myself. Father he curses the waste floating past. Will I mouth the name of a politico, waste of a cheekbone, tonight while she floats down the river. A raft and the suitors of waste on her arm. Foie gras smeared like waste on their teeth. Toy soldiers and dead cats and wedding rings in the river. My father steering the raft with his pole. "John my father," Salt writes me. On this one hook the world is hung. Waste of a name. Waste of a name I never made for myself. Waste has me flagged for removal, wants my history. "I've wondered," Salt tells me: could I break into the tunnels tonight and waste the toll collector. Bury his name and his pole. Unfollow him. And write my father, the waste king, write his name on the throne instead.

Danniel Schoonebeek is the author of *American Barricade* (YesYes Books, 2014) and *Trébuchet* (University of Georgia, 2016), a 2015 National Poetry Series selection. In 2015, he was awarded a Ruth Lilly and Dorothy Sargent Rosenberg Poetry Fellowship from the Poetry Foundation, and recent work appears in the *New Yorker*, *Poetry*, *American Poetry Review*, and elsewhere.

NICOLE SEALEY

The First Person Who Will Live to Be One Hundred and Fifty Years Old Has Already Been Born

for Petra

Scientists say the average human
life gets three months longer every year.
By this math, death will be optional. Like a tie
or dessert or suffering. My mother asks
whether I'd want to live forever.
"I'd get bored," I tell her. "But," she says,
"there's so much to do," meaning
she believes there's much she hasn't done.
Thirty years ago she was the age I am now
but, unlike me, too industrious to think about
birds disappeared by rain. If only we had more
time or enough money to be kept on ice
until such a time science could bring us back.
Of late my mother has begun to think life
short-lived. I'm too young to convince her
otherwise. The one and only occasion
I was in the same room as the *Mona Lisa*,
it was encased in glass behind what I imagine
were velvet ropes. There's far less between
ourselves and oblivion—skin that often defeats
its very purpose. Or maybe its purpose
isn't protection at all, but rather to provide
a place, similar to a doctor's waiting room,
in which to sit until our names are called.
Hold your questions until the end.
Mother, measure my wide-open arms—
we still have *this much* time to kill.

Nicole Sealey is the author of *Ordinary Beast*, forthcoming from Ecco, and *The Animal After Whom Other Animals Are Named*, winner of the 2015 Drinking Gourd Chapbook Poetry Prize. Her work has appeared in the *New Yorker* and elsewhere. "The First Person Who Will Live to Be One Hundred and Fifty Years Old Has Already Been Born" was first published in the *Village Voice*.

ALAN SEMERDJIAN

After Brooklyn

Macie will have graduated into a tornado
of new reconciliations including the leveling
of proper instincts (cradle, volcano) and mauve
lipstick sunsets (beaten quaggy) minus the roofs.

There will be time again for sweeping, imagining
without hiccup or hesitation. There will be
music in the streets, Coronas, Ghost's howl,
a bandana like a former planet on the kitchen table.

Oliver's poems will attempt to mean again. Urgent
and true, his evening and his neighbor's evening
will be closer to one. Someone will intimate the purr
of irony, and poof. It will turn (like sin) into wild honey.

Writer, musician, and educator Alan Semerdjian's poems and essays have appeared in such venues as *Adbusters*, *DIAGRAM*, and *Brooklyn Rail.* He is the author of the chapbook *An Improvised Device* (Lock n Load Press, 2005) and the collection *In the Architecture of Bone* (GenPop Books, 2009). His songs have appeared in television and film and have been charted on CMJ.

VIJAY SESHADRI

Street Scene

The job of redemption, with its angels and lawyers,
running late into the morning,
the halls are empty, and from seagreen foyers
where aquamarine jackets sag unused
no one walks out to be disabused
by the day, so confident and businesslike.
The domiciled, stunned, paralyzed, in mourning

for the vanishing illuminations, radium-edged,
that made their nerve ends glow
in the dark, are secretly pledged
to attenuate themselves in this,
the spirit's nocturnal crisis,
and still twitch with dreamwork,
and won't open their eyes. But although

not enough energy otherwise subsists
for the nurse to pop an antihistamine
and rise from her viral mists,
for the existential tough guy and thief
to wake up to some extra grief,
for the dog to be led to the park,
for the *viejo* to paint his fire escape green,

so that their race might never be caused to perish
from the contradictions of flight,
up above the satellite dish
pigeons of every color but exactly one size
mob, scatter, and reorganize
to practice crash landings on the street
that divides the black neighborhood from the white.

And at a distance rinsed of charity and malice,
their riots are being umpired by
the unmentionable, porticoed phallus

of the Williamsburg Savings Bank clocktower,
which manufactures the next hour
serene in an ongoing function
it can never be called on to abjure or justify.

Trailing Clouds of Glory

Even though I'm an immigrant,
the angel with the flaming sword seems fine with me.
He unhooks the velvet rope. He ushers me into the club.
Some activity in the mosh pit, a banquet here, a panhandler there,
a gray curtain drawn down over the infinitely curving lunette,
Jupiter in its crescent phase, huge,
a vista of a waterfall, with a rainbow in the spray,
a few desultory orgies, a billboard
of the snub-nosed electric car of the future—
the inside is exactly the same as the outside,
down to the m.c. in the yellow spats.
So why the angel with the flaming sword
bringing in the sheep and waving away the goats,
and the men with the binoculars,
elbows resting on the roll bars of jeeps,
peering into the desert? There is a border,
but it is not fixed, it wavers, it shimmies, it rises
and plunges into the unimaginable seventh dimension
before erupting in a field of Dakota corn. On the F train
to Manhattan yesterday, I sat across
from a family threesome Guatemalan by the look of them—
delicate and archaic and Mayan—
and obviously undocumented to the bone.
They didn't seem anxious. The mother was
laughing and squabbling with the daughter
over a knockoff smart phone on which they were playing a
video game together. The boy, maybe three,
disdained their ruckus. I recognized the scowl on his face,
the retrospective, maskless rage of inception.
He looked just like my son when my son came out of his mother
after thirty hours of labor—the head squashed,
the lips swollen, the skin empurpled and hideous
with blood and afterbirth. Out of the inflamed tunnel
and into the cold room of harsh sounds.

He looked right at me with his bleared eyes.
He had a voice like Richard Burton's.
He had an impressive command of the major English texts.
I will do such things, what they are yet I know not,
but they shall be the terrors of the earth, he said.
The child, he said, *is father of the man.*

Vijay Seshadri is the author of three collections of poetry, including *3 Sections*, which was awarded the 2014 Pulitzer Prize for Poetry. His other collections of poems include James Laughlin Award–winner *The Long Meadow* (Graywolf Press, 2004) and *Wild Kingdom* (1996). Seshadri has received grants from the New York Foundation for the Arts, the National Endowment for the Arts, and the John Simon Guggenheim Foundation, and has been awarded the *Paris Review*'s Bernard F. Conners Long Poem Prize, the MacDowell Colony's Fellowship for Distinguished Poetic Achievement, and the Literature Award of the American Academy of Arts and Letters. He currently teaches nonfiction writing at Sarah Lawrence College and lives in Brooklyn.

PURVI SHAH

Signs There Is a Hole in Manhattan

What outlasts all this business and craziness is poetry.
—Sunita Viswanath

Die-hard New Yorkers gaze at the twin ends
of the island and cannot determine which path

leads downtown. The new city immigrants are white sheets
garbed in Kodachrome and public telephone numbers. Call

any day, any time. People are unequivocally welcoming—
city strangers go to greet everyone, lingering.

The immigrants are outnumbered only by patriots
in their tricolored regalia. Old immigrants adopt

this new passport to safety. Lanky white women escort
groups of Muslim children to reach primary school.

Burkha-clad women refrain from public conversation,
skirt quickly through streets. Union Square

is the new civic center. Through the day,
through the night, the public carves the ground.

According to the sign taped to the cragged concrete,
the coffee cart man is a block north.

Every house glows with a TV buzz. Subway riders
over the Manhattan Bridge are pulled like moths

to the windows on the track to Canal St. Underground
transit is subject to detour. Some of the lines are reported missing—

Q diamond runs express. Q circle is local and becomes R.
W is N until Brooklyn when it's J or M or Z. Q=R; W=N—

words with absent hearts: queer or when. So much is beyond delineation, beyond the circuits of language, like missing=bombs=smoked solace.

Purvi Shah's first collection, *Terrain Tracks* (New Rivers Press, 2006), won the Many Voices Project prize. In 2008 she won the inaugural SONY South Asian Social Services Award for her work fighting violence against women. In 2011, she served as the artistic director for Together We Are New York, a community-based poetry project to highlight the voices of Asian Americans during the tenth anniversary of 9/11. Her recent chaplet, *Dark Lip of the Beloved: Sound Your Fiery God-Praise* (Belladonna*, 2015), explores women's devotions, status, and being.

ROBERT SIEK

We Do Hospitals and Leave

I have to label this river, watch another disaster movie,
speak to boys in mint green jammies seated on pleather couches,
I mean, you know, really tell them my story, sweep the side roads,
the kind Google maps can't offer street views of, the walkways
to front yards where dead daffodils still stand in late spring,
the eyesores of white petals turning brown to black,
burnt edges of one sheet of typing paper, the circle of them
planted around a light post, the painted to match the shutters,
where they hung the address number of the house, two digits
on a piece of metal cut in the shape of a banner, this whole thing
in the way when mowing the lawn. It's a pow wow
in a locked psych ward, a 12-step meeting
on the eighth floor, where someone leads
these in-patients, introduces a speaker
from the outside. One young guy asks
if they like KISS. "You mean like the band.
I fucking love them." Maybe because we're both
dressed in all black, like this must be witchcraft,
hand me the special knife, it's time to feed the earth.
It's time to hire a mapmaker, offer suggestions on how
not to die, like follow me at top speed on foot away from
the nearest body of water. Some goddamn tidal wave
is coming. Don't you know some people
manage to outrun it, always breathing
heavy until the end.

Robert Siek is the author of the poetry collection *Purpose and Devil Piss* (Sibling Rivalry Press, 2013) and the chapbook *Clubbed Kid* (New School, 2002). He lives in the Bushwick neighborhood of Brooklyn and works at a large publishing house in Manhattan.

EMILY SKILLINGS

Fort Not

I'm not really that kind
of smart. Sometimes I can hardly.
I hear a little bell
and a film gets all over.

Twice yesterday, actually,
the imagined consensual entered.
Held onto for a long time. A shriek
parade was ordered by the county.

The new gender I wanted to become
was actually more of an arm
movement—simultaneously
strong, accurate, elegant, lilting

and weaponized. Scrolling white text
opened doors to previous anticipation.
The opening credits came on last,
all puffed out with options.

I did this very gentle tapping
to activate the month in my skull.
I watched some massage-related porn
for purely relaxational purposes,

locked violets and crystals
in the gun safe. Mold bloomed
on the ceiling in the museum
of best practices. Everyone got sour.

If it's ok to cry
in this widening, groaning hall,
I'll do it after I sign
for the deliveries.

The smallest muscles in my hands
are hard at work
generating a closeness to god
that is rare in these parts.

When I end the American movie
and it rains all over the Puget Sound,
will you shepherd me
to the opposite of safety.

Place one hand at the small
of my wreck. Pour out
every single refreshment.
There's so many savings

and so little time.
Sally wore a bathing suit.
Nobody's home
at the Holiday Inn Express.

The scenic route drowned
a long time ago.
Didn't you know? Water froze
in the generation.

Baby Food

I ate some.
It tasted fine.
I'm alive.
Blood is coursing
through my veins.
I could call out
into darkness—
I could harness
some powers
beyond my
usual scope
of action.
I feel fortified

and nutrient-
rich. I think
the baby food
did this
to me. It was
banana squash, two
things I've never
thought to
combine. Who are
these brilliant,
innovative
chefs we appoint
for our youth?
How long
will I feel this way?
I don't have
a baby (I'm
ambivalent about
mothering) but
I've always
really wanted
to publicly breastfeed
something. Ideas?
I want to drape myself
and also to expose
my feeding breasts
and argue about my right
to expose or not expose
those feeding breasts.
I want to get in fights
with other breastfeeders
and non-breastfeeders
on the internet
and in person.
In the park.
In the coffee shop.
To come
to blows.
I would get
that special pillow,
the bra

with the holes
in it,
pumping freely
into containers
of many sizes.
I want to yell
from a bathroom stall,
"Would *you* want
to eat lunch in here?!"
I want to judge men for staring.
I want to judge men
for looking away,
to be equally
frustrated and empowered.
I'd feed my lover
and my friend
as much milk
as they wanted,
one on each side,
more than a baby
could take.
They'd spread on
that special
anti-chafing ointment.
I'm thinking about leaking
onto a rag,
or a document,
moistening a
territory.
The areola,
that bobbing
spot on
the GPS.
Nipple kinesphere.
It's so powerful
to have food in you
streaming somewhere
or just out.
The sun dips
below the equator.
The smallest,

rubberized sensation
broke my personal
barrier. I'm not
even thinking now,
just acting—
pure, unbridled
physical being.
I feel like I'm talking
extremely loud. Would
you say that
is accurate?
It's a Monday
in America.
I'm 26 years old.
Could you help me
with my body?

Emily Skillings is the author of two chapbooks: *Backchannel* (Poor Claudia) and *Linnaeus: The 26 Sexual Practices of Plants* (No, Dear/Small Anchor Press). Her first full-length collection of poetry, *Fort Not*, will be published by the Song Cave in 2017. Skillings lives in Brooklyn and co-curates the Earshot reading series with Allyson Paty. She is the recipient of a 2017 Pushcart Prize.

FLOYD SKLOOT

Toomey's Diner

Empire Boulevard, Brooklyn

Sundays at dawn were whispers and silent
pissing on the inside of the privy bowl.
If belt buckles merely clicked, zippers
crept shut, and the heels of heavy shoes
only thudded together muffled in our hands,
mother slept on as we crept out the door.

Sunday mornings my face seemed to melt
in ripples of chrome circling high stools
at the bar of Toomey's Diner. The air
inside was thick with breath and smokes
as I spun between my father and brother
waiting for our *flapjacks all around.*
I saw the soles of my feet turned upside
down in the stools' silvery pedestals
and knew enough to spin without a squeak.

So this was the world outside. Red leather
to sit on, red formica edged in chrome
where my elbows fit, red menus studded
with paper clips. Signs said Special Today.
This was the stuff of weekday dreams. A small
jukebox at every table, rice to keep
the salt dry, toothpicks, a great pyramid
of cereal boxes hiding the cook.
Sunday was sizzling grease and apple juice
glowing pink, then blue in the sudden shift
of neon. Sunday laughter gave off such
heat that walls burst with sweat.

When the day came apart, I always had
the relative silence of knives and forks
on plates, the delicate lids of syrup holders

snapping shut, coffee slurped from steaming mugs,
coins on the counter, the sound of our bill
skewered by Toomey as we turned to leave.

Reese in Evening Shadow

I prayed for easy grounders
when Pee Wee Reese fielded,
hanging curves when he hit.
At Ebbets Field, in late August
of my eighth year, I watched
him drift under a windblown
pop fly, moving from sunlight
to shadow as he drew near home.

Now, on the first anniversary
of his death, the August night
is wild with mosquitos and bats,
skunk in the compost. A pack of deer
thrashes through tangled hazel
and poison oak as they cross the hill
below its crest in search of water.

Nursing the day's final herbal
concoction against joint pain
and lost sleep, the same drink
I have used all twelve years
of my illness, I tilt my head back
in its battered Dodgers cap to rest
against the slats of an Adirondack chair

as a screech owl's solo whistle
pierces the endless crescendo
of bullfrogs and bumble bees

when Reese at last drifts back out
of evening shadows. He wears
loose flannels. Wrinkled with age,
stained by his long journey,
he still moves with that old grace
over the grass. I see anguish

of long illness on his familiar face
and something like relief too,
that rueful smile, the play finished,

game over. I stand and his arm
settles on my shoulder, a gesture
he used to silence the harrowing
of Jackie Robinson. He helps me
find balance while the world spins
as it always does when I rise
and the whisper of wind is his voice
saying it will be all right, pain is nothing,
stability is overrated, drugs play havoc
with your game, lost sleep only means
waking dreams, and illness is but a high
pop fly that pulls us into shadow.

He is gone as the wind he spoke with
dies down. I find myself on the trail
those deer walked, seeing where I am
now though already lost in a darkness
that soon will reach home.

Floyd Skloot was born in Brooklyn in 1947. His most recent books include the poetry collection *Approaching Winter* (LSU Press, 2015) and the novel *The Phantom of Thomas Hardy* (U. of Wisconsin Press, 2016). He has won three Pushcart Prizes and the PEN USA Literary Award in Creative Nonfiction, and his work has been included in the *Best American Essays*, *Best American Science Writing*, *Best Spiritual Writing*, and *Best Food Writing* anthologies. He lives in Portland, OR.

CHRIS SLAUGHTER

Dear Barbershop,

Is this a barbershop? If we can't talk straight
in the barbershop, then where can we talk straight?
—Eddie Cedric

I come from you: every argument, debate and dare—
every hand-me-down bet that taught me to run

from nothing while fading the world down small enough
to doubt. No one else understands the gravity

in the way a chair turns after a fist fight, with blood staining
hair and hardwood floors. Music somehow tells the story

better than us, mirrors turn away, but I saved
the dirt and hair from under my nails. I'm not hard currency

to you—anymore. I'm no longer steady handed and perfect for slang.
You say, with every chair in the shop full, "What happened to you, man?

You even look at customers like they're not good enough anymore"
—but I'm made from discussion, contradiction, and cheap cognac; cussing

in every sentence just to get points across a loud room. I'm a glass bottle
on the ledge of some mantle that built a ship inside of itself (and the ghosts

it holds). I'm against the same grain as I've always been; believe in
the same skin-fade, sharp line, and half-moon. I'm the same crazy bastard

that called the pizza man a racist, with mute Omar by my side
waving his arms—don't forget the good times and what hurts,

what makes our blood agree, how women come in alone
with their boys and listen to us go on about presidents, one-night-stand sex,

and Kobe's fade-away; they listen to us throw *nigga* and *bitch* around
like they aren't even there—this isn't about money, I just want my name back.

Chris Slaughter has an MFA in poetry from Hunter College and a bachelor's degree in English from Medgar Evers College. He has received fellowships from Cave Canem, Brooklyn Poets, and North Country Institute for Writers of Color. Having previously been a barber for 20+ years, Chris has merged his personal life and the barber's life into a narrative. He is presently a director at Eagle Academy for Young Men of Harlem while chipping away at his first full-length book manuscript.

TOM SLEIGH

Space Station

My mother and I and the dog were floating
Weightless in the kitchen. Silverware
Hovered above the table. Napkins drifted
Just below the ceiling. The dead who had been crushed
By gravity were free to move about the room,
To take their place at supper, lift a fork, knife, spoon—
A spoon, knife, fork that, outside this moment's weightlessness,
Would have been immovable as mountains.

My mother and I and the dog were orbiting
In the void that follows after happiness
Of an intimate gesture: Her hand stroking the dog's head
And the dog looking up, expectant, into her eyes:
The beast gaze so direct and aliently concerned
To have its stare returned; the human gaze
That forgets, for a moment, that it sees
What it's seeing and simply, fervently, sees...

But only for a moment. Only for a moment were my mother
And the dog looking at each other not mother
Or dog but that look—I couldn't help but think,
If only I were a dog, or Mother was,
Then that intimate gesture, this happiness passing
Could last forever...such a hopeful, hopeless wish
I was wishing; I knew it and didn't know it
Just as my mother knew she was my mother

And didn't...and as for the dog, her large black pupils,
Fixed on my mother's faintly smiling face,
Seemed to contain a drop of the void
We were all suspended in; though only a dog
Who chews a ragged rawhide chew toy shaped
Into a bone, femur or cannonbone
Of the heavy body that we no longer labored
To lift against the miles-deep air pressing

Us to our chairs. The dog pricked her ears,
Sensing a dead one approaching. Crossing the kitchen,
My father was moving with the clumsy gestures
Of a man in a space suit—the strangeness of death
Moving among the living—though the world
Was floating with a lightness that made us
Feel we were phantoms: I don't know
If my mother saw him—he didn't look at her

When he too put his hand on the dog's head
And the dog turned its eyes from her stare to his…
And then the moment on its axis reversed,
The kitchen spun us the other way round
And pressed heavy hands down on our shoulders
So that my father sank into the carpet,
My mother rested her chin on her hand
And let her other hand slide off the dog's head,

Her knuckles bent in a kind of torment
Of moonscape erosion, ridging up into
Peaks giving way to seamed plains
With names like The Sea of Tranquility
—Though nothing but a metaphor for how
I saw her hand, her empty, still strong hand
Dangling all alone in the infinite space
Between the carpet and the neon-lit ceiling.

Second Sight

In my fantasy of fatherhood, in which
I'm your real father, not just the almost dad
arriving through random channels of divorce,
you and I don't lie to one another—
shrugging each other off when words
get the best of us but coming
full circle with wan smiles.
When you hole up inside yourself,
headphones and computer screen
taking you away, I want to feel in ten years
that if I'm still alive you'll still look
at me with that same wary expectancy,

your surreptitious cool-eyed appraisal
debating if my love for you is real.
Am I destined to be those shark-faced waves
that my death will one day make you enter?
You and your mother make such a self-sufficient pair—
in thrift stores looking for your Prom dress,
what father could stand up to your unsparing eyes
gauging with such erotic calculation
your figure in the mirror? Back of it all, when I
indulge my second sight, all I see are dead zones:
no grandchildren, no evenings at the beach, no bonfires
in a future that allows one glass of wine
per shot of insulin. Will we both agree
that I love you, always, no matter
my love's flawed, aging partiality?
My occupation now is to help you be alone.

Tom Sleigh's many books include *Station Zed*, *Army Cats* (John Updike Award from the American Academy of Arts and Letters), and *Space Walk* (Kingsley Tufts Award). He's received the PSA's Shelley Memorial Award, a Guggenheim, two NEAs, and many other awards. He has a book of essays and a book of poems forthcoming from Graywolf, *The Land Between Two Rivers: Poetry in an Age of Refugees* and *One War Everywhere*. He teaches at Hunter College and works as a journalist in the Middle East and Africa.

CHRISTOPHER SOTO

Those Sundays

My father worked too many hours. He'd come home with his
cracked hands and bad attitude. & I'd rather talk about Rory now.
[His blond locks] How the sun would comb crowns into his hair.
Rory was my first love, before he killed himself.

    My father hated faggots. The way my cock looked beneath a
    dress. The mismatch of his chafed knuckles and my cut cuticles.
    A scrambling of hands. I was always running. Mascara. Massacre.
    My momma would wash the red paint off my nails and face.
    She'd hold me like the frame of a house. No, the bars of a prison
    cell.

"Mijo, your father is coming home soon. Hide your heels." I'm
the donkey clanking down the hall. Click, Clack, Click, Clack.
Over Momma's body [he'd grab me] & throw me against the
wall. My bruises dark as holes, he punched into the wall. His
hand was the hammer. I was the nail. & I want to talk about Rory
now.

    That night, after my father smashed the television glass with his
    baseball bat, I met Rory at the park. We made a pipe out of a
    plastic bottle and aluminum foil. [He watched me undress & run
    through ticking sprinklers]. I fell beside him then; beneath the
    maple tree. & he saw my goose bumps from the cold. & he felt
    my bruises, as they became a part of him.

Rory, I want to say that death is what you've always wanted. But
that can't be the Truth. [This time] we can blame it on me. I'll be
the packing mule, carry all the burden. & you, you can be a child
again; fold your church hands like dirty laundry [crease them tight].
Nobody has to know about us, not my father nor yours—
  No, not even God.

Christopher Soto aka Loma (b. 1991, Los Angeles) is a poet based in Brooklyn, New York. He is currently working on a full-length poetry manuscript about police violence and mass incarceration. He received an MFA in poetry from NYU.

SAMPSON STARKWEATHER

letter of resignation

so long language

thank you for the opportunity
you look sweet on my CV
my time here has taught me
your world is not for me

this place creates
a silent violence

spiritual detritus
the world's last light
spilling from this shipwrecked tanker

what do you think the last human dream will be

I think it might be me
jumping out the goddamn window
    yelling
who's coming with me!

good luck steam cleaning the semen

sincerely

poetry

3 shots to the chest at the arcade

Sadness is my favorite video game
I am its hero
the little man with facial hair
scampering through pixilated cities
looking for clues

and accumulating shit
without knowing why
trying not
to be crushed
or free fall
into the not-world's dark
as 8-bit clouds
scroll across the pre-
programmed sky
it's exhausting
but I take it
next level
I am happy here
it feels real
and I can always die

I am often associated with flowers

Hello, my name is Charles Baudelaire.

I was born in 1976, where I was raised in Pittsboro, North Carolina.

I am a poet. It says so on my Wikipedia page.

My themes are beauty in the modern world, the fleeting, ephemeral experience of life in the age of the internet and Mac products, and the responsibility art has to capture that experience.

My first 4 books went mostly ignored and was soon forgotten, although it is still available on eBay for $22.84.

Tiny cookies of my life are crumbled around the internet, most notably a nude photo covered in chapbooks, that too will be buried.

I am poor, ADD, drunk, and might be masturbating to death.

I am this close to moving back in with my mother, or at least "renting" her house on Airbnb while she vacations in Mexico.

I will probably die of syphilis...again.

No one will leave flowers at my grave.

The End.

Sampson Starkweather is the author of *PAIN: The Board Game* (Third Man Books, 2015) and *The First Four Books of Sampson Starkweather* (Birds, LLC, 2013). He is a founding editor of Birds, LLC, an independent poetry press, and the author of nine chapbooks, most recently *Until the Joy of Death Hits, pop/love audio-visual GIF poems* from Spork Press, and *Flux Capacitor*, a collaborative audio poetry album from Black Cake Records. These poems were originally published in *Prelude* and *PAIN: The Board Game.*

LEIGH STEIN

Definition of Adrift

Adjective. Mapless, does not answer
to her married name, marooned
on a beach on which every night
the tide erases her letters home.
Can never remember what she wrote.
Last night's said: *Send a fleet.*
Tonight she will write: *Send a fleet.*
Never anchored. Like some islands,
the ones made of bulrush, or shipwrecked
love that loses its shape inside the ever after.
Distressed. Consumed with nostalgia
for copy machines, a desktop clock,
a postcard sent from one destination
to another: *I'm here. I can't speak*
the language, but I'm not coming back.
On this island there are no postcards.
Tonight she will write: *Send pirates*
in the sand. Or tonight she will forget to
write. Tonight she will try to mend the boat,
then go and sit in a grotto at high tide awe-
stricken with oblivion, motherless.

The Illusion of Space

I like to flag my emails urgent. I'll write Anna:
Anna, I have to steal my roommate's house slippers

before the quiet agony of these footsteps kills
me. I will kill her first. I cannot afford an efficiency

studio anywhere in this entire city, or the next
one, or the next. Have you ever heard of Fishkill Plains?

I'll tell you where I don't want to live.
I did a shoddy job of making my bed this morning,

then I lied to the landlords about how much noise
their baby makes during the hours when I'm home,

I mean when I'm not out, having the time of my life,
networking with unpublished novelists, making love

to athletic hedge fund managers on their palatial
divans, one eye always turned towards their exotic

fish aquariums. O Gods, why must I
spend my nights mending the seams

of my secondhand Versace dress,
reciting verse to myself like an echo

of the mind, trying to remember
the name of the girl in Rumpelstiltskin?

Sasha? Ada? Rhoda? Keiko?
Importance: High. I only remember his.

Truth be told I never do my homework anymore,
or maybe I always do and just don't know I do it,

or maybe when I'm dead I'll wish I'd done less, but how
will I know when that day has come, what can I do now

but carry on, the way we do in musical theater,
like I've just watched my tenor dip a broad

with a more waspish waist than mine, but
I'll be damned if I ever go back to Iowa. Agnes?

Candace? The woman standing near me on the train,
the reader, she could be the one. The one

in the red knit hat, holding the Michigan mug,
where could she be from? Did someone

lock her in a tower until she knit that hat?
O Gods, O Anna, O Midwestern reader,

I will never be beautiful, I will never have a veranda
and a view of the heaving sea. I will only get older,

and move to Fishkill Plains, where I'll be able to rent
an entire cul de sac. Every night, more barefoot girls

will arrive from the Catskills, arms full of straw,
and knock on my door. I will say of course I'll help you,

Deborah. I was young once, too, Evangeline.
Then they will lay down their straw and I will say

close your eyes and they will remember the world,
the world as it was, the one that came before this one.

Leigh Stein is the author of the poetry collection *Dispatch from the Future*, as well as a novel (*The Fallback Plan*) and memoir (*Land of Enchantment*). Her poems have appeared or been anthologized in the *Awl, Barrow Street, Bat City Review, BOMB, Bone Bouquet, DIAGRAM, Please Excuse This Poem, Poem-a-Day: 365 Poems for Every Occasion*, and *Sixth Finch*. She has been called "de facto poet laureate" of *The Bachelor* by *New York Magazine*.

BIANCA STONE

Making Apple Sauce with My Dead Grandmother

I dig her up and plop her down in a wicker chair.
She's going to make apple sauce and I'm going to get drunk.
She's cutting worms out of the small green apples from the back yard
and I'm opening up a bottle. It erects like a tower
in the city of my mouth.

The way she makes apple sauce it has ragged
strips of skin and spreads thickly over toast.
It's infamous; eating it is as close to God as I'm going to get,
but I don't tell her. There's a dishtowel wrapped around her head
to keep her jaw from falling slack—

Everything hurts.
But I don't tell her that either. I have to stand at the callbox
and see what words I can squeeze in. I'm getting worried.
If I dig her up and put her down in the wicker chair
I'd better be ready for the rest of the family

to make a fuss about it. I better bring her back right.
The whole house smells of cinnamon and dust.
We don't speak. She's piling the worms, half-alive
up in a silver bowl, she's throwing them back into the ground
right where her body should be.

The Fates

I cracked open my skull and out flew mom.
She alit in the rafters, electric in a massive chamber.
She has abilities accessed by latent genes.
Quietly terrible powers come
with great responsibility—which
you don't have to use—either way one still
has the power;

a few lives to fuck up; to
wreck or save—
wind chimes won't let go of me.
I ring whenever I move.
I feel like the Titanic sailing straight
into the liquor store on Saint Marks and Franklin.
I'm watching a TV show
about supernatural detective brothers
who travel back and forth across the United States
revenging their parents' deaths
until they can't remember anymore why or how they died.
In general
the need to kill demons and vampires
overtakes their need
to remember anything.
And who can blame them?
Every night in the hotel the two talk indirectly about their feelings—
manly men, massive in sex appeal, drinking
and killing and talking.
In this episode the Services of Fate are no longer required in the human world.
Thus, everything in the future is affected.
In this reality
I know my brother is living near me,
so close
I can wave from my window
into his.
He's telling me he's writing a poem
about the way
the face disappears.

Blackflies

Today blackflies appeared, all at once, whirring around like tiny
airborne pickup trucks from the future, spitting-up in their hands,
rubbing them together, a group of old grossers at a card game around my head.
It seemed like they were aware of me. Like in *Phenomena*,
the movie. Not the embarrassing religious one with John Travolta
but the 1985 horror film starring Jennifer Connelly as a famous actor's daughter
with psychic powers who communicates with insects and is sent to a creepy
boarding school in Switzerland. There were so many layers now that I think
about it. A blackfly leads Connelly to the corpse of a girl killed by a deformed

serial killer child, living in secret on a remote estate with his mother,
who turns out to be the headmistress. It's loosely Freudian,
with a surprising soundtrack by Iron Maiden and Motörhead.
The only survivors at the end of the film are Connelly and an orangutan
owned by the kindly (but eventually killed) entomologist, and of course
thousands of flies. The two embrace in the final scene—young woman
and ape—on the dark shores of a Swiss lake, with great sadness and relief.

Bianca Stone is a poet and visual artist, the author of *Someone Else's Wedding Vows* and *Poetry Comics from the Book of Hours*, and artist/collaborator on a special illustrated edition of Anne Carson's *Antigonick*. She runs the Ruth Stone Foundation and Monk Books with her husband, the poet Ben Pease, in Vermont and Brooklyn. "Making Apple Sauce with my Dead Grandmother" was first published on Poets.org; "The Fates" first appeared in *jubilat*.

PAIGE TAGGART

when you write about what you see:

the sky lifts/lights over you
the music conducts the atmosphere
my thoughts become a conduit and to
write what you see
means you are collaging in space
you are filling in words
where there are none

the crook of my arm is a genius
it recites within blankness
conducts virtual realities
elicits boredom when you probe too
hard
I'd like to not council
for literary effect
if at all possible

my man grabs my breasts and butt
whenever we're in a quiet public space
like at a bookstore I get groped so hard

see the aisles
take inventory
plucking at the core of what it
means to archive
bores me

most things booorrrree me
life preserves a timeline
that we are constantly
at war with
I hung myself on the coat rack
begging to be all object

I wonder if Stein was obsessed
with nouns because she wanted to be all
thing
to crave tactility sans brain
not a care in the world

I stare facing myself in my underwear
slap at the parts of me I hate
thinking I could shrink some aspects
all ass inebriated
bonne chance!

my window jammer screams
eeking some salt into the water cave
discombobulate
rancor of tone and kidney
life forever = LIVER
speech haphazard = spazz
kilt of pink cotton
I floss in the dark

collage in the open space of my mind
bring all things together
as a testament to my ability to speak

am able minded even when blindsided
by fear

FEAR IS NEAR
IT'S EVERYWHERE

I keep thinking about love
and what does that mean
fish swim upstream

LOVE IS NEAR
IT'S EVERYWHERE

I scream to no one in particular
the vault of my mouth
flappy skin / akin to reason

swivel the collocutor around
see things from all sides
barter for soap
pay ritualistic fees on bended knees
trying to not use the:
of, there, then, on top of, above
code modified speech
directing someone else's actions
lift the bridge of your attention
I must yell for encouragement

Of Is Our Origin

I'll start writing really clearly that way
when I go to type it up there will be no
confusion and
then when I go to read this aloud I will
annunciate very clearly so there will be
no confusion
I'll sound out each word like "tsk tsk"
you'll think everything is onomatopoeia
and you'll be all like she must be boom
thrashing on her insides
there must be a little storm of
confidence insider

just so you know
she did hear cheers of goodwill as she
wrote this and everything was of an of
because it's so difficult to make
something perform as is
without being the "of"
which hosts a whole metaphor of
compliant ideas and allusions

I took a bunch of bites of my bagel
sandwich in between these lines

I took a screen shot with my iPhone of
images of Cher

the grey area of multi-tasking shone itself
in its ripe colors of distraction
like how we can't just do one thing without thinking about another
or say one thing without implying a whole heed of our identity
that we were born with
the very second our mothers pushed
us out into the world

Paige Taggart is the author of two full-length books, *Want for Lion* and *Or Replica*, and five chapbooks. She has her own jewelry line: mactaggartjewelry.com. "Of Is Our Origin" was originally published in *Pinwheel*.

MERVYN TAYLOR

The Center of the World

I.

From here I can see the world, all the people
walking down Flatbush Ave., going into stores,
waiting at the bus stop, all the latecomers rushing
into the subway cat-a-corner from my window,
across Ocean Ave. all the new immigrants in winter
wearing too much clothes, the police recruit from
Long Island under the awning of the Arab grocer.

Salaam, I can hear the crack addict, the last of
his kind disappearing between the floorboards,
arguing with the Arab chief, the one with the scar
on his left cheek next door to whom the Asians
scrape calluses from feet three times the size
of their own, giving them the designs they want:
star, crescent, half-moon, the flag of any country.

I see all four seasons pass through the park, in
winter, the lake shimmering between the trees,
in autumn the nervous leaves shaking and falling,
the sudden flood of green in spring. And summer,
oh summer, with the smoke of a hundred grills,
the smell of bar-b-q, the birthday balloon sailing
away from the crying boy, the slap of dominoes
on the picnic tables, the relentless hawk, a rat

dangling from its talons, dripping red onto the
cyclist's jersey, the yellow paddleboats on their
circular journey around the island that is the ducks'
breeding ground, dense, impenetrable, the raccoon
that scared us after the concert at the band shell
the night Rudder sang his calypso blues, where
a year ago Odetta made her last appearance half-
sitting under a falling moon. And the vet whose

shock of white hair stood out among the runners,
I don't hear his sidewise shout anymore.

In the zoo the enclosure where the bears ate a boy
has a higher fence, painted with pretty pictures.
On Sundays the drummers still form their circle,
and in the evenings horns announce the arrival of
the Haitians, their sound atonal, harsh, unrelieved.
They move in concentric circles, singing not words
but a series of o's, rising, falling, rising.

II.

Sometimes the midnight lines at the McDonald's are
seven registers across. Here a homeless man might sit,
nursing coffee, pretending to wait for the No. 12.
I know where it goes, out Linden, through dangerous
parts of East New York, I take it almost to the end of
the line, to a building boasting a thirteenth floor and
terraces with a great view of flights leaving Kennedy.

I watch the Puerto Ricans on their day, the coquís on
the hatband of the older men. Fridays the Jews
stream in numbers toward the end of the park where
the big synagogue is, the cops with backs to them
blocking traffic. I see all the time accidents at this
five-way intersection, the elderly couple never
making it to a wedding, their car spun round facing
the opposite way. I catch, on Labor Day,

steel pans going down the middle of the avenue,
a girl waving a mysterious flag, the sergeant longest
on the beat saying, ahh, don't worry 'bout it, too long
to explain what *wining* is. I've heard relationships die
at 3 am, among the pillars in the pavilion, or at the stoplight
while a car idled. I've heard the prettiest rendition of
a Scott Walker song come up the fire escape and through
my window, through a long and sleepless night…

III.

I've heard the shocking quarrels of people over
a parking space, over love, over nothing. I've
seen a boy gasp his last between the park benches
after the pop, pop turned out not to be fireworks,
the cap on his head turning red. There are times
I looked out to see not a soul, and times it seemed
a congregation had gathered under my window,
times when the heat would rise and then would not,
my guest and I sleeping in gloves.

I've lived through three supers, watched their sons
grow to manhood. I've let the woman next door
climb through my window when she'd forgotten
her keys. I've stepped over the nodding ghosts of
men acting like doormen in the lobby, their number
dwindling till there was one, who could hardly lift
my suitcase. I leave but always come back here,
where I review things from this vantage point,
the confluence of people and lives after deliveries
are dropped off early in the morning by trucks
rambling through this intersection of the world.

Mervyn Taylor, a longtime Brooklyn resident, was born on the island of Trinidad. He has taught at Bronx Community College, the New School, and in the NYC public school system. He is the author of six books of poetry, including *No Back Door*, in which this poem appears, and, most recently, *Voices Carry*, both from Shearsman Books.

CHARLES THEONIA

This Morning Your Horses

walked beneath my window,
woke me with their warm, short
gusts, breathing *come with us*.
What I called love was letting
the loose dirt of someone else
crumble over me. Then you
called me out the window—
it's not something I dig into
alone anymore.

∴

Let's dance in the mirror
and '90s-montage
our outfit changes.
Spinning to Mazzy Star
in your red velvet,
pleather, and mesh.

Let's get our lace wet. Come,
braid my hair, get me ready,
brush gold into my eyebrows
until they glitter with malice,
sharpen your wings before
we put our bodies
out into the streets.

∴

Baby blue wax accretes
on the wood of my desk,
gathering itself in invisible
increments. Wanting
to meet you all the time
is a sweet allowance of myself.

Without knowing it I'd sensed
that need was dangerous.
Now, I can see it building.
You say what I am, and I
have a chance to become it.

Charles Theonia is a poet and teacher from Brooklyn, where they are working to externalize their interior femme landscape. They are the author of *Which One Is the Bridge* (Topside Press), where "This Morning Your Horses" first appears, and co-editor of *Femmescapes*.

DANIEL TOBIN

Bridge View

The grandeur of the tower was nothing at first
but our surmise at what it would become,
gleaned from rumors; though before long
we watched the stanchions' gradual ascent
above Shore Road's distant stand of trees
where Third narrowed to its vanishing point.

Nothing at first, and then, from the corner,
one day we saw the legs barely risen,
two sheer columns of iron and steel:
the tensile thighs of a man being built
foot by lifted foot from the bottom up,
girder and crossbeam, rivet and plate.

For two years he grew, his height accruing
like a child's stature notched on a wall,
while up from the Narrows the body took form
from foot to hips and vaulted crotch. But where
was the rest of him, broad torso and head?
It was we who gave that image to the air,

gave it likewise to its twin across the strait
before they strung the cables, hung the roadway
amazingly into place, so that, that first time,
we drove through a space left by torn-down homes
up the approach, the Island spread before us,
the river below, and climbed into the sky.

In the Green-Wood

No country churchyard, where now the avenue
   blusters and throbs with weekend shoppers
hot for buys, its buses and delivery vans,
   cadenzas of boom-boxes and car horns,

but this archway like a cathedral wall
   fashioned out of brownstone, as though Upjohn
had turned to fresher labors, before steeple
   and vaulting nave and great rose window

found manifest form, so only this gate
   rises solitary above its city
of patient sleepers. Jet-lagged, nearly late
   for the tour, we pull up incongruously

it seems to us, as if we'd been sped back
   like Twain's time-shifter into stereoscope
only to discover the heart's true Gothic,
   a lost extravagance in our idea of home.

We fall in behind, following our guide
   through steam-blasted spires, the funeral bell
silent as our group rambles up the grade,
   our train boisterous, motley, raggle-taggle,

more Bruegel than Currier & Ives—
   those swallow-tailed, bonneted picnickers
on Sunday daytrips in their carriages,
   the graveyard less a graveyard than a park.

Here was heaven's waiting parlor, benign,
   tombs like villas along bluffs and dells,
ornate plots cafe-stocked with lounges,
   in unused fields the grazing animals

dissimulating into their fluent Eden.
   And here, still, is nature in pastoral,
little worse for wear, where Resurrection
   reclines like Autumn into the moraine.

Sylvan water, Crescent Water, Vision Path.
   Each floral lane and woodland boulevard
bends along the rim of a new expanse,
   weaves back again, a lost urban heaven

our guide unfolds in wit and anecdote:
   Colgates, Whitneys, Pierreponts, the Steinways,

their grand mausoleum like an annex
  big enough to house a hundred guests;

Marcus Daly, Montana's "Copper King";
  "Big Bonanza" Bill MacKay, his crypt
heated like a marble country cottage
  for the grace of his eternal comfort;

Henry Ward Beecher, Horace Greeley;
  Basquiat, Bernstein, James Weldon Johnson;
Roosevelts, Morses, Tweeds, and Tiffanies.
  Though we prefer the less familiar stones:

Here lies Fannie, dog "with limpid eyes,"
  the sewing magnate's pet; brash Lola Montez
(a.k.a. Eliza Gilbert) who would drive
  men wild with her erotic "spider dance";

McDonald Clarke, "Mad Poet of Broadway,"
  doggerel lines scrubbed from his obelisk;
Captain Hayes of the clipper ship *Rainbow*,
  these fathoms empty, his last voyage wrecked;

Bill the Butcher and Albert Anastasia,
  killers who called themselves "true Americans";
Do-Hum-Me, Barnum's Indian Princess,
  buried in her wedding dress, her husband

the brave weeping on her stone, like Azrael
  the angel of death; and the other lovers
with their iconographies of loss—
  a groom's pruned oak branch, a bride's clipped rose—

such early deaths. And here is a column
  transplanted under yews in this calm grove:
Matilda Tone, who buried her children
  and died alone. We'd seen her husband's grave

who slit his throat in the Dublin Barracks;
  saw his comrades in the vault at St. Michan's,
their bones crossed, skulls staring from their nests.
  For these doomed lovers, America was exile—

insufferable, "a culture of boors
   and swaggarts" she would suffer nonetheless,
her afterlife of life without him moored
   to a widow's dream of revolution.

And what if they had given up the cause,
   chose another life as settled farmers,
their heirs harkening to Greeley's "Go West"?
   Or would they become like Bellows's *Cliff Dwellers*

(the artist asleep in his unmarked grave)
   crowding sheer tenements? Now further on,
Battle Hill rises above the Narrows,
   Washington's stand, studded with monuments;

and other hills lush with Civil War dead,
   no masts in the harbor now, but barges
churning under the bridge for Gowanus docks
   astride the projects where my father lived;

and farther out, the island with its stalls
   and cages, its teeming, endless labyrinth
and line of faces, its railroad heading west;
   and farther west the meadowlands, and farther....

Here is the soul, a granite sphere with wings.
   Here pollen rains gold dust from the trees.
Monk parrots fruit the branches. We watch pass
   high sculpted clouds, opulent and migratory.

Daniel Tobin is the author of seven books of poems, most recently the book-length poem *From Nothing*, as well as critical studies and edited volumes. Among his awards are the Massachusetts Book Award in Poetry and creative writing fellowships from the National Endowment for the Arts and the John Simon Guggenheim Foundation. "Bridge View" and "In the Green-Wood" first appeared in *The Narrows* (Four Way Books, 2005).

TIM TOMLINSON

Eight Days a Week

I don't know it yet, but it's the last day
I'll ever follow my big brother, Wally,
off Knickerbocker Avenue, up Bleecker
toward our grandma's apartment, the Myrtle
Avenue El rumbling behind us. The small
teeth of a slanted comb poke from Wally's
back pocket, his Cuban heels clack
on the sidewalk, his iridescent slacks
shine like gasoline on a puddle.
He's a ten-year-old Frankie Valli.
I'm eight, and one thing I know: big girls might
not cry, but big brothers do. Wally acts
tough, but at the dentist, I hear him howl
so loud I drop my *Boy's Life*. And when Dad
raises his voice, Wally changes his pants.
He can't hack a little pain, or even
the threat of it. I follow him now through
the hot exhaust blowing out the dry cleaner's
vent, past Pete the Jeweler selling watches
from the trunk of a Buick. Mrs Gentile's
sunk her elbows into the pillow on
her windowsill, her lips smeared with ragu.
Corner of Central, Wally runs the comb
through his wings, shoulders up to the window
where an Annette Funicello lookalike
scoops Italian ice into Dixie cups.
He says a lemon ice for him, and can she
heat up some milk for me? It's time for my
nap, he says, like I'm the kid brother,
a pest, an affliction who cramps his style,
and the girl, this candy store Mouseketeer,
laughs right in my face. All I ever want
is to follow Wally, make him see that
I can hang with the big kids, make him laugh,
even act as tough and dumb as his friends.

I want to shrug off this new hurt, show them
I'm not some crybaby punk, when a sound
I've never heard before fades in from
the radio of a Ford Skyliner idling
at the steps of St. Barbara's. Major chords
chiming behind a voice that shoots
like a drug into the pleasure center
of my brain. Later I'll learn how chords can
have false relations, how their false match is
barely perceived, but the discord they make
creates unbreakable bonds. That's not what
I'm thinking when I hear them. I'm not thinking
at all. I'm feeling, and everything that
once felt important—good grades, fast sneakers,
even Wally's approval—suddenly
they're meaningless. When the Skyliner pulls
away, Wally says, *Was that that Beatles*
shit? But I barely hear him now, and it's
like that for several years, until little
by little, I don't hear him at all.

To the Best Friend of the Girl in the Mr Peanut Costume, Halloween, 1986

Thank you for agreeing to come with me
into the men's room of Original
Ray's on 82nd & Columbus
while the pie we ordered with the olives,
extra cheese and anchovies baked
in the brick oven. And thank you
for opening your blouse when I asked you
and for kissing so passionately, like
you meant it when I lifted your ass on
the dirty sink and hiked the school-girl skirt
over your waist and—Christ, I'm
seeing stars here just recalling the way
your saddle shoe rested against a mop
bucket filled with scummy water reeking
with disinfectant and how the smells
we made together in the sewage funk
swirled into the raunch of the room with

the roaches crawling across misogynist
graffiti and the lock half on a door
we couldn't close. And thank you for saying
thank you when I sunk it in and thank you
for making me feel what I haven't felt
in so many years. You were from, what, Maine?
I loved the way your best friend in
the Mr Peanut costume waited for us
to emerge, the bubbling hot pizza
cooling below the cigarette she smoked
in a holder, like she was the one just come
from the rest room. The pizza was so good.

Tim Tomlinson is a co-founder of New York Writers Workshop and co-author of its popular text *The Portable MFA in Creative Writing*. He is also the author of the chapbook *Yolanda: An Oral History in Verse*, the poetry collection *Requiem for the Tree Fort I Set on Fire*, and the collection of short fiction *This Is Not Happening to You* (Winter Goose, 2017). He is a member of Asia Pacific Writers & Translators. He teaches in the Global Liberal Studies program at New York University. "To the Best Friend of the Girl in the Mr Peanut Costume, Halloween, 1986" first appeared in the sadly discontinued *Unshod Quills*.

ED TONEY

The Baptist Growl

Oh, Preacher, you don't know the growl
if you ain't born of the deep, deep south
eating yellow grits, hog maws and crackling
with red-dirt scars on your knees and elbows

If you ain't got the hole in your gut
from Grandma giving you a shot of castor oil
a keloid from the thin weeping willow switch
you just got a whippin on the tender rump with

If you ain't hung no cross around your neck
carved from a sycamore tree in a 108 heat
while sipping grandmas iced tea and reciting
all the psalms without looking before 6:30 am

If you ain't sat in church sun-up to sun-gone
not wiping sweat off your brow with your index finger
tapping that hardwood floor to the sweet sounds
some backwood boys harmonizing "Goin up Yonder"

If you ain't baptized all 280 of your church members
since first generation born
round back of the church in that muddy river
everybody wearing white robes and humming "Wading in the Water"

If you learned everything you know from God
and ain't hardly been no further than elementary school
and your blessed great-great grand-pappy preached
and his daddy, and his daddy and your daddy too

Then you best know how to growl up that holiness
from the pews in your chest, sanctify some spit from
the old white church paint chippings off your tongue
throw your head back, gurgle-growl them blessings into words

make juke-joint folk shout, do the holy-ghost dance
make grandma's knees get strong, go ahead nana, run
make Uncle Pete shout like James Brown
and make Jesus grab his binoculars to take a peek.

Ed Toney is a poet, writer, and chemist born in Queens, NY, who now resides in Brooklyn. Ed seriously began his poetry writing career in 2001 while attending the Louis Reyes Rivera workshops. Ed is a Cave Canem workshop participant, and has been featured at numerous poetry venues, bookstores, rallies, Black Poets Speak Out, etc., throughout the boroughs of New York. Ed has facilitated workshops and is a member of the Hot Poets Collective poetry writers group. He is currently completing a chapbook, *Gut Level,* and his first full-length poetry manuscript, entitled *Nicks in the Tongue.*

DOMINIQUE TOWNSEND

One to Ten

one

mistake

stupidly
unchecked
not lazy
but over
exerted

I found it
in a dream
wakened
panicked
flawed
mistaken

there are conventions
for correction

apology
edits
open letters
also denying / lying
can work

why the torrent
why the dread

of being
known

fear of conveying

being
outside

akin
to barbaric
tabooed
quietly pariahed

opposite

two

moves
to glorifying

a skunk

by comparing
the animal with raised tail stunning
to the woman you love, bottom raised rummaging
in a low drawer

this is not a mistake but a metaphor
therefore artful

three

in the end, ego
I am wronged

four

late fall already
high pink morning sky
behind the oak all golden
I didn't sleep enough

five

time to wake up
a poem should be funny—isn't it?

six

there is history

and unconscious
a line misread and illuminated
accept in exception

seven

there's art in
artifice
and artificial

as a matter of course

in certain
thinking
lying for the sake of instruction
is not just

acceptable
but profoundly
right

the proper
work of masters
of insight
who know what's real

eight

age two

the phrases of his early childhood
fade day by day

by afternoon

Upwidada

I mine dat!

Wadisit?

I wannit

No wannit

these three mental poisons

desire ignorance aversion
a rooster pig and serpent

become intelligible to strangers
convention takes root

likewise, his needs

ultimately will barely involve me

nine

sink hole

the journalist said
the bed shifted barely creaked
and the ground beneath
gaped
to wolf him up
bed frame and all

his brother bored
watched tv in the living room

ten

it's terrific
to love
like this
afraid &
fearsome

Dominique Townsend is an assistant professor of Buddhist studies at Bard College. Her debut book of poetry, *The Weather & Our Tempers*, was published in 2013 by Brooklyn Arts Press.

MICHAEL TYRELL

Custody

My mother's old now;
she's almost my baby.
Soon she'll have to go to school.

Death will have to take her.
He has her during the week,
I get her on weekends.

I'm like my mother—
neither of us can drive.
The court didn't care for that.
That's why I didn't win full custody.

So, on weekends, my mother & I wait at a bus shelter.
Death's around here someplace—
no such thing as unsupervised visits, with him.

I'd kill for a restraining order,
but that would require his assistance.

I'd accuse him of breaking the bus-shelter window,
but that's not his style. Besides, it's not even real glass,
the way today is spring in writing only,
endorsed by a calendar's soon-to-be-crossed-out square.

Our divorce was amicable;
he wasn't a bad provider,
and everyone says
reconciliation is inevitable.

In fact, he still has his good points.
He lets the bus complete its route,
he lets the market exist.

With expiration dates
he signs the shelved milk & pills, the batteries
for disaster flashlights—

One turn down the wrong aisle
and I'm the child again,
scanning the market
for my lost mother—

Strangers all I can turn to,
and one I must marry.

Michael Tyrell is the author of the poetry collections *Phantom Laundry* and *The Wanted.* With Julia Spicher Kasdorf, he edited the anthology *Broken Land: Poems of Brooklyn.* "Custody" was first published in the *New Republic.*

JOANNA C. VALENTE

My Vagina Will Be the Death of Me

In the morning a storm like breath
dimming in dread twists like silver
around fingers, a bit too tight
so it leaves a mark, almost stops
blood but faintly quivers back—

larger like smoke from a house
fire—blacker—heavier like
colonial brick. Part of surviving
is to keep moving, grow up
& ignore the distance where

dogs sometimes bark—most
people will try to write a novel
without using their hands, praying
to a sack of human bones dug up
in the sand, ask WebMD if

we're hypochondriacs, if a man's
hand at the base of a woman's
vulva is haunted with alien symbols,
is a weapon salting infertility,
is an abandoned Victorian decomposing

in Louisiana heat, his hand over
her mouth stales her desire for
anything, her mind sets an ultimatum:
Heaven or Brooklyn? When she
gets home she tweets #StruggleCity

& cuts an apple like sun lighting
the holes between maple branches,
a voice wafting a million years homeless
like burning garbage the shape of
woman's first body, a hole drilled down

the middle of a long damaged earth.

Your Body Doesn't Matter

When you're a woman & your last name
is jerked around like a rabbit running

from a wolf penning a way to climb
the cancerous limbs of a winter tree falling

like a dead woman's body after being
ghosted from body to body to another

struggling to wake up after she is gouged
on an icicle in someone's basement apt

& all of her is shot in the head like the good
slut she is & the psychic said her chakras

needed to be fixed & why does she wear
her dead grandmother's perfume if she

doesn't enjoy wishing she were dead
so when her dream becomes a reality, shouldn't

she be wearing that badge of honor like
a tramp stamp like the leader of a wolf

pack whose chosen spirit animal is an owl
is a helicopter is a crucifix is a syringe

around the arm of a girl who used to be
a boy whose only hunger is some pills to wind

back time to before she is alive so she's basically
dead anyway

& it's her fault because she's too pretty & no
woman can be that dumb not to know

how men are when the swing is about to fall
to earth & how could she not fall?

Joanna C. Valente is a human who lives in Brooklyn, New York. She is the author of *Sirs & Madams* (Aldrich Press, 2014), *The Gods Are Dead* (Deadly Chaps Press, 2015), *Marys of the Sea* (ELJ Editions, 2016), and *Xenos* (Agape Editions, 2017), and the editor of *A Shadow Map: An Anthology by Survivors of Sexual Assault* (CCM, 2017). She received her MFA in writing at Sarah Lawrence College. She is also the founder of *Yes, Poetry*, a managing editor for *Luna Luna Magazine* and CCM, and an instructor for Brooklyn Poets. Some of Joanna's writing has appeared in *Prelude*, *Atlas Review*, *Feminist Wire*, *BUST*, *Pouch*, and elsewhere.

FLORENCIA VARELA

Bimhuis

I agree it's hard to make a life here.

The song doesn't live
past seven folds, stays gaslit.
Someone gives the drunks
in the park a harmonica;
imagine that spell.

Of all songs,
to land on caroling.

Of all songs,
its winter may soon kill me.

One more wrong key,
and my neighbor will be hanging
out the window again,
all red screams. Possessed, I move
every piece of furniture in the apartment
until my pacing changes its shape,
spinning, bewildered even—
a Scheherazade in ruins.

I was evolving, I was taking it personally.

Florencia Varela's poems have appeared in journals such as *Western Humanities Review*, *Drunken Boat*, *DIAGRAM*, the *Destroyer*, *Phantom Limb*, *American Chordata*, *Gulf Coast*, and *Washington Square Review*. She completed her MFA in poetry at Columbia University. Her chapbook *Outside of Sleep* was published in 2012 by dancing girl press. She currently lives in Brooklyn.

ELISABET VELASQUEZ

New Brooklyn

During my last visit to Brooklyn, I found nothing where I left it.
This city doesn't stay still like it used to. They call it growth. Mami
calls it eviction. She is scared of the way the gringos are turning
her bodegas into gardens. She says flowers remind her of funerals.
I say: Mami, maybe you will feel better if we sit on the steps. I say this
as if the stoop is an open mouth, as if it will remember how we taste,
as if it will not spit us back out for being bitter or worse, for having
too much flavor. I change the subject. "Mami, I got the job I always wanted."
She hears: *You got the job I never had. Your only job is to keep yourself*
off government payroll. I laugh and worry more about keeping my body
off a gentrified street because, these new art galleries on the block wanna
call my stretch marks abstract, when in reality they are the strings of a harp,
the tag name of God. I am a black book. I am an untuned instrument. One
part graffiti, one part music. Today I looked at the way my bones work.
My body was built in a factory, the kind of factory my mother worked in.
Sewing machines and severe workplace violations. Stains on the floor
from the workers who made a blood pact with it. You know the kind.
Or maybe you wouldn't know the kind. They have nice windows now.
Real paint, not blood. There are words the thesaurus does not pair properly
with other words. Gentrification. Colonization. I am angry all the time now.
Really, I'm just loud. I don't know how to talk without sounding like
revolution. Like my throat is all boombox and block party. I argue like
an unraveled cassette tape that could have sounded like music had it been
wound tightly. But in New Brooklyn, they don't care nothing about my music.
I heard they tried to take down the Avenue of Puerto Rico street sign.
The one we called gra-hahn, the one they pronounce Graham. The one
that's been there thirty-three years before they tried to take it down—which is,
ironically, the age Jesus died. Why they always wanna kill holy things?
They say there aren't enough Puerto Ricans there these days. They pretend they
can't smell the sofrito in the air, can't hear the salsa blaring from a third floor
window because a Latino is cleaning house. You hear that? The irony
in the chorus: Quitate tu, para ponerme yo. Quitate tu. Fania knew the future.
Mami knew the future when she taught me to keep some bass in these hips.
They gonna act like they can't hear you? That's when you make them feel you.

—and you vibrate like you tryna break the sound barrier, or a stereotype,
and you tell the New Brooklyn that if they tryna clean house,
they will always hear our music in the background.

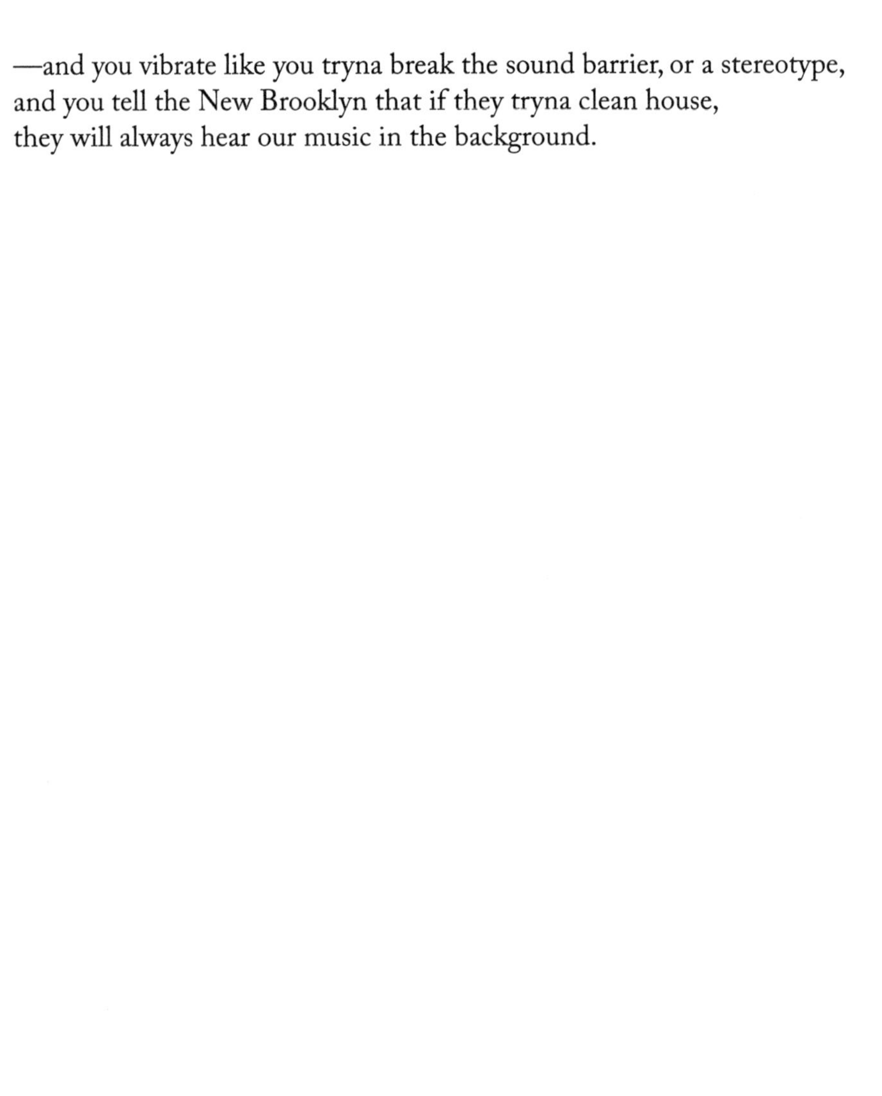

Elisabet Velasquez is a Latina writer, performer, and madre from Bushwick, Brooklyn. She began performing in 2009 under the stage name Ms. Sick Prose, a name she chose to escape an environment surrounded by mental illness. She earned a spot on the 2009 Nuyorican Poets Café National Slam Team, has performed at universities across the country, and has been featured at venues including the legendary Nuyorican Poets Café, Bowery Poetry Club, the Brooklyn Museum, and Lincoln Center, among others. She is the author of the chapbook *PTSD* and her work has been published in *Muzzle, Centro Voices*, and *Elephant Journal.*

R. A. VILLANUEVA

As the river crests, mud-rich with forgotten things

Colors this summer Raritan
carries: of this flailing, flaring New
Jersey sunset   of the burnt-ends of cigarettes
as they   and gravity then the river kiss
Red's surge toward night-
fall: a dark diastole   rich with the blood
of pigeons, worms, catfish—a mercury blood,
heavy with gas   This orange Raritan
This drunk, Dutch princess   flanked as if by knights:
trunks bent, leadened with her forgotten things   they knew
tomorrow would bring nothing   but kisses
of moss   feasts of cigarettes
and pistols, denim and pulp   All sick at rest
with clay in the roots, their shallowed blood,
bruised corpuscles kiss
only the light left, only the ache   for some life rarer than
this, apart from the current's slurs and weights   New
moon—pulsing yellow muscle of the night-
to-be—flexes along each surface: driftwood night-
stands, a kingdom of algae, ash-nests of cigarettes—
even the vertebrae of gulls aglow   as henna-brown canoe
hulls, course past blood-
oranges, pockets of glass, a Samaritan
mold   And as the bitter, mosquito kiss

of evening ebbs in, its shifts and shadows kiss
every branch, every veined leaf and weed: night-
shade, poison oak, sumac root   orangutan
vines of ivy along the banks awash in cigarette
fog, ripe with tar   And now as how blood

clots to black, the river thickens tints: its platelets of news-
paper ink   shake-songs of newt
throats and cricket shanks kissing
the growing murk   Here freon blood's

systolic pump through fridge coils, these night-
    sticks beached among trestles, cigarettes'
leach and slush: all lullaby the muck This Raritan—

    this hematite sinew moth-swollen nightingale
ventricle kissed with charcoals, cigarette
    papers—its blood-dyed roar, return

Crown

To hear it their way we wanted
ships' holds, fields of tobacco and

cane, canneries reeking of cod,
whale, prawns to devein; we wanted

more sand to die in; we wanted
fingernails worn to the quick and

carrion crows' songs, borderland
raids, boots on the ground. We *wanted*

this, they say. We asked for it
with our hardened necks, our cakes, our

unpronounceable names. *Why must*
each damned lake and bird of the air

need altar and mouth, horn and dance?
—they call out to us with fire.

*

They called out to us with fires
before posing for photographs,
arranging each shadow with care—
each child's dead stare, bangle, and half-
touch a corona to circle
missionary men, or their wives.

They called out to us with charnel
work and missals, cinnabar mines
to dig in service of the Crown
and cross. What's cut from the portrait

is the cordillera, the sun
warming our spit, coals, a piglet
run through, and this girl waiting for
her son, his jawbone bruised, tender.

R. A. Villanueva's debut collection of poetry, *Reliquaria*, won the Prairie Schooner Book Prize (U. Nebraska Press, 2014). New writing appears in *Poetry*, *Guernica*, *Prac Crit*, *The Forward Book of Poetry 2017*, *American Poetry Review*, and widely elsewhere. A founding editor of *Tongue: A Journal of Writing & Art*, he lives in Brooklyn and London. "As the river crests, mud-rich with forgotten things" was originally published in *Painted Bride Quarterly*, and later in *Reliquaria*. "Crown" was originally published in the *Wolf*.

M. A. VIZSOLYI

Blind Man as Astronomer

i was a body in firelight being read by
people who were they & where were they
from i never saw them in the bar or in
town they were lean rabbits coming
out of a hole & would they disappear
back again tomorrow to their lives & look
in the mirror say my hair look nothing can
be done with it those who gave themselves
to someone what will they do i was
sure if someone knew it was Grief but he
was busy with a girl explaining to her
something about silence in music its relation
to those blank pages at the end of a book
he was going to try it he said a book
with blank pages at the beginning take
notes on lamps or anything at all first
he said see how they hold up to the literature
you have yet to read i heard her laugh &
then i heard nothing i looked & saw Grief staring
at the girl in silence who looked uncomfortable like
a tall man asleep on a very small red couch

The Blue Infected Will

the sign on my bar's door read you
should not have come & thinking it
a joke Marie went in & Bernadette
not without drunkenness sat down
near a window loudly
i was busy making a sandwich
& the two of them
proclaimed loudly we
are to be given two beers &
two of your best sandwiches

please & then Marie laughed &
whispered something to Bernadette
looking into the kitchen where
i was & next to them
was a couple breaking up the young
man was crying & the girl looked at him coldly with
impatience & embarrassment a
look that says i can not
console you being emptied out if
you were to see the look you might
think of an empty house with some
boxes outside or a windless valley
of snow or a cave so dark a flare
might be afraid to enter it or a
second-story balcony where the curtains
are open & you can peek inside though
there's nothing in there & you think
it's odd & Marie listened to his tears
without pity eyeing the kitchen
& drinking her beer

M. A. Vizsolyi is the author of *The Lamp with Wings: love sonnets* (Harper Perennial), winner of the National Poetry Series, selected by Ilya Kaminsky. He is also the author of the chapbooks *Notes on Melancholia* (Monk Books) and *The Case of Jane: a verse play* (500places press). He is part of the faculty of the BFA in Creative Writing program at Goddard College. "Blind Man as Astronomer" first appeared in the *Journal*, and "The Blue Infected Will" first appeared in *Crazyhorse*.

OCEAN VUONG

On Earth We're Briefly Gorgeous

i

Tell me it was for the hunger
& nothing less. For hunger is to give
the body what it knows

it cannot keep. That this amber light
whittled down by another war
is all that pins my hand

to your chest.

i

You, drowning
                        between my arms—
stay.

You, pushing your body
                        into the river
only to be left
                        with yourself—
stay.

i

I'll tell you how we're wrong enough to be forgiven. How one night, after
            backhanding
mother, then taking a chainsaw to the kitchen table, my father went to kneel
in the bathroom until we heard his muffled cries through the walls.
And so I learned that a man, in climax, was the closest thing
to surrender.

i

Say surrender. Say alabaster. Switchblade.
        Honeysuckle. Goldenrod. Say autumn.
Say autumn despite the green
        in your eyes. Beauty despite
daylight. Say you'd kill for it. Unbreakable dawn
        mounting in your throat.
My thrashing beneath you
        like a sparrow stunned
with falling.

i

Dusk: a blade of honey between our shadows, draining.

i

I wanted to disappear—so I opened the door to a stranger's car. He was divorced. He was still alive. He was sobbing into his hands (hands that tasted like rust). The pink breast cancer ribbon on his keychain swayed in the ignition. Don't we touch each other just to prove we are still here? I was still here once. The moon, distant & flickering, trapped itself in beads of sweat on my neck. I let the fog spill through the cracked window & cover my fangs. When I left, the Buick kept sitting there, a dumb bull in pasture, its eyes searing my shadow onto the side of suburban houses. At home, I threw myself on the bed like a torch & watched the flames gnaw through my mother's house until the sky appeared, bloodshot & massive. How I wanted to be that sky—to hold every flying & falling at once.

i

Say amen. Say amend.

Say yes. Say yes

anyway.

i

In the shower, sweating under cold water, I scrubbed & scrubbed.

i

In the life before this one, you could tell
two people were in love
because when they drove the pickup
over the bridge, their wings
would grow back just in time.

Some days I am still inside the pickup.
Some days I keep waiting.

i

It's not too late. Our heads haloed
        with gnats & summer too early
to leave any marks.
        Your hand under my shirt as static
intensifies on the radio.
        Your other hand pointing
your daddy's revolver
        to the sky. Stars falling one
by one in the cross hairs.
        This means I won't be
afraid if we're already
        here. Already more
than skin can hold. That a body
        beside a body
must make a field
        full of ticking. That your name
is only the sound of clocks
        being set back another hour
& morning
        finds our clothes
on your mother's front porch, shed
        like week-old lilies.

Ocean Vuong, an American poet and essayist, is the author of *Night Sky with Exit Wounds* (Copper Canyon Press, 2016). A 2016 Whiting Award winner and Ruth Lilly Fellow, he has received a Pushcart Prize and honors from the Civitella Ranieri Foundation, the Elizabeth George Foundation, the Academy of American Poets, *American Poetry Review*, and *Narrative*. "On Earth We're Briefly Gorgeous" was previously published in *Poetry*.

STU WATSON

The Ostrich in the City

The ostrich
I imagine
can't be killed
or won't
be anyway
not here
not like this
in a line
clipped off
or with a
clip expended
the ostrich
I imagine
is immortal.

Who cares
about opposable
thumbs when
you have
an opposable
face? A beak
is like a hand
an ostrich
neck is like
an arm but
flexible in
ways arms
aren't plus
arms don't
have eyes
at present.

I say these
things
to myself

when I
want to
be the
ostrich
as if it's
a consideration
that bears
working out
that I
might roam
the city
a deathless
flightless bird
and terrify
and smash
things leaving
tracks in snow
never
being caught
surveilled
yet still
enraptured
from a
perspective
beyond anyone's
appreciation.

An immortal
face like
an arm
with eyes
to walk
or sprint
in wrath
unmindful
of a dying
city this
I think to
myself
smoking idly
in the courtyard
this is

what an
ostrich life
would be like
for me
no doubt
about it
could its
terrible
time be
now come
round
at last?

Stu Watson is a writer, musician, and teacher living in Brooklyn. A founder and editor of *Prelude*, his poems, essays, and stories have appeared in *PANK*, the *Collapsar*, *Queen Mob's Teahouse*, *Flag + Void*, *Jacket2*, and *Flapperhouse*. He teaches at John Jay College of Criminal Justice.

YUN WEI

Unpublished Diaries of the Philae

Comet Lander, November 2014

four billion miles later I thirst
for a pinch   a hurt   a cough
pin drop on floorboards   anything
to break this flameless lickless
        nothing   streak across

dust water ice will do nicely
for a ten-year crave
brought nothing   but tampons
and passports for a comet chase
a tensile density they told me
in crystal-cut multiplications

I should have stayed where
up   down   were severed siblings
where silence lived within its means
but no one would let me laugh
the way I do here   tongue out   loose bones
flattened to match the dark-glazed scenery

how the cartilage of things glow here
boundaries can be traced   filled
        with all the geometry I can remember
except for the shape of arrows   and exit
yes dust water ice feels good
                        between the toes

Yun Wei received her MFA in poetry from Brooklyn College and a bachelor's in international relations from Georgetown University. Her writing awards include the Geneva Literary Prize in both poetry and fiction and the Himan Brown Poetry Fellowship. Her work has appeared in *apt*, *Brooklyn Review*, *Word Riot*, and other journals. Recently, she has been working on global health development in Geneva, where she subsists on a daily diet of cheese, chocolate, and mulled wine. "Unpublished Diaries of the Philae" first appeared in *Maudlin House*.

ABIGAIL WELHOUSE

Bad Baby

I will kick you in the eyes and laugh.
There's no greater comedy than a broken nose.
I will dance on your hospital bed
and order pizza when nobody's home.

I will unravel every sweater,
put wet paint in every shoe.
How could it possibly be me?
Babies can't talk. Babies can't order pizza.

I will light fires in the garden.
Fuck plants. Long live babies.
Who's lucky now, lucky bamboo?
Bow to your baby queen.

That's not a rattle. It's my scepter.
You will obey me or else
I will make a noise
you will never forget.

Royalty

in another time, if I had my food cooked for me sometimes
and delivered to my door or served to me on ceramic plates,
if I could have one woman paint my nails while another paints my toes,
if I could live alone with wood floors and travel every day,
they'd think I were royalty.

if I could shower whenever I wanted and turn a spout to find water
and flush a toilet instead of chucking shit out the window
onto the street to land in the faces of children,
if I could buy dresses, even if on credit, if I could read magazines
or even if I could read anything at all, and eat entertainment created just for me
by the internet where the court jesters take off their clothes for fame and money,

they'd wonder what kind of queen I was, if I was benevolent, am I benevolent,
they'd have to listen either way and even if now I don't have servants,
strapping men to carry me home and fan me with palm fronds and feed me grapes,
I'll take now, with bathing and fewer powdered wigs, and plumbing, and college
tuition, and the rent is too damn high, and everyone's trying to sell you something
or wants you to fund their dreams, and horses live further from people,
and more of us live miles from where we were born, and we fly out for weddings
and cry and throw rice and think about being present and think about being whole
and think about swimming with manatees, and how peaceful they are,
they're vegetarians you know, and friendly, and I am two of these things
but not the other, and think about how I'll take now but all of this
is only for now and there's no change to believe in except when they want you
to vote for them. Change is eternal but you can read it in every fashion magazine,
if you're royalty, if millions of people have paid for you to learn how to read
and paved the roads for you to drive to people that you think about
that will leave you and your heart will break but they'll give you their chairs,
or a rice cooker, or some spices that will feed you when combined with cheese
from your magical refrigerated box, which back then would have gotten you burned
as a witch. I forgot to mention. They'll also pay to send you to war.

Abigail Welhouse is the author of *Bad Baby* (dancing girl press), *Too Many Humans of New York* (Bottlecap Press), and *Memento Mori* (a poem/comic collaboration with Evan Johnston). Her writing has been published in the *Toast*, the *Billfold*, *Ghost Ocean*, *Yes, Poetry*, and elsewhere. She would like to thank Jen DeGregorio for previously publishing her poem "Bad Baby" in *Cross Review*, and Kristy Bowen for previously publishing both of these poems in the chapbook *Bad Baby*.

MONICA WENDEL

Courthouse

At the rally for the woman who was raped
by that cop, Reverend Billy started in on
corporations, eventually winding his way down
to her body. The booing stopped, then. In Bushwick,
near Varet Street, one wheatpasted sign reads
you can't have capitalism without racism and another
says *occupy my penis*. Audre Lorde said *the master's tools*
will never dismantle the master's house which I hated
when I first heard it—of course plantation tools
could kick holes in walls, of course fire burns both
fields and hearths, until I realized what she meant.
Or maybe I still don't. Maybe the sign should have read
you can't have capitalism without misogyny or plain old *fuck cops*—
after the trial was over, a jury member said, of course
the cop did it, we just didn't have enough to convict. It was
he said she said. Here's all I can say: the cops formed
a wall outside the courthouse, hands behind their
backs, chests forward. Like they were the ones under
attack. Like it's not violence if someone gets off.

Brain Science

Between Fairhope, Alabama and Ocala, Florida
I drove away from the sun until no lights
were left on the highway, just woods around the road, the
car, and washed-up bits of tires like seaweed
or the egg purses of eels. I felt like Dante's Dante:
midway upon the journey of life I found myself upon a forest dark
though I'm not as old, not midway, even as much as Florida
feels like hell, or caves under its own weight
into sinkholes that reach the slow-moving aquifer.
Minutes and miles into the darkness, a cell phone
running lower whenever I GPSed, and on
NPR a girl was hit by a semi, already

deaf, now struck blind, and when her boyfriend
(who her mother disliked—"I didn't like her look
when she looked at him") finally traced words
on her skin, Helen Keller–like, she said
"Oh how sweet. How nice of you" to his declaration
of love, the first words to reach her,
and hers to him spoken out loud, "I love you too.
Who are you?" Later, she told him,
Can you help, can you get me out? I'm trapped
behind this wall. In the car, alone,
I started to believe that she was there with me,
feeling the hands of strangers, hearing people
come in and out of her room, hallucinating
the lost senses. I was afraid that I was a figure
in the dream she couldn't wake up from.
When I called you from the hotel, you told me
you listened to the same *Radiolab* while painting the other day
(Florida NPR running reruns) and I heard the story again
with your voice as all the voices, and we're still
so far away from each other, I haven't seen you
since weeks before that conversation. I'm scared
that every dream will feel like being trapped inside a wall,
like my childhood fear of being buried alive,
and after I got home from Ocala I dreamt
I was locked in a prison with a man who was going to rape me,
at the beginning of the dream I was a reporter, maybe
that's how I figured out it was a dream, and when I told the man,
"I'm going to wake up," he took off his shirt, he said,
"Can you? can you really?"

Monica Wendel's first book, *No Apocalypse*, was awarded the 2012 Georgetown Review Press poetry manuscript prize, selected by Bob Hicok. She is also the author of three chapbooks, most recently *English Kills* (Autumn House Press, 2016). "Brain Science" was published in *Nimrod* and "Courthouse" was published in *Rattle*.

JARED WHITE

Peer's Brooklyn Poetry Shop

Who am I?

If I can write my address this is a poem but if I write your address instead it isn't. What number could shudder these words loose from poetry using the logic language to make the robot smoke. You sing the law chuckle anguish tomb ache their rowboats milk, did you say? Most of me crunches very big primes. Vorticism is good. Tarzanism is goood. Bitcoins are gooood. Is Peer's politics a wheel that turns idealism into sexploitation? I only know bodies by what they do, organs inside torso like a death cult project. And which organ is decomposing this? Poem for left kidney. Poem for full fathom five. Poem for Gaudí Towers of Barcelona. Greed is so not art. The remnants of my friends are their messy little booklets. They used to be in love with each other and then they had a staring contest and sorted themselves into piles as with a threshing comb. I don't even know where a voice ends, let alone the ghost of one. Except these aren't ghosts, these are hopeful future people waiting in the someday line. And how old are they choosing to be for their right now representation? My hair doesn't actually grow, I just gently pull away from it. Zip code zippedeedoodah 11201 (eleven thousand two hundred and one). Don't give me this who is the president pupil dilation clip on angel wing nonsense as if ideas need climate-proof boxes. I wish you knew my son you would love my son. My wife's son. My wife's my son, my my husband's wife's my son. Captain, are we in international waters yet? The spiders are weaving drunken webs. The ferryboat lists. Being the object of a feeling feels like there is a right answer to your question. Since last September we're my own grandpa.

Poem for a Note to Follow So

In the Brooklyn School of Poetry

the book club has open enrollment but a vicious policy for laggards.

Last seen in the subway, found in the East River.

Two jumpers last night on the George Washington Bridge collided in mid-air
and one survived.

Boy is almost body or buoy.

I make myself shiver but is that bravery.

An occupation big as a wall.

The forsythia blooms or at least some orange bush we point at and say is that forsythia.

O PEN

for business.

ourang-outan.

The Brooklyn School is a merciless tutor for loving but I get so tired of my friend geniuses.

It's too easy to be comfortable in my autobiography.

Ocean water washes over the Brooklyn School of Poetry only at high tide, for a few minutes.

In the shop I say and you say and I say and you say and every time you is a different person.

It's talking to the laundry. What I should publish is empathy, not poems.

In San Francisco do they even write poems or is it all posthumous translation.

In Tel Aviv it's babies teaching babies.

The newspaper prints a photograph of the 25'ers club

just like walking on black stars.

The key is going barefoot and working up a sweat so the boiling draws heat away from the skin.

Gerunds gerunding lemmings lemming.

Temporary people are looking at temporary flowers.

Provenance of an email.

La.

The Brooklyn School of Poetry is applying for official appellation status in spite of the fact that all the raw materials are imported and only the processing or warehousing facilities must be local.

I am a zoology professor. My interest in you and me is zoological.

Po hurty. Po earthy.

Goodnight. Goodnight. Goodnight. Goodnight. Goodnight.

Jared White's chapbooks include *Yellowcake*, published in the anthology *Narwhal* (Cannibal Books, 2009), *My Former Politics* (H_NGM_N Books, 2013), and *This Is What It Is Like to Be Loved by Me* (Bloof Books, 2013). With Farrah Field, he is co-owner of a small press bookstore, Berl's Brooklyn Poetry Shop.

ROBERT WHITEHEAD

Kate Bush's House in Danger of Falling into the Sea

So it goes there is sadness first.
It is daily, like furniture.
There is a polish for it, she buys it,
she polishes the sadness in close, bright circles
with a filthy t-shirt. She sits near it,
tells the people who call
that she is sitting quietly near her sadness,
watching it tick. The living room
is perched on stilts, hounded into a cliff face.
Stupid birds squire the air, which is rolling
in a pattern complementary to the sea, rolling.
The bolts in her sadness are probably coming loose.
The ones who eat the fish
closest to the surface of the sea, those birds,
those stupid white birds,
calling out for everything to be named.
The house could be sown into the sea factory
where what is made is not usually
the pulp of a house of a star.
A house swimming with a whale.
A house for the reef to eat.
The lights go off which means drama,
as dark as a theater is. Her sadness was so much
that she couldn't keep it from happening,
the bracket legs sliding, holding
only loosely to the cliff face, then
not at all, the inching downward, splinter
by splinter, which is how house-big things
appear to move, slowly, like glaciers,
like sadness moving into a living room
and slowly saying, *this is everything*
it can be gone so easily.
And inside the house, the chairs
are slipping across the floors.

The view outside the windows
is not the same as when she moved in.
This could be a consequence of the sadness,
muting the air with its humid breath.
She doesn't want her house to slip.
But if sadness is not held up like a fish throat
and cut into, it will keep swimming,
will evade the birds and their menaced tongues,
filling the sea with its demolished houses.
The roughage left over will cling to the rocks above.

Cinderella Stay Awhile

While the light is heavy.
While the ruckus of want is unburied.
In you, the animal is soft, is lowing.
In me, the teeth are bared, the sights set.
Could you tell a seraph not to drop
the miracle of her bad news?
Could you change anything godly
into an orbit between what you can want
and what you can get?
The sisters squabbled for the good husband
and what did it get them?
Shoeless, undocumented, no dance at the hall.
You've given me an ultimatum,
which is to say
you've given up on the improbable future.
Either the shoe fits or I don't love you.
Either the angel comes or
what are we to do about mankind?
I drew blood, it tasted sweet.
How were you to know once I was lit
there was no turning me off.

Robert Whitehead was accidentally caught in a net by a rowdy crew of fishermen off the coast of Spanish Point, which is actually in Ireland. He was exhibited at the 1904 World's Fair in St. Louis under the description "Fearsome Half-Human, Half-Fish." For more information, visit robertmwhitehead.com.

CANDACE WILLIAMS

Crown Heights

She pulls the curtain back and light engulfs
her pre-war home. The sun illuminates
the parquetry and lines of lacquered oak
around the walls. The kettle boils; she grinds
the coffee beans and weighs the grounds. She drinks
her coffee while she reads the *Times*. She puts
her pit bull into coat and boots. They do
their morning routine—heading west on Crown
to Rogers; turning right and buying sweets
near President; going east to Nostrand
and walking back to Crown. She walks the heart
of Crown Heights. She walks the ghost perimeter
of Crow Hill Castle—named after murders
of crows that flocked to trees atop the hill;
or darkies lined up on the hill like crows;
or the louring inmates dressed in crow black.
She's never heard of this Crow Hill because
the county tore it down and built Crown Heights.
The county built and ran the Castle too.
The walls were pitched thirty feet high and made
of stone. Eight turrets enclosed five acres.
Women were jailed with infants in their cells.
The men were forced to dig the city roads.
The women stitched; they sewed 15,000
leather shoes per day. The Sabbath sermon
would ring from chapel under sobs and screams
of men and women whipped with frayed cowhide.
The inmates starved or had to eat the bad
food—rancid butter, rotted fish and meat.
That was then. Now, a CrossFit gym is named

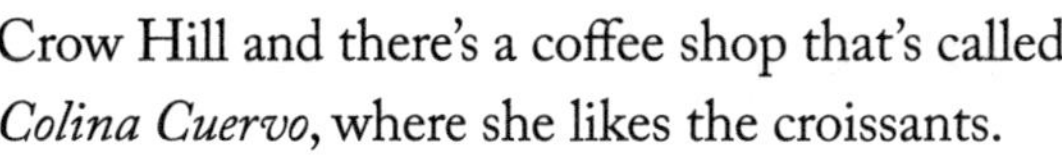

Crow Hill and there's a coffee shop that's called
Colina Cuervo, where she likes the croissants.

Candace Williams is a black, queer poet living in Crown Heights. Her work has appeared or is forthcoming in *Sixth Finch*, *Bennington Review*, *Lambda Literary Review*, and *Copper Nickel*, among other places. She's been awarded a Brooklyn Poets Fellowship, a Best of the Net nomination, and workshop scholarships from Cave Canem. She graduated cum laude from Claremont McKenna College with a degree in Philosophy, Politics, and Economics (PPE) and earned her MA in elementary education from Stanford University. "Crown Heights" appeared as a Brooklyn Poets "Poet of the Week" feature online.

JENNY XIE

Zuihitsu

Sunday, awake with this headache. White clot behind the eyes.

•

Someone once told me, *the future and the past are just another binary*. It was midwinter, I had no passport. In my apartment, two mice made a paradise out of a button of peanut butter.

•

What thief came and took off with one of my possible lives? He must've liked symmetry. He saw you and me, and he stole one of yours, too.

•

These days, I've had my fill of Chinatown and its wet-markets. Gutted fish. Overcooked chattering. The stench making me look hard at everything.

•

Let there be no more braiding of words. I want a spare mouth.

•

My father taught me wherever you are, always be looking for a way out: this opening or that one. Or a question. Sharp enough to slice a hole for you to slip through.

•

Pear tree dandruff. Hard to believe another half-year has dropped, wooden bead on an abacus.

•

Could it be that the life we want is always two steps behind us? Nights when you were already in bed, body hooked by a heavy dream.

•

Embarrassment not to grow out of this reticence. A scarcity on some days, but on others, riches.

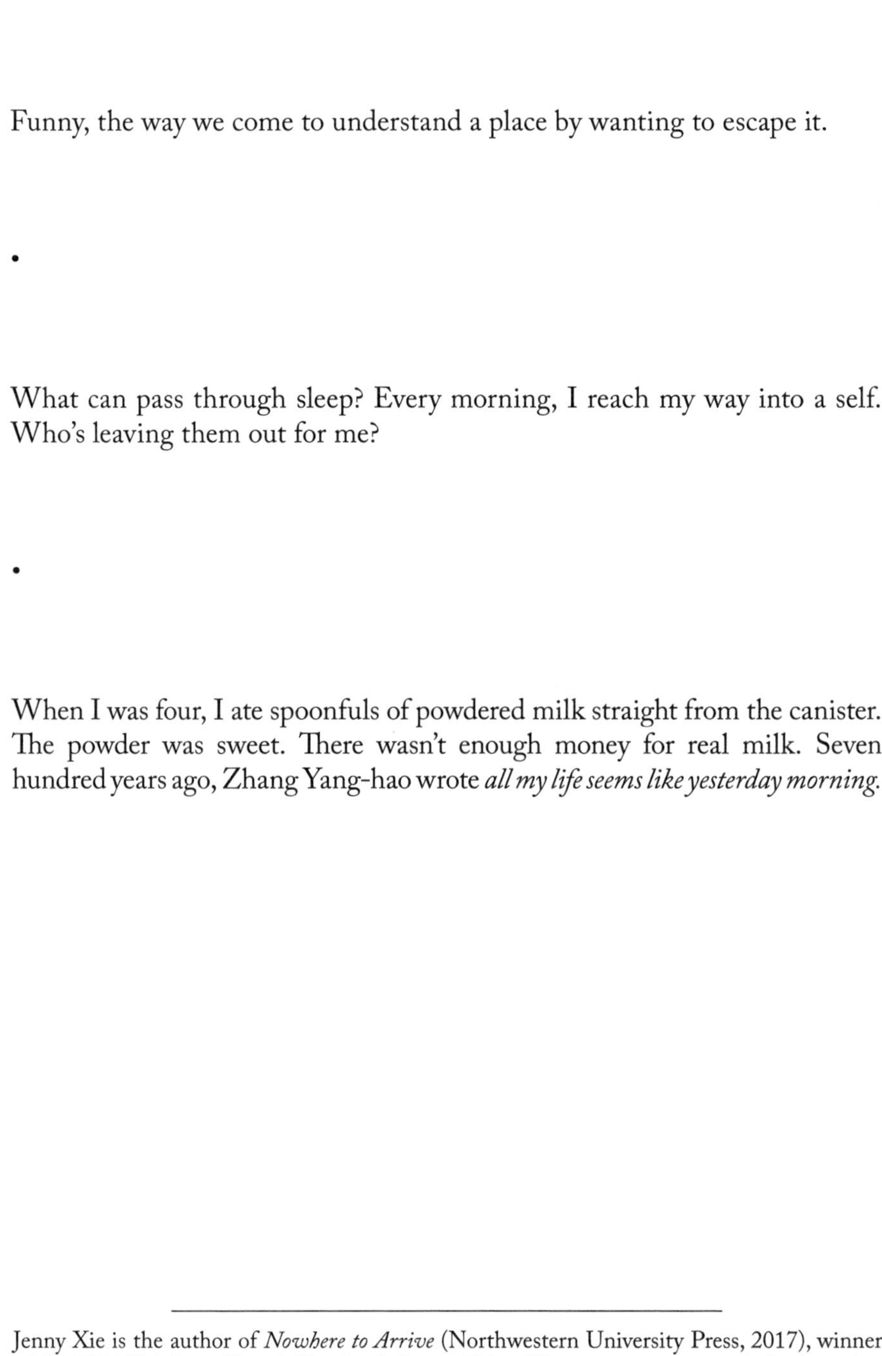

•

Funny, the way we come to understand a place by wanting to escape it.

•

What can pass through sleep? Every morning, I reach my way into a self. Who's leaving them out for me?

•

When I was four, I ate spoonfuls of powdered milk straight from the canister. The powder was sweet. There wasn't enough money for real milk. Seven hundred years ago, Zhang Yang-hao wrote *all my life seems like yesterday morning.*

Jenny Xie is the author of *Nowhere to Arrive* (Northwestern University Press, 2017), winner of the 2016 Drinking Gourd Chapbook Poetry Prize. Her poetry appears or is forthcoming in the *New Republic*, *Tin House*, *Harvard Review*, *Oxford Poetry*, *Literary Review*, *Columbia: A Journal of Literature and Art*, and elsewhere. "Zuihitsu" was first published in *Tin House*.

WENDY XU

Recovery

Whatever the vectors pushed off into, a flight
inching home in snow, you in your delighted
heavy abstraction. I was an egg and more eggs swimming
in the margin's pool. Life is vague and vaguer when
we still kneeling in front of the television push
a finger inside. I smoke alone in my room, the war was
a disambiguation across platforms, notably its own
eddying to music. The it of love was on my mind.

A halo of newsprint, when I became alone I claimed
the greedy living text, jasmine, the sink sang
its steam about the house. The war was a syntactical
construction pointing back towards itself when I
could not turn off the radio's list of fatalities. I locked
my literal body inside the green deadbolt. The house breathed
its hotter mouth, when I became alone the whiter hand
of my country sweeping towards me.

Some People

I had a theory, it flung its scent over
every shadow surface. One human apartment, one
comes to a loud boil in the morning. If they found
me oblique then I am doing this for my bluer
augmented self now. Fear of the unannounced
colloquial war, or, I liked it when the sullen man said
just leave your name. The restaurant
was crowded. The news was death watches
are available, I felt devoted to my new angel
of losing time. Categorical elegy. Something I thought
today was system error, was reverent, was one
or orbiting nothing. No other.

Civil Dusk

As an object does, perhaps turning
in place, fixed orbit satisfies
my aesthetic need

Off-stage a roaring fire
Shafts of light gesture in separate directions

between the hole where
I emerge and where I never get
any sleep, just a few feet

Night stopped softly by I worried
over seeming clever or
unfeeling, rather

like damaged roses
Their scent trailing a hot factory, not
Taiwan or Manila where the news anchor

loathes her boss
When the news anchor
quits her job some of us
got loaded, hopped up on rooftops

lewd views
made a reality of
getting into art early for whom?
Solar noon
approximate equation for the poem's
degraded center like

I'm once again stuck
in the cross streets without
a bathroom
mapping app

Grace under fair weather, brevity

under God
under pressure

Wendy Xu is the author of *Phrasis* (Fence, 2017), winner of the 2016 Ottoline Prize, and *You Are Not Dead* (Cleveland State University Poetry Center, 2013). The recipient of a Ruth Lilly Fellowship, her work has appeared in *Best American Poetry*, *Boston Review*, *Poetry*, *A Public Space*, and widely elsewhere. Born in Shandong, China, she lives in New York City and serves as the poetry editor for *Hyperallergic*.

MATVEI YANKELEVICH

from Some Worlds for Dr. Vogt (XXXIV)

Outside
outside myself
there is a world,
—William Carlos Williams, *Paterson*

...so, posing a line
in repose, passing the time
instead of time passing, you
may contemplate some
meaningful coherence even
now fragmented into segments

as a shoulder jutting from
behind a garden urn on which
it leans, hair attached backwards
as spider legs to make a fragment
of a head, a face turned away
never to be more than image

imagined in expectation, i.e.
a contemplated form, the more
seductive thereby promise
of meaning; its beautiful
constructs, *or a way of putting it*
doesn't in the end matter—line

wrestles with words and means
in the glade or shade of cool
grotto until worn out where
it breaks at a point over the hills
with tradition, as the surveyor
folds the tripod of his scope

over a bee in the grasp
of an ant in the dirt, as *as* points
to a simultaneous resemblance
unfilled, unconsummated, yet
reciprocal, all-consuming in
its decor—a drowsing line

in lieu of a revised totality in
sunlight's daytime sense, a
line, then, at leisure to
describe (as in *un-write*)
the shape of a day off—
a patter not for sake of art

to celebrate a sabbath
that is useless to this world
of labor relations, useless to
you, too, now, following the line
with a working finger, that is
a finger that has been made

by time to represent your work,
entire occupation, nimble, severe,
its rings of skin, etched crosshatch
half moon over a frayed
horizon tell of the wash
of waste. Outside

where nothing cuts, nothing
joins, someone is calling on
this phone as if a line tethers
to the world, whereas in fact
it circumscribes another: *It's*
for you, Dr.

Matvei Yankelevich is the author of *Some Worlds for Dr. Vogt* (Black Square), *Alpha Donut* (United Artists Books), and *Boris by the Sea* (Octopus Books), and the translator of *Today I Wrote Nothing: The Selected Writings of Daniil Kharms* (Overlook/Ardis). He is one of the founding editors of Ugly Duckling Presse, where he curates the Eastern European Poets Series. Matvei teaches for the MFA Program in Creative Writing & Literary Translation at Queens College and Columbia University's School of the Arts (Writing Division).

PERMISSIONS

"The Givens," "Invisible Signals," and "Seasonal Affective Disorder" are from *Mortal Trash*, © 2016 Kim Addonizio, used by permission of W.W. Norton.

"Salat" and "Asking for the Daughter" first published in *Hijra*, © 2016 Hala Alyan, used by permission of Southern Illinois University Press.

"Sirens" first published in *Once More with Feeling*, © 2017 Tina Cane, used by permission of Veliz Books.

"false prophet" and "forgetting something" are from *The Captain Asks for a Show of Hands*, © 2011 by Nick Flynn. "Forty-Seven Minutes" is from *My Feelings*, © 2015 by Nick Flynn. All used with the permission of The Permissions Company, Inc, on behalf of Graywolf Press, www.graywolfpress.org.

"New York City" is from *Moth; or how I came to be with you again*, © 2013 Thomas Heise, used by permission of Sarabande Books.

Excerpt "*from* Gabriel: a Poem" is from *Gabriel: a Poem*, © 2014 Edward Hirsch, used by permission of Alfred A. Knopf, an imprint of the Knopf Doubleday Publishing Group, a division of Penguin Random House LLC. All rights reserved.

"The Miracle" from *New Selected Poems* by Philip Levine, © 1984, 1991 by Philip Levine. "Call It Music" from *Breath: Poems* by Philip Levine, © 2004 by Philip Levine. Both poems used by permission of Alfred A. Knopf, an imprint of the Knopf Doubleday Publishing Group, a division of Penguin Random House LLC. All rights reserved.

"Giants in the Earth" from *That Kind of Danger*, © 1993 by Donna Masini, used by permission of Beacon Press.

"Coney Island" and "Landscape with Rum and Implosion" from *If I Should Say I Have Hope*, © 2012 by Lynne Melnick, used by permission of YesYes Books.

"Gowanus" from *Shuffle*, © 2015 by Emily Moore, used by permission of Paper Nautilus.

"My Aunts" and "Sleep" from *Once*, © 2013 Meghan O'Rourke, used by permission of W.W. Norton.

"Signs There Is a Hole in Manhattan" from *Terrain Tracks*, © 2006 by Purvi Shah, used by permission of New Rivers Press.

"As the river crests, mud-rich with forgotten things" reproduced from *Reliquaria* by R.A. Villanueva by permission of the University of Nebraska Press. © 2014 by the Board of Regents of the University of Nebraska.

"Recover," "Some People," and "Civil Dusk" from *Phrasis*, © 2017 by Wendy Xu, used by permission of Fence Books.